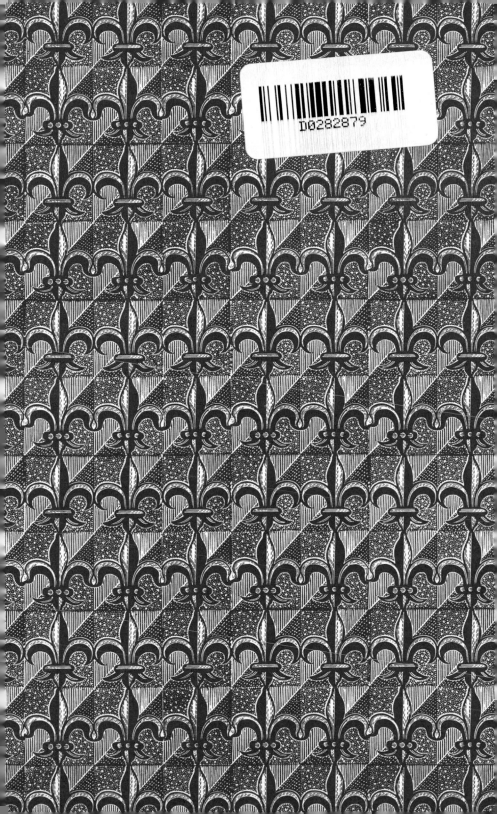

A WORD IN TIME

A WORD IN TIME

Philip Howard

WITH ILLUSTRATIONS BY
GED

SINCLAIR-STEVENSON

First published in Great Britain by
Sinclair-Stevenson Limited
7/8 Kendrick Mews
London sw7 3hg, England

Copyright © 1990 by Philip Howard
Illustrations © 1990 by Ged Melling

British Library Cataloguing in Publication Data

Howard, Philip, *1933*–
A word in time.
1. English language
I. Title
420

isbn 1-85619-017-x

Photoset by Rowland Phototypesetting Limited
Bury St Edmunds, Suffolk
Printed and bound in Great Britain by
Clays Limited, St Ives plc

CONTENTS

For the English Muse

Multa novis verbis praesertim cum sit agendum
propter egestatem linguae et rerum novitatem.

(Especially since we often have to use new words because of the poverty of the language and the novelty of our topics.)

Lucretius, *De Rerum Natura*, I, 138–9

INTRODUCTION

L ANGUAGE IS THE only full democracy. It is open for
anybody who wants to use or abuse it. No two people
use English in exactly the same way. A person's idiolect is
his or her individual linguistic system, which differs in
some details and idiosyncrasies from those of all other
speakers and writers of the same language. We can recognize the handwriting, or the lisp, or the turn of phrase of
someone we love out of all the other millions of hands,
and lisps, and idioms in the world. So we all have a voice
in making and changing the English of our times. Of
course, in this democracy of Babel, some people have
louder voices than others. Poets, imaginative writers,
bestselling authors, pop singers and other cult figures,
broadcasters of all media, politicians, celebrities and such
cattle have more influence on the language than mute

inglorious Miltons, because their words are more widely broadcast. Modern communications spread the word faster than ever before, drum it in more repeatedly and emphatically than ever before, and so change it faster than ever before.

Some people, like the Prince of Wales, feel threatened by the change in their language, as they read and hear the verities they were taught at school eroded and ignored by the rising generations. But language has to change continually, to meet the new needs of the new world and the new inhabitants of the world. To resist linguistic change is as doomed to failure as the exemplary effort of the Prince of Wales's ancestor, Canute, to stop the tide coming in at Westminster – or was it Southampton? It is more profitable to observe the change, to lie back and enjoy it, and if possible to steer it in a helpful rather than an unhelpful direction.

Observing the changing language is as endless a job as painting the Forth Bridge. The proverb is something musty (*Hamlet* – Shakespeare was an obsessive word-watcher and word-innovator) in a concealed quotation, which is part of the changing face of English. That Forth Bridge in the cliché is now a hundred years old, and no longer a wonder of the newspaper-reading world, having been replaced in celebrity by the road bridge opened in 1964. And, in any case, the twenty-eight men employed by British Rail continually to paint the cantilever railway bridge of 1890 do not start at one end and work their way across to the other, and then go back and start again. They go at it piecemeal, attacking the places that look most in need of a touch of paint.

As soon as the Forth Bridge is painted, it starts to rust or wear out, or whatever painted bridges do. As soon as English is observed, in a dictionary or a book like this, it just carries on changing, making the book out of date. The early letters in the second edition of *The Oxford English Dictionary*, some of which have not been revised since 1884, are now grotesquely out of date.

Nevertheless, we must look at the language. It is our most precious common possession. And this is a good time to look at it, as we rush, chattering and scribbling and 'destroying' the language towards the second millennium Anno Domini (or, if you prefer, of the Common Era): one of the topics in this book is the small but knotty problem of dating. *A Word In Time* is a serious (but not solemn) survey of the state of English at the end of the twentieth century. It covers the field from spelling to uneducated new pronunciation, and from grammar to the etymology of new slang. It asks which of the new words of the Nineties are going to find a permanent place in the language, and which are going to fade away like mayflies: thumbs up for 'bimbo', thumbs down for 'Thatcherism'. It examines the changing grammar of tiny words such as 'a' and 'on', and the semantic reasons for describing a flower as a 'non-edible vegetable' in Eurojargon. It deals with big matters such as the divergence between American and British and all the other Englishes, and small matters such as the change in semantics and idiom that makes a rude double entendre out of Parson Woodforde's diary for January 9, 1765: 'Mr Bridges Priest Vicar of the Cathedral at Wells called upon me this afternoon. I took him with me up to Mr Clarke's where we supped and spent the evening. Mr Bridges made himself very disagreeable to all the Company and exposed himself much.' Is the notion that you must never split an infinitive as old-fashioned as the notion that you should never strike a lady? And should we be calling her a lady in the first place, before we strike her, anyway?

As the diplomats say, in another phrase that is showing its age, it is a *tour d'horizon* of English as it is today. It takes the robust view that we live in exciting linguistic times, but that our language is evolving for the new world of the Twenty-Ones, or whatever we decide to call the next century, rather than decaying. Some of the chapters and themes first appeared as warning-shots in my 'New Words for Old' column in *The Times*, and have been expanded, corrected, improved and enlarged with the magic new ingredients from the correspondence they provoked. Readers of *The Times* are still keen word-watchers. Many of them have become friends as well as arguers and mentors. I salute all such good friends and wordsmiths, in particular: Denis Baron, Paul Beale, Peter Brown, Henry Button, Robert Burchfield, Bert Canning, Frank Collieson, Gay Firth, Roy Fuller, Peter Glare, Patrick Hanks, John Harris, David Hunt, Peter Jones, Bernard Levin, Edwin Newman, Edward Quinn, Anthony Quinton, Randolph Quirk, Isabel Raphael, Cormac Rigby, Alan Ross, J. M. Ross, William Safire, Christopher Sinclair-Stevenson, John Sykes, Laurence Urdang, David West, and Laurie Weston.

1

THE PAST PERFECT

Delusions of Grammar

The English have no respect for their language, and
will not teach their children to speak it. It is impossible
for an Englishman to open his mouth without making
some other Englishman hate or despise him.
Pygmalion, preface, 1912, by George Bernard Shaw

W HEN, IN HIS latest populist tirade at the end of 1989,
the Prince of Wales complained about the 'dismal
wasteland' of modern English, he was talking unhistorical
and Old-fogeyish rubbish. His is not a new grumble.
People have been whingeing that the English language is
going to the dogs, and that the young are no longer taught
to speak or write proper, ever since English has been
written down. When you consider how in its history English has changed from being a fully inflected language,
losing almost all its declensions, conjugations, and com-
parisons, the dual voice, and many other fine grammatical
inflexions, it is remarkable how little anxiety that English
is somehow decaying or even dying has found its way into
the records.

Our original Anglo-Saxon language-fathers were illiterate pirates when they waded ashore in Kent and Essex in
the fifth century. But they already had rune-masters who
kept the alphabet and other sacred traditions of the tribe.
No record survives, but the existence of rune-masters
implies that they were there to preserve the status quo of

language, and tick off the young for making a dismal wasteland of traditional English.

King Alfred the Great asserted that English was taught bloody badly in his preface to his translation (the first into English) of Gregory's *Cura Pastoralis* (before AD 896). A copy was sent to each bishop, with a view to the spiritual and linguistic improvement of the clergy. Much of the rest of Alfred's *œuvre* is devoted to repairing 'the decay of learning' in England, indicating that his grasp of how language works was almost as shaky as that of his descendant, the Prince of Wales. In 1066 the Norman Conquest transformed the English language as well as the English kingdom. For nearly three hundred years Norman French was the official language, and French literature was dominant in Europe. In their settlements the peasant Anglo-Saxons still spoke their regional varieties of English, but for official business of law or feudal duty or government, they had to use French. You can see English going to the dogs in the texts, for example with the introduction of the Romance *qu-* to replace the Old English *cw-*. No doubt Old English Fogeys of the period regarded this as a horrendous solecism, though interestingly no trace of their horror survives.

Printing, personified by Caxton (c. 1422–91), opened the gates of English to more mischievous foreign influences, sending it farther to *les chiens*. The Renaissance, a time of linguistic as well as cultural and religious ferment, took two opposing attitudes to the decay of English. On the one hand innovators such as Sir Thomas Elyot (1499–1546) tried to save English from what they described as 'barbarousness' by introducing 'eloquent' new foreign words from the Classics and the Continent. On the other hand conservative scholars such as Sir John Cheke (1514–57) rejected what they described as 'inkhorn' terms, and urged a return to the 'pure currency' of native English words. You can see the contemporary argument being dramatized in *Love's Labour's Lost*. Shakespeare, wonderful wordsmith, always on the lookout for a plot or a theme, made the best of both sides in his contemporary war of the words. Nobody used more, or stranger, or more un-English words (33,000 compared with Racine's spare vocabulary of 2,000). Nobody could use the common Old English monosyllables to greater effect.

Dryden took the side that English was going to the dogs. In his dedication of *The Rival Ladies*, 1664, he wrote: 'I have endeavor'd to write English as near as I could distinguish it from the tongue of pedants and that of affected travellers. Only I am sorry that (speaking so noble a language as we do) we have not a more certain measure for it, as they have in France, where they have an Academy erected for that purpose.' Jonathan Swift was also an 'English is going to the dogs' grumbler. In 1712 he published his *Proposal For Correcting, Improving and Ascertaining the English Tongue*, putting forward numerous misguided suggestions in the continual quest for the fool's gold, of 'ways to fix it for ever'. It is a perennial delusion that it is possible or desirable to fix English for ever. Each new generation naturally needs to change it to suit its new needs. The only 'fixed' languages are described as dead, because nobody uses them for everyday purposes any more.

Samuel Johnson started as a going-to-the-dogs fixer, and was spacious-minded enough to recognize his delusion. In *The Rambler* of March 14, 1752, he was a fixer and purifier: 'I have laboured to refine our language to grammatical purity, and to clear it from colloquial barbarisms, licentious idioms, and irregular combinations.' One of the principal reasons for which he started his *Dictionary* was to stop the decay of English once and for all; but he came to recognize that decay is a daft metaphor for a living language: 'If the changes that we fear be thus irresistible, what remains but to acquiesce with silence, as with the other insurmountable distresses of humanity? It remains that we retard what we cannot repel, that we palliate what we cannot cure.' Because it is such a mongrel language from all the dogs that bark around the world, English more than any other language is full of barbarism, colloquialism, licentious idiom, and irregular combinations. The characteristic sound of English down the centuries is cacophony and uproar. As Shakespeare recognized, the thing to do is to make use of the novelties and barbarisms that express your purpose. Those that are found useless or ugly or boring by the democracy of English speakers and writers are going to drop out of the language anyway.

The great Victorian educators saw their function as instilling cold baths, Christianity, cricket, and 'correct' grammar. Thomas Arnold (1795–1842), the hidden hero of *Tom Brown's Schooldays*: 'As for rioting, the old Roman way of dealing with that is always the right one; flog the rank and file, and fling the ringleaders from the Tarpeian Rock.' Other eminent Victorians saw the advantages of the flexibility of English. That wild and endearing genius, Samuel Taylor Coleridge: 'It may be doubted whether a composite language like the English is not a happier instrument or expression than a homogeneous one like the German. We possess a wonderful richness and variety of modified meanings in our Saxon and Latin quasi-synonyms, which the Germans have not.' By now American English was becoming dominant in the growth of English, by sheer weight of numbers. Contrary to the snobbish and insular fears of the fixers, this is a great strength, not a weakness. Walt Whitman took the point in his *Slang in America*, published in 1885: 'View'd freely, the English language is the accretion and growth of every dialect, race and range of time, and is both the free and compacted composition of all.'

The argument about whether or not English is going to the dogs has been around for donkey's years. For centuries atrabilious Robespierres have been calling for the return of 'correct' grammar, spelling, and (if they were Dr Arnold) the birch for offenders against either. It is worth asking these gloomy pseudo-grammarians when exactly, pray, was this golden age of grammar. When were the vintage years of English syntax? They always turn out to have been when those who think English is going to the dogs were at school themselves, being taught 'correct' English grammar, and (if they went to the sort of private schools to which the Prince of Wales went) being whacked when they got it wrong. The rules of grammar are so fundamentally impressed upon them that they can still feel the sting in frosty weather. It is significant that these grumblers about the decay of the English language are all white, almost all men, almost all middle-class and (in the United Kingdom) privately educated, and all middle-aged, temperamentally if not temporally. They find themselves surrounded by new ideas, new culture, new books, new art, new language, new and younger rivals, and a new world they find threatening. The only thing they feel qualified to pontificate about is the English language. But when they say that English is going to the dogs or decaying, and that the young do not use it properly any more, and that the new words are ugly and the new grammar simply wrong, they are transferring their general *Angst* by displacement to the only common target that belongs to everybody who uses it: the language. Their problem is not the death of English, but what is described (in a shocking new metaphor) as the male menopause.

At one of the Prince of Wales's old schools, we were taught English grammar on strict lines derived from Latin grammar (conditional and final clauses, subjunctives, and so on) and interminable spelling bees of impossible words. It was quite fun for those of us who were good at it. I can still spell *diarrhoea* and *eschscholtzia* (better with the t, though it is sometimes omitted, to preserve the name of the German botanist and nomenclator who gave the Californian poppy his name in 1821) without pausing for thought. No doubt this is a remarkable talent. But it is a useless one, because this is the first time I have had to spell those words for years. It is simply not true that English is being used less well than it was a generation ago. We may not have a first division poet at present, but those are rare birds who come not in battalions, but single spies, and when the spirit moves. But more poetry, and more varied and intelligent poetry, is being published in English than ever before. Ten times as many books are being published as were published a generation ago. Although most of them are a great waste of trees, in some categories (general fiction, genre fiction, school and university textbooks, biographies, children's books) the quality of the language seems vastly improved (which simply means that it is more appropriate to our age).

The cure for nostalgic admiration for the English of the past is to read it. A generation ago the general quality of tabloid pop newspapers was absurdly genteel, written by shop assistants for shop assistants as the snobbish Press Baron observed, impossible to read today without a snigger or a shudder. (We have reacted too far from their gentility, so that today the pop tabloids seem to be written by sex-crazed lager louts for sex-crazed lager louts.) Even in such a minor literary and oratorical form as royal speeches, the standard of the English has improved greatly, so that the British royals actually talk like real people sometimes, and even dare to imitate popular radio shows.

It is simply not true that the young are using English less well than they used to. They are just using it differently. A generation ago in darkest Suffolk and elsewhere, adult illiteracy was widespread. Most children left school at fourteen, just about able to read and recite by rote well-loved passages of the Bible and English literature, and went straight onto the land or into the factory or shop.

What happened was that a generation saw the world and got some education during the Second World War. After the war there was a necessary reaction against the absurdly narrow and élitist teaching of English grammar, spelling, and literature, as though the only respectable kind of English was what is described as the Queen's English (oddly, since the Royal Family have not been in the least literary since George IV, or possibly Charles II), as pronounced and written in the better boarding schools and older universities, and in middle-class homes in the south-eastern corner of England.

As always with necessary reactions, some enthusiasts for change went too far in the opposite direction, throwing out basic grammar and spelling in favour of a sloppy, let-it-all-hang-out self-expression for children. Anything that anybody said or wrote was deemed as 'correct' as anything else. This is not true. Of course there is a lot of slop, and cliché, and obfuscation, and illiteracy, and incoherence around. There always has been, dear Prince. The cure for supposing that our ordinary forefathers used English better than we do is to read them. Usually only the writings of good writers survive. But there are substantial records of ordinary men and women speaking preserved, for example from the time of the English Revolution in the Putney Debates; and pretty sorry, ungrammatical stuff it is.

What we need now is a sensible middle of the road between the absurd old Victorian rigours that treated English grammar like square-bashing on the parade ground (if you passed out in your final parade of grammar and pronunciation, you had worked your way into the middle class), and the new encouragement of children to express themselves, building on the grammar and vocabulary of past generations, but finding their new language for the Nineties. That is the way that language works, and has always worked. The English language itself is just fine. Reports of its death have been greatly exaggerated.

2

NINETIES NEOLOGY

Global Warming to Dead-Cat Bounce

Good to see a return
to old Norman words
and values.

MENDICANT
PLEASE HELP

GED.

Master, master! news, old news, and such news as
you never heard of!

The Taming of the Shrew, III, 1594,
by William Shakespeare

A S WE MOVE into the Nervous (or Nicer, or Neighbourly,
or Nebulous) Nineties, let us do some linguistic archaeology on the new lex that is coming into the language.
Words are fossils. They carry their histories on their backs

for the archaeologists of language. For example, 1066 was a turning-point in the English language as well as for English history. From that date you can mark the arrival in English of such Norman-French words of government as advice, command, commons, country, court, govern, parliament, peer, people, Privy Council, realm, royalty, rule, and sovereign. From that revolutionary date also most of our Old English words for war were replaced by the new French words such as battle, conflict, strife, and war itself. At the same time with the arrival of Norman values our original words were replaced by miserable, poor, poverty, pauper, mendicant, and so on. Anglo-Saxon was a primitive, tribal language. It had to borrow terms for its general and abstract concepts from older and more sophisticated French. So Old English had lots of words for colour, but none for colour itself. It had specific words for many types of movement, from running to swimming, but none for the notion of movement generally.

All historical periods leave their marks on the English language, though none as deeply as the Norman Conquest. For example, when R. W. Burchfield began his *Oxford English Dictionary Supplement* in 1957, as a pilot experiment he listed twenty-one key words that he reckoned would unlock the language of the twentieth century for him: action painting, automation, chain reaction, cybernetics, disinflation, ionosphere, jet (-engine), megaton, meson, morpheme, myxomatosis, nylon, paratroop, penicillin, plutonium, radar, self-service, skiffle, sound-barrier, trafficator, welfare state. Not surprisingly, most of them came from science and technology.

Our language has moved on again since then. Since Volume I of Burchfield's *Supplement* was published in 1972, some 5,000 new words from 'yuppification' to 'perestroika' have established themselves firmly enough in the language to be recorded in the second edition of the *OED*, published in 1989. Not surprisingly, far the biggest category of these new words (1,200) came from the sciences. The arts and social sciences also did well. There were 175 new words introduced into English from politics, 95 from economics, 57 from linguistics, and 74 from the law.

As we march into the Nineties, making up words as we go, we can begin to ask which words are going to stick with us to define the Eighties, as 'gig' and 'mini' (both skirt and car) define the Sixties. I can see that this is a disobliging observation for the political classes, who think that all history is politics: political eponyms have a short shelf-life. 'Thatcherite' and 'Reaganomics' will be as meaningless to the next generation as 'Foxite' and 'Peelite' are to ours, apart from historians of the early nineteenth century. *Res publica brevis: lingua longa.*

'Thatcherism' has made it into the dictionaries for future historians to represent shorthand jargon for the political and economic policies advocated by Mrs Thatcher, especially as contrasted with those of earlier Conservative leaders. The first recorded citation of the word comes from *The Times* of 1979: 'The party was fighting off the shrill divisiveness of Thatcherism, with its simple monetarist policies.' In addition, 'Thatcherite' has come into English to mean either a supporter of the views or policies of Mrs Thatcher, or, as adjective, of, pertaining to, or characteristic of Mrs Thatcher or Thatcherism. Again the *OED* gives an early and inadequate citation from *The Times*: 'The Thatcherite philosophy can be summed up in two words: non-interference.'

There have been other eponyms spinning off from the name of the Prime Minister who has marked the dictionary as well as the decade. 'Thatcher's girls' is slang for prostitutes, because Mrs Thatcher's policies were believed by her opponents to have caused widespread unemployment, forcing women on the breadline to seek work in the only field available, the sex industry. A week is indeed a long time in politics. All these eponyms and 'Maggie' variants are likely on past precedent to be as forgotten as last year's headlines as soon as Mrs Thatcher retires. The same goes for the 'Iron Lady' sobriquet, which was originally coined by the Soviet magazine *Red Star*, gratefully adopted, and became a seven-day slogan. 'Iron Lady' was rejected by the *OED* as being too short-lived to be recorded for all posterity, already made obsolete by the Prime Minister's new 'caring' image. *Le Quotidien de Paris* dismissed the 'Iron Lady' label as being too base a metal; she was, instead, it wrote, 'a woman of uranium, with peculiar irradiations'.

Policies live longer than people. The new words of policy jargon will rumble around for longer than the Prime Minister herself. 'Monetarism' has established itself in English during the Eighties. Professor Paul Samuelson is cited in the *OED* as calling monetarism a disease, and defining it as a pathological belief that only the rate of growth of the money supply can affect significantly the rate of inflation or the level of unemployment. 'Sado-monetarism' and other related derivatives from the policy argument of the decade in other countries as well as the United Kingdom are living and evolving in the lexicon, and will be there for the historians. 'Conviction politics' has replaced consensus as a catchphrase for the 'chattering classes', who are themselves a catchphrase of the Eighties and Nineties. 'Fudge and mudge' is the new (otiose) doublet jingle to slag off policies of which one disapproves. Oddly enough, the words of the Thatcherite revolution that are likely to live the longest are the most frivolous, language being no respecter of politics. 'Wet' and 'dry' are short, sharp, Anglo-Saxon epithets to hurl at two opposing attitudes in politics. 'Dry', meaning a politician (especially a member of the Conservative Party) who advocates economic stringency and individual responsibility, and uncompromisingly opposes high government spending, was first spotted by the *OED* in *The Times* of 1984: 'It is hard to see economic dries such as Mr Ridley buying the channel tunnel arguments now.' A 'wet' as a politician with liberal or middle-of-the-road views on controversial issues (often applied to members of the Conservative Party opposed to the monetarist policies of Margaret Thatcher) was recorded by the *OED* in *The Times* of 1980: 'Who are to be counted among the wets? The answer seems to be anybody who crosses the Prime Minister in fashioning a particular policy.' I am sure that this particular use of wet goes back to English boarding schools; but the political twist is Thatcherite. There is no sense of propriety in language. Prime Ministers live in the dictionary for accidental trivialities. Mrs Thatcher would live longer in the language if she could feature in some lurid journalistic scandal all over the front pages of the tabloids, or if she could carry a bag like Gladstone, or invent a boot like Wellington.

Gorbachev will probably make it as a word in his own right as well as a personal name into the next edition of the *OED*. And the Ayatollah has already made it, as a nasty fossil to remind us of the Eighties. Other celebrity words of the Nineties, such as Arafat, Crocodile Dundee, and Charles and Di may not be so durable. Expect to read and hear a lot more of those Green words in the Nineties. From muesli to jogger's nipple, and from the greenhouse effect to global warming, the Nineties are going to go down in the dictionaries as the decade that started to worry about the future of the planet. Green itself as a political label in English is coming to mean humourless, bespectacled, neurotic, and sanctimonious, in a new version of the old English voice of Puritanism.

The Eighties and Nineties are going to be remembered in lexicography by many new words to do with the deregulation of the money markets, from arbitrageur to junk-bonds to the weasel word 'unbundling' (a euphemism for asset-stripping) to 'dead-cat bounce' (a deceptive temporary recovery in share prices in a stock market whose price-level is generally low, because even a dead cat will bounce up from the sidewalk if dropped from a sufficiently high window in Wall Street), to all those jocular new compounds made of gold, from gold card to golden handcuffs.

Computers are marking the lex of the Nineties strongly, from wetware to laptops. To err is human, but really to foul things up requires a computer. Customer: 'Excuse me, sir. Do you have any user-friendly sales reps?' Electronics shop manager: 'You mean consumer compatible liveware? No, it's his day off.' Computers affect our lives in many departments, not least in our language. Some computer jargon may be ugly or silly. It would be a miracle if it were not, jargon tending to be coined by busy people on the run. But quite a lot of it seems to me to be rather good, taming the technological revolution with homely or joky metaphors. For example, a 'mouse' is computerese for the little hand-held thingy that is moved by the operator over a flat surface to produce a corresponding movement of a cursor or arrow on a VDU. Your mouse usually has finger-tip controls for selecting a function or entering a command. A 'breadboard' is an older computerese metaphor, taken from radio jargon, to mean the board on which something like an experimental electric circuit is set out. It is an old and endearing human characteristic to take the sting out of the unknown by pet names. So the ancient Greeks called the vengeful and terrifying Furies 'the Nice Ladies'. As we advance into the Nineties, more of us are going to have to keep our eyes open as we 'boot' the 'micro', call up a 'window', and set up the 'mouse' on its 'tablet'. A glance at the manual will tell us that this machine not only has an amazingly small 'footprint', but boasts both a main and an auxiliary 'handshake'. Luckily mine doesn't yet say, 'Have a nice day' – but they're working on it. What shall we select from the 'menu'? I spotted an advertisement for an 'intelligent breadboard' in *Scientific American*. I should like one of those, I think. Perhaps it makes us feel better to treat our computers as humans. I scream with frustration when System 6 'crashes' at *The Times*, usually at a crucial time on a Wednesday evening when we are about to 'shoot' the Books Page. Perhaps it humanizes the frustration to talk about a system 'crash', or a program 'falling over', in the same words that we might use for such disasters befalling one of our children.

Metaphor is an important source of semantic change in computerese and the other technical jargons, and outside too. Here are some examples of new metaphors changing the way we speak in the Nineties. 'Guilty *leakers* have been known to get the sack, but strenuous efforts are usually made to keep this out of the papers.' 'Mao's proclaimed policy was *to lean to one side*, though he was careful to maintain his balance.' 'This lousy *lemon* we took in trade on a Buick.' 'The guy who's keepin' us *lidless* – free to ride as we decide.' 'Because Governor Dukakis stands 5 feet 8 inches tall, cruel Republicans are already playing on the ancient phrase with "Beware of Greeks wearing *lifts*".' 'She began her campaign being carefully coached by her *minder*.' 'The meeting consisted only of Marge, Sonia, Ernie Mason – the poetic *munchkin* – and Eli Hurwood.'

Metaphor has given us such combinations redolent of the Eighties as the Teflon presidency and golden handcuffs. From intelligent breadboards to poetic munchkins, from 'whiskerless mice' (or mouses?) to four-wheeled lemons, our language advances into the Nineties with evolving metaphors. 'My computer dating agency came up with a perfect woman; still I've got another three goes.' By far the biggest category of new words of the Nineties, as usual this century, will come from medicine and the other sciences. By far the most interesting will be the few general words that stick. Will 'bimbo' become a permanent piece of the English vocabulary, once Gary Hart, Ollie North, and Ralph Halpern are ashes under Potomac and Tamesis? We shall see. Meanwhile, tomorrow to fresh words and phrases of the Nineties.

3

LINGO

Why Mongrels Make Better Poets

What's this penchant for etymological doublets?

GED.

The Italian is pleasant, but without sinews, as a still reflecting water; the French delicate, but even nice as a woman, scarce daring to open her lips for fear of marring her countenance; the Spanish majestical but fulsome, running too much to the *o*, and terrible like the Devil in a play; the Dutch manlike, but withal

very harsh, as one ready at every word to pick a
quarrel.
Epistle on the Excellency of the English Tongue, 1605, by
Richard Carew

Spanish is the language for lovers, Italian for singers,
French for diplomats, German for horses, and English
for geese.

Spanish proverb

MARIE-LOUISE DENIS was Voltaire's niece, for a time his
mistress, and kept house for him in his old age. She
was a sparky French woman, a *femme du monde*. During an
English lesson she grew impatient with the difficulty of
pronouncing the words of this uncouth language. She
exclaimed to her teacher: 'You write *bread*, but say *bred*.
Wouldn't it be simpler just to say *du pain*?'

Pace Mademoiselle Denis, mongrelism is a strength of
the English language, as it is of the English nation. Celts,
Romans, Anglo-Saxons, Norsemen, Normans, Huguen-
ots, Eastern European Jews, East and West Indians are
in the melting-pot that makes the versatile nation. Their
combined and interacting languages make the vocabulary
of English three times larger than that of any other
language, with variants and ambiguities not available in
other tongues. That is one of the reasons why English is
so apt for poetry. Much of the poetry and many of the
jokes in Shakespeare come from the juxtaposition and
contrast between long Latinate words and short Germanic
ones.

In the violent tides of history that created the English
and their mongrel language, sometimes the same word
came in twice by different routes and in different forms.
For example, English adopts a French word derived from
Latin, and also adopts the original Latin word from which
the French word was derived. The philologists call such
pairs of words of identical origin 'etymological doublets'.

The partners in a pair of etymological doublets never mean exactly the same. There is no such thing as an exact synonym, because as soon as it comes into the language and starts to be used, each word builds up its individual history and network of connotations. But quite often each leg of an etymological doublet means roughly the same, not surprisingly, since they both come from the same origin. Part of good writing is picking exactly the right word for your purpose and context, hitting the bull's eye of meaning rather than the inner, or in hustling journalism the magpie.

For example, the Latin *fragilis* (liable to break, from *frangere* to break) has produced the etymological doublet of *fragile* and *frail* in English. Their meanings overlap in a Venn diagram. But the two words are seldom interchangeable. The good writer will pick the right one, the careless writer will bung in whichever comes to mind first. *Frail* is three centuries older in English. It came from the Old French adaptation of the Vulgar Latin *fraile*, which has become *frêle* in modern French. *Fragile* was borrowed from written Latin by the French scribes in the Middle Ages, and was soon cribbed by the thieving English. Both words refer to things that are easily broken, from their ultimate Latin root.

Fragile is the most general umbrella word, and suggests weakness and delicacy as well as liability to break: a *fragile* glass; the transport of *fragile* materials; his *fragile* health; a *fragile* red-figure vase with a curious foot. *Timon of Athens*: 'Throws/That Nature's *fragile* vessel doth sustain/In life's uncertain voyage.'

Frail carries its particular implication of slenderness or enfeeblement, as well as suggesting that something is weak or easily broken. *Fragile* can often be a compliment; *frail* seldom. So, a *frail* hedge; *frail* columns bearing the architrave; made *frail* by persistent bouts of malaria. If thinnish is what you mean, *frail* not *fragile* is your word. 'The wicked grow/Like frail, though flowery, grass.' The American slang use of *frail* to mean a woman is a male chauvinist

A WORD IN TIME

use of the adjective to indicate the supposedly weaker sex: 'She's a swell dish – a lovely piece of *frail.*' Peter Cheyney, and dated. Today he would have written: 'A lovely *frail.*'

Here are some other etymological doublets, from Latin directly and mediated through French:

Fabrica, in Latin a craft or art, specifically metal-working or building, gives English both forge (*ab* having shifted to *av* then to *au* then to *o*) and fabric. As a general rule, the more a borrowing has shifted from its original, the older it is likely to be in English and the more likely to have been borrowed through French.
Traditio in Latin gives English both treason and tradition.
Redemptio gives ransom and redemption.
Securitas gives surety and security.
Radius gives ray and radius.
Species gives spice and species. Spice had a curious journey into English. In Late Latin *species* acquired the *specific* sense of articles of merchandise, especially aromatics and spices, perhaps by analogy with the Late Greek development of the plural of *eidos*, a form, to mean groceries. Hence it passed into Old French as *espice*, lost its initial *e* by aphesis, and came into Middle English, with gradually narrowing sense to mean spice.
Pauper gives poor and pauper.
Abbreviare gives abridge and abbreviate.
Appretiare gives appraise and appreciate.
Here is an etymological triplet:
Ratio gives reason (French), ration (Latin with a French suffix), and ratio (pure Latin).
And here is an etymological quadruplet:
Gentilis (belonging to a Roman *gens* or clan) gives English gentle, genteel, gentile, and jaunty.

Users of English have more and more delicately specialized tools in their word-box than users of any other language.

English is the greatest magpie language, borrowing words from every other language it meets, and making them its own, often with doublet and triplet variations.

The process works the other way too, as the Académie Française tries to stop, as vainly as Dame Partington at Sidmouth in 1824, trying to push back the Atlantic with her mop. The ceaseless flow of words and ideas is as wonderful as the tides, and sometimes as strange. The flow is not just between the old and the big languages, such as Latin and French, but between the little and new ones as well, the small seas as well as the big oceans. For example in Krio, the lingua franca of Sierra Leone and adjacent parts of West Africa, *bakanti* means a scissors-kick, back over the head and spectacular if it comes off (which it seldom does), at football. How come? Something to do with back-to-front? Surely nothing to do with drunken revellers from Ancient Greece? Only remotely. The word is derived from HMS *Bacchante*, whose sailors first demonstrated the scissors-kick in Sierra Leone.

Japanese is a language that has grown prodigiously from foreign borrowings in the past few years, perhaps in step with Japan's startlingly rapid economic growth since the war. Naturally enough, the Japanese have adopted words to identify things not indigenous to their own country; for example, *hanbaga* to mean hamburger; *tabako* for cigarettes; *arubaito* for a part-time job; and *sakka* for football. Interestingly the American import, baseball, has been given a word of its own, *yakyu*. With the Japanese passion for making things smaller, they have taken some English words, and shrunk them: *wapuro* for word processor, and *Loli-kon*, which is short for Lolita complex, and is used to describe a man with a liking for pre-pubescent girls. In some instances, perhaps significantly, the native Japanese words have been replaced by foreign imports: *communication*, *bijinesu* (business), *shoppingu*, and *orientation* are all now used as often as, if not more often than, their original Japanese equivalents.

Cypriot is another localized language that is exposed, like all languages, to the tides of imported foreign words. It is a highly flavoured register of Greek, enriched by Italian because of the long Venetian connection, and by Turkish.

Aphrodite's island was ceded to the United Kingdom for administrative purposes by the Sultan in 1878, since when Cypriot Greek has taken on board and adapted its share of English. When people mix, their languages are bound to mix also. For instance, the Cypriots soon caught on that their new masters were obsessed with the word 'gentleman'. But they did not realize that the word was marked for the masculine. So in Cypriot *gentleman*, pronounced *chendliman*, means something really beautiful, the tops, ace; and it can be applied to men, women, animals, or inanimate objects. You can say: 'Marika is really *gentleman*' (i.e. beautiful); or: 'This bicycle is *gentleman*' (i.e. perfect). *Revolver* is another English word that has been taken into the Greek spoken on Cyprus, but not, I think, into the Panellinios Demotiki, the modern Greek spoken in Greece. Because of differences between English and Cypriot habits and dispositions to pronunciation, it comes out on Cyprus as *livorvoro*. As you would expect, the British military garrison on Cyprus has introduced over the years a number of martial English words into Cypriot Greek:

O *sárgis*: the sergeant.

O *cópros*: the corporal.

O *coronéllos*: the colonel (this could be from Italian).

O *brigadías*: the brigadier.

O *absentís*: the absentee, or the soldier who has taken French leave, and let us try to keep the French out of this.

I *Náfi*: our own beloved NAAFI, purveyor of snowballs (coconut buns) and beer to the troops; genitive: tis Náfis, etc.; there is no plural.

I *cantína, tis cantínas*, etc.: the canteen.

Apart from garrisons, the other traditional British export has been football. Accordingly, English football terms have been taken into Cypriot Greek, as they have into Krio and most languages of the world:

O *foúrbos, tou foúrbou*, etc.: the football. Interestingly, and perceptively, in Cypriot the word also means the idiot and the dupe.

O referís, ton referín, tou referí, oi referídes, etc.: the referee.
O láisman (the same for singular and plural): the lines-
man.
O mpak: the back.
Hands as a verb: to foul or give away a penalty.
O portaris (the porter or doorman): the goalkeeper.
Other English words that have been imported into
Cypriot include:
To vérikon: a variety of grape, probably from 'very good'.
To lordikon: a choice variety of pear, from your English
lord or lordly.
To rállin: the bicycle (Raleigh).
Ta sklips: bicycle clips.
To séif: the safety catch of a gun.
And, for a philosophical rather than a practical word,
To fríoul: the free will.

There are many more loan words and adopted words
travelling in both directions between two old languages
with such ancient connections. It is a natural process, a
sign of health and growth, not of decay.
Consider another old and localized language, Welsh.
The English have a bad reputation for linguistic as well as
political imperialism in Wales. Until quite recently schoolchildren in Wales were punished with placards around
their necks and worse for speaking their native language
in school. As is natural when two languages are spoken
next door to each other, Welsh words have been adopted
into English, or more accurately survive in English as
archaeological remains of the language of these islands
before the Romans came: for example, *hwyl*, the sporting
cliché to describe the emotional exuberance of Welsh for-
wards at Rugby Football, and, more anciently, such place
names as *Kent*, the *Thames*, and probably *London* itself. The
Eisteddfodau, with their druidic fancy dress invented by
Iolo Morgannwg in the nineteenth century, seem a bit of
a joke to the insular English, and the poems declaimed
there by the bards seem unconscionably long and banal.

And yet, even in translation into English, some of the work of modern Welsh bards such as that grand old man Saunders Lewis is clearly the right stuff. Welsh poetry has been recorded uninterruptedly since Taliesin, *floruit circa* 550, at a time when the Anglo-Saxon forefathers of the English were illiterate pirates.

It is a common error by speakers of a dominant language like English to suppose that less widespread, dwindling languages are primitive, or in some way less sophisticated as languages. Perhaps it is not surprising that Eskimo has dozens of different words to describe ice, a far richer vocabulary than English, from *migalik*, pancake ice, circular pieces of young ice up to six feet in diameter with raised rims, to *uguruguzak*, grease ice, the earliest stage of freezing, which causes wind ripples to disappear from patches of the water surface. English makes nothing like such fine distinctions about ice, because it does not need to. But apart from the needs of local geography, some of the vanishing AmerIndian languages like Shoshone have verbs that conjugate with a vast number of forms, and grammars of a complexity that makes English look clumsy and primitive. It is a mistake to suppose that primitive people communicate by bestial grunts. Peoples who have not yet discovered metals or writing or television can invest more of their creative energy into the art of language and poetry. It is Western Europeans and Americans, living in a highly technological civilization, accustomed to computer and mathematical formulae and advertising slogans, who could be said to be reducing language to a series of inarticulate grunts.

Look at the significant difference between the English and Welsh words for administration. The English word comes from Latin via French, and it came in with the Normans, who introduced many abstract words into primitive Old English. It is a bossy word, as the Normans were the new bosses. That *ad* carries the implication that administration is something that you do *to* other people, from on high. *Richard II*: 'Swear by the duty that you owe to heaven/To keep the oath that we administer.' The English word 'administration' is management, government, the ministry, officialdom, something that 'they', or the Men in Whitehall, do to us. The Welsh for administration is *gweinyddiaeth*, defined by the dictionary of the University of Wales as the act of ministering, attendance, service; and secondly, as a body of ministers to whom is entrusted the government of a country, the ministry, or an administrative department of government. A related and more general word for service is *gwasanaeth*. *Gweinydd* is service or ministry in the personal sense, for example of a public servant or a clergyman, to or for someone. The adjective is *gweinyddol*. The standard (pre-1988) Welsh Bible uses another word, *gweinidogaeth*, for the Authorized Version's ministration (e.g. *Luke* I, 23; *Romans*, XII, 7, etc.). The *Beibl Cymraeg Newydd*, the New Welsh Bible of 1988, has *gwasanaeth* and the verb *gweini* for ministration and to serve respectively. The root of *gwasanaeth* is *gwas*, a male servant or lad. This common old Celtic word shifted across the border to give Middle Latin *vassus* and hence the English vassal. Welsh is even more flexible than English at constructing compound nouns and adjectives from verbs and nouns. The root of *gweinyddiaeth*, the Welsh for administration, is a worker or farmer; one working under authority; one who is serving somebody or upon something; in the biblical sense (especially in the feminine) it is somebody who looks after others, visiting the sick, helping the poor, a deaconess. Words are formed by the many accidents of history, geography, propinquity, and culture. I much prefer the Welsh *gweinyddiaeth* to the Norman-English word administration as a description of the activities of Our Masters in government and elsewhere: Your Obedient Servant, as opposed to the Man in Whitehall Knows Best.

Sam Johnson, great and funny English chauvinist, who used English like an angel trained in the classics, was visiting North Wales with friends, and asked: 'Has this *brook* e'er a name?' He was assured that it was called the

River Ustrad. 'Let us jump over it directly,' he said to his companions, 'and show them how an Englishman should treat a Welsh river.' Unlike rivers, languages flow in both directions.

4

TIME WARPS

Gay Howlers

> Time is like a river. As soon as a thing is seen it is
> carried away and another takes its place, and then
> that other is carried away also.
>   *Meditations*, iv, *circa* 170, by Marcus Aurelius

TIME, LIKE AN ever-rolling stream, bears all our words
away. *Tout passe, tout casse, tout lasse*, in language as
in life. The English of somebody born a generation before
us is already beginning to sound dated. That of a century
ago needs glosses for anybody who is not a historian
of the period. That of five hundred years ago needs a
translation, and that of a thousand years ago is another
language.

One of the ways that language is continually changing
is by indirections and absurdities. Howlers can become
'correct' if enough people persist in making them. This has
finally happened to 'prestigious'. Until a century ago it was
used only in its etymologically correct meaning, 'practising
juggling or legerdemain', related to 'prestidigitation'. Since
then, in spite of the protests of pedants, the British have
persisted in using it in an 'incorrect' sense to mean 'having
or giving prestige', the magic quality of the twentieth
century for which we have no other adjective. 'Prestigious'
is still a hollower quality than 'distinguished', but the
howler has become correct, and if you use 'prestigious' in
its old juggling sense of conjurer's tricks, you will be

misunderstood. That is a howler that has been enthroned because it fills a gap.

Other howlers arise by simple muddle between two words that sound the same, for example 'appraise' for 'apprise', and 'mitigate against' for 'militate against'. Confusing 'flaunt' with 'flout' was popularized by Noël Coward in a song, and by the former British Prime Minister, Edward Heath. The howler is not established yet, and should be resisted.

'Infer' is widely used to mean 'imply' (and has been in the past by writers as eloquent as Thomas More, Milton, and Walter Scott). This is widely regarded as a howler, and it would be a pity to lose the useful distinction we have evolved between 'infer' and 'imply'. 'Disinterested' is often used to mean 'uninterested' and is widely regarded as a howler. In fact the first recorded uses of 'disinterested', by John Donne and Junius, are to mean 'uninterested' – half a century before 'uninterested' came into English. These are howlers between words that have similar meanings as well as similar sounds, and the boundaries between which will always tend to be fluid and disputed. But where a useful distinction has been evolved between two such related words, it is prodigal and wanton not to observe it. Sometimes a howler wins through by adopting by analogy the wrong preposition from a similar word; though I hope that 'comprised of' and 'inflicted with' can continue to be branded as howlers for a few more years, common though they have become.

We may (and do) deplore many of these changes; but if the tide of *vox populi* has set on a change, in the long trawl not even the strongest swimmer can fight against the tide. Prestigious people, from our best writers to pop singers, have more influence than most in changing the language. But language grows from the bottom up as well as from the top down. Lexicographers and linguists record the grunts and snorts coming up to them from us, established 'howlers' and all. *C'est leur métier*. It is the job of teachers to teach the best contemporary English in its many registers, and to expunge howlers, aware that today's howler may eventually become correct. English is a matter not of morality but of usage.

There is a new howler, which it may already be too late to nip in the bud: there is a creeping confusion between *prevaricate* and *procrastinate*. Here are two recent examples from *The Times*. 'Some fear the Minister will *prevaricate* (without doing anything about computer hackers) until the next election.' And here is the Professor of Law at London University, in an article: 'But still the Government *prevaricates*. It will now await the views of Parliament in the autumn before deciding whether to introduce legislation (about war crimes).' His *prevaricate* made it (disgracefully) into the headline.

The words are both quadrisyllables beginning with 'pr'. But their roots and meanings are quite different. That *cras* in *procrastinate* means tomorrow in Latin; and the word means time-wasting, or putting off until tomorrow. *Prevaricate* means to evade the truth in ways short of lying, to be economical with the truth, and its roots come from walking crookedly. *Varicare* in Latin means to spread the legs apart, to straddle; *varus* is bow-legged. In Latin *praevaricari* meant first to straddle across anything, and then by metaphor in legal jargon for an advocate to act in collusion with his opposite number in order to secure a particular outcome to a trial. Cicero often accuses the other side of *prevarication*: 'He took money from Catiline on condition that he *prevaricated* disgracefully.' *Procrastinate* is the attitude of *mañana*: never do anything today that you can postpone until tomorrow. *Prevaricate* ranges from economy with the truth to falsehood. There is an interesting little incipient division between American and British use of *prevaricate*. In America *prevaricate* has acquired and retains a strong sense of lying, or at least fiddling with the truth. In British English the word has softened and slipped in the other direction, to mean nothing much worse than 'shilly-shally'. This, no doubt, helps to explain the confusion with *procrastinate*. It is a fertile new little source of misunderstanding between

American and British English. *Prevaricate* and *procrastinate*
are still quite distinct. To muddle them is still a howler,
and all good men and women will rally round to maintain
the useful distinction.

But if enough professors of law and sub-editors on *The
Times* carry on using *prevaricate* where they mean *procrastinate*, the next edition of *The Oxford English Dictionary* will
have to record the howler. If Latin were more widely
taught, there would be less barbaric (should that be barbarous?) confusion about the roots of our language. Many
popular modern howlers, for example, spelling Phillip
with two ls, 'miniscule', and pronouncing the word 'dis-
sect' as though it were spelled with a single s and rhymed
with bisect, arise only from barbarous (should that be
barbaric?) ignorance of our grandmother tongue.

Time makes a monkey of our quotations as well as
our syntax and semantics. A quotation is something that
somebody once said that seemed to make sense at the
time. But times and idiom change. If he were composing
today, I do not think that Henry Vaughan, the Welsh
mystic poet, could write: 'How brave the prospect of a
bright backside!' It was too much for the Rev. H. F. Lyte,
anyway: in his edition of Vaughan he amended the last
two words to 'traversed plain'. This fundamental erosion
of idiom occurs mostly in translation these days, as in the
engraved brass plate outside the Mosel riverside hotel at
Cochem, which translates: *'Nacht Eingang auf der Rückseite
bitte* – Night entry at the backside please.'

I do not suppose that Elizabeth Barret Browning would
put it exactly the way she did in 'Wine of Cyprus':

> Our Euripides, the human,
> With his droppings of warm tears,
> And his touches of things common
> Till they rose to touch the spheres!

Time has eroded and custom coarsened some of those
words. Would Trollope, if he were writing *The Eustace
Diamonds* today, put it: 'As he sat signing letters at the

India Board, relieving himself when he was left alone between each batch by standing up with his back to the fireplace, his mind was full of all this.' 'To relieve oneself' has become a common euphemism, and most of us would face the fireplace. Here is another quotation, coarsened by time, from Churchill's *Life of Marlborough*: 'In his last years he had woven Marlborough into the whole texture of his combinations.' And here is H. G. Wells making an anachronism in chapter 14 of *The War of the Worlds*: 'His landlady came to the door, wrapped in dressing-gown and shawl; her husband followed, ejaculating.'

The passage of time and the change of idiom stick out like reefs in books written only a generation ago. The most obvious example of changing idiom rendering quotations offside is the use of 'gay' as a less hostile description of homosexual than 'queer'. This was first recorded in underworld slang in the Thirties, but since the last war 'gay' has become widely idiomatic in this sense on both sides of the Atlantic. Consequently, a range of famous quotations from Eng. Lit. have become impossible without schoolboy sniggers from the roughs at the back of the class. For example, it is no longer possible for Chaucer's Wife of Bath to ask in her prologue: 'Why is my neighbour's wife so gay?' without some risk of double entendre. The same embarrassment has come upon *Samson Agonistes*:

> But who is this, what thing of sea or land?
> Female of sex it seems,
> That so bedeck'd, ornate and gay,
> Comes this way sailing
> Like a stately ship of Tarsus.

And how about Iago, praising women to Desdemona and Emilia: 'She never lacked gold, and yet went never gay'? In his poem 'The Menagerie', one of William Vaughan Moody's characters advises: 'If nature made you so graceful, don't get gay.' And what are we to make of Yeats's assertion in 'Lapis Lazuli': 'They know that Hamlet and Lear are gay'? Samuel Rogers: 'There's such a charm in melancholy, I would not, if I could, be gay.' Scott in *Guy Mannering*: 'Sophia, as you well know, followed me to India. She was innocent as gay; but, unfortunately for us both, as gay as innocent.' At Christ Church, Oxford, according to Christopher Hobhouse's *Oxford* (1939): 'The life is easy-going and tolerant; the company is intelligent and gay.'

Poetry in particular treads a perilous tightrope between sublimity and bathos. I know that beauty is in the eye of the beholder, and double entendre in the ears of the Lower Fifth. But there are some words that have become so dodgy because of changing slang that the prudent tightrope-walker avoids them. Take 'pants'. Since about 1840 these have become colloquial for the undergarments that were previously called drawers. This has undermined a series of famous quotations. 'Kubla Khan': 'As if this earth in fast thick pants were breathing.' Shelley in 'Epipsychidion': 'The slow, silent night/Is measured by the pants of their fast sleep.' In *Othello* Cassio prays that Othello might 'make Love's quick pants in Desdemona's arms'. In *Antony and Cleopatra* Antony tells the wounded Scarus to 'leap thou, attire and all,/Through proof of harness to my heart, and there/Ride on the pants triumphing'. Francis Thompson, in 'A Corymbus for Autumn', declares that 'day's dying dragon is panting red pants into the West'. I am trying as hard as I can to be high-minded about this, but I cannot help twitching at those red pants. I am afraid that 'pants', like gay, is a coarsened word that has been ruled out of bounds by the passage of time.

Once you have started spotting double entendres, litera-ture becomes a minefield. *Paradise Lost*: 'And leave a singed bottom all involved with stench and smoke.' *Vanity Fair*: 'Amelia wept confidentially on the housekeeper's shoulder, and relieved herself a good deal.' *Uncle Tom's Cabin*: 'Mrs Shelby stood like one stricken. Finally, turning to her toilet, she rested her face in her hands, and gave a sort of groan.' Literature is as booby-trapped as life.

5

PRONUNCIATION

It's Not What You Say,
It's How You Say It

You can't be happy with a woman who pronounces
both *d*s in Wednesday.
      Sauce for the Goose, 1981, by Peter De Vries

I T IS A formidable controversy, inherent with genuine furore and dilemma, that our pronunciation is deteriorating. Never mind the meaning. Read that first sentence aloud, and see whether you have any doubts or hesitations about how to pronounce and where to stress the eight polysyllabled words in it.

Language purists and reactionaries get more excited about what they consider mispronunciation (i.e. pronunciation different from what they were taught as children) than about almost any other kind of sin or error by the media. Old fogeys complain that they cannot understand what the young are saying any more. A certain amount of old-fashioned snobbery comes into this. Educated Received or Standard British English (i.e. the form spoken by a person born and brought up in one of the Home Counties, educated at one of the established southern universities, and not so pig-headed as to suppose that the way he speaks is the only correct sort of English) is a strong class shibboleth in the United Kingdom. Let us try to sort out what is happening to our pronunciation.

Until recently, the pronunciation of a word took at least fifty years to change, and even longer before the change was accepted by linguistic shellbacks. All language is changing, all the time. But change in pronunciation is the most egregious, because it is the one that we meet most often in the hubbub and twitter of the day. For example, armāda was pronounced to rhyme with 'raider' until about 1880. You still occasionally meet a conscious antiquary of enunciation who pronounces armada that way, but the standard pronunciation has come to rhyme with 'larder' over the past century.

The speed of linguistic change, particularly in pronunciation, has been greatly accelerated by the vast expansion of broadcasting since the Second World War. Before 1939 it was exceptional for a household to own a television set, and middle-class to own a wireless or gramophone. Today a television, video recorder, radio, and music centre are common necessities over most of the world, and the broadcast babble never ceases all round the clock. Accordingly, fashions in pronunciation, as in other things, spread around the global village in the twinkling of an eye or the twitching of an ear. 'Celebrities' with regional, or uneducated, or incorrect pronunciations are imitated by their fans. Since most celebrities come from the United States, American tendencies are accentuated.

But there are older factors than random celebrity-worship at work on our pronunciation. English tends to concentrate the stress and accent on a single syllable, and leave the others to take care of themselves. This is in marked contrast to a language like French, which enunciates and stresses each syllable with beautiful clarity. English uses a practice called the recessive accent, the tendency to get in early and put the stress early in a word. French words like *château, charlatan, nonchalant, garage* and *menu* put at least as much stress and accent on their last syllables as on any other. But as soon as we Brits have borrowed the words, our ancient Germanic pronunciation tendency shifts the stress back to the beginnings of the words, and we start to say shátto, gárridge, shárlatan, and the like.

Working against these tendencies is the difficulty of skipping through a dance of light, unstressed syllables in polysyllabic words, after we have got rid of the big bang on the first syllable. We are taught that the correct pronunciation is to put the stress on the first syllables of words like kílometre, lámentable, fórmidable, láboratory, ádversary, Déuteronomy, and on the second syllable of words like recrímination (a prefix is not normally stressed). But this rapid dance of unstressed syllables after the early stress is difficult to pronounce. So we solve the tongue-twisting problem by dropping a syllable or two (lábratri, gúvment, jóolry, dísplinri); or by introducing a second stress (dísciplínary, Déuterónomy); or by shifting the stress forward again (labóratory). Any of these pronunciations is likely to offend at least half of its auditors, because they belong to a different pronouncing tribe. In the end with some words (like armada) we may reach a temporary consensus on the pronunciation that suits our generation best. But don't count on the support of subsequent generations in this matter.

Even in a single generation, for most words there is a large variety of pronunciations, formed by national, regional, dialectal, educational, and personal differences. It is rash, and possibly offensive, to pontificate about other people's pronunciation. Because of its size and mongrel origins, English naturally admits more varieties of pronunciation than any other tongue since Babel. Pronunciation is a notorious field for the old English wargames of class distinction and social shibboleth: for example, how you pronounce *how* is reckoned (by snobs) a sure divining-rod between U and non-U, to sort the sheep from the goats. Albert Chevalier, the Cockney music hall artist, had a famous song, 'Aitches don't make artists – there ain't no H in Art'. Horatio Bottomley, the rogue British journalist and financier, called to see Lord Cholmondeley, and pronounced the name as it looks when written down.

'Lord *Chumley*, sir,' corrected the butler.

'Oh, all right,' said Bottomly. 'Tell him that Mr Bumley would like to see him.'

It is offensive and rash to pontificate about pronunciation. So, here goes.

There is a lot more public pronunciation around these days, because of that increase in broadcasting, popsongs, and mass tourism. A century ago, most people heard the pronunciation only of their immediate circle of family, friends, neighbours, and villagers. An alien voice even from the neighbouring county was a rarity. Today we all hear a much wider range of regional and class accents. They come into our living room at every hour of the day. In the process, some useful distinctions in pronouncing, which have been established over the years, are being eroded, to the detriment of us all.

For example, there is a useful tendency in English to distinguish between nouns on the one hand, and verbs and adjectives on the other, when they are spelt the same, by pronouncing them differently. A general rule has been established that the noun accents the first syllable, but the verb, and to a lesser extent the adjective, stress the second. Thus, the president and his cónsort. But, do not consórt lubriciously with presidents' cónsorts. She is an expért gardener. But, she is an éxpert (noun) at the names of flowers. We have a cónflict here. But, that headline con-flícts with the text. This is only a rough éstimate. But, I estimáte that the multitude is about five thousand men, besides women and children.

This distinction in pronunciation is a nice one, and it is not fully established with some words, for example, in-cline, construe, excerpt. With words of more than two syllables, such as compliment, practice varies widely; but there is still a useful tendency to put the stress on the first syllable when the word is a noun, and to splash the stress around a bit when the word is a verb or an adjective. This distinction seems to be being widely ignored by broad-casters, and so eroded. Presenters and reporters on the BBC and other broadcasting organizations continually pro-nounce such words as íncrease, éxport, ímport, and ésti-mate always as nouns, with the accent on the first syllables, even when they are using them as verbs. So a handy little marker distinction is being worn away. If you wanted to hoist the black flag of prescriptivism, you could say that this is pure ignorance, and that people who make their living from broadcasting words should take the trouble to pronounce them correctly. Speakers on Radio 3, the British highbrow channel for serious music and talk, often manage to refer to compáct discs. Speakers on pop channels like Radio 2 and 4 almost always pronounce cómpact as though it were a noun.

The tendency of broadcasters to put the emphasis on un-important little words such as prepositions, particularly 'of', and in particular to give heavy emphasis to the little indefi-nite article, saying it as 'ay', may be because this is thought to sound posh; it may be because it lends an air of portentous importance to the pronouncement; it may be just to make a brief pause, while the broadcaster thinks what he is going to say next in the intolerable stream of non-stop verbosity. But it can be irritating, particularly first thing in the morning, as can uneducated pronunciations like 'drawring' and 'the idearof'. Trick stresses such as 'The Prime Minister WILL go to Ireland on Friday', and 'The clouds IN the West WILL move across Britain' are heard every minute of the day and night, and are affecting the way that the rest of us pronounce. Another broadcasters' trick is the loss of t, d, and other dentals before vowels, so that the Tube becomes the Choob, and dukes are jukes. (I have seen the converse effect of the latter when a reviewer wrote of what is known as 'the juke box theory' as 'the duke box theory'.)

Similarly irritating, no doubt, are pronunciations that sound through the shaving soap like 'ladies (latest) forecast', 'speouze (spells)', 'Wayouze (Wales)', 'violing (violin) concerto', 'rape (rate) payers', 'hegwaters (headquarters)', 'I wamp frim (I want for him)', 'crab (crowd) problems', 'lashir (last year)', and the Juke of Kent. Such mispronunciations may be inevitable in the intolerable wrestle to keep talking and sound natural. But they can lead to confusion, where a pronouncing distinction has been evolved to mark the difference between words that look alike but mean different things. For example, there are two suffixes in British English, '-meter' and '-metre', which are derived from the same root, and are pronounced identically, but spelt differently (except in the United States), and have quite different meanings. The '-meter' suffix, almost always preceded by the letter o, means a device for taking measurements: thermometer, barometer, odometer, hydrometer, etc. These words put a stress on the o. The '-metre' suffix refers to a basic unit of length, which in the metric (SI) system may be preceded by a number of prefixes, indicating multiples or submultiples of that unit. These words referring to metric length put a stress on the first syllable of the word. But one of the possible prefixes is kílo-, meaning one thousand times the value, which unfortunately ends in o.

A WORD IN TIME

This leads, by analogy with barómeter and the like, to widespread mispronunciation of kílometre by broadcasters as kilómetre. This sounds as though it should mean a device for measuring 'kils' (whatever they are). No engineer should be in doubt about the correct pronunciation, for he/she should be familiar with the two words 'mícrometre' and 'micrómeter'. The former is the SI unit measuring the millionth part of a metre (or the thousandth part of a millimetre). The latter is a device for measuring very small distances. There is an example of the way in which mispronunciation by professional broadcasters is obfuscating a useful distinction.

Wok can we do about these common mispronunciations? Play music on Radio 3? These broadcasting pronunciations do not always obscure or distort the meaning. But the fashionable chimera, kilómetre, and the loss of the distinction between pronouncing nouns and verbs do, and should accordingly be resisted and corrected by all who care for the huge range of possibilities in English. This is not a recommendation that everybody should speak the Queen's English with an upper-class, south-of-England, prunes-and-prisms, elocution-educated accent, formerly called an Oxford Accent, or, better these days, Received Pronunciation. Let a thousand regional accents flourish. But where we have evolved useful distinctions in pronunciation, and particularly in accent, stress, and emphasis, let those of us who care for English fight to maintain them.

6

SPELLING

Get It Write

Orthography is so absolutely necessary for a man of
letters, or a gentleman, that one false spelling may fix
a ridicule upon him for the rest of his life; and I know
a man of quality who never recovered the ridicule of
having spelled *wholesome* without the *w*.

Lord Chesterfield, letter to his son,
November 19, 1750

LORD CHESTERFIELD, OF course, was a crashing social
and intellectual snob. Peter Sellers once received a
letter from a fan of the *Goon Show* asking for 'a *singed*
photograph of yourself'. Egged on by Harry Secombe,
Sellers took the writer at his spelling. With his cigarette
lighter he burned the edges of one of his publicity photo-
graphs, and sent it off to his fan. A week later the fan
wrote back: 'Thank you very much for the photograph,
but I wonder if I could trouble you for another as this one
is *signed* all round the edge.'

Spelling, formally called orthography in the jargon, is a
minor department of the English language, of far less
importance than grammar, logic, originality, composition,
orthoepy, and the other departments. Shakespeare was a
notoriously erratic speller. He could not even make up his
mind how to spell his own name. The notion that there is
only one correct way to spell an English word was

introduced in the eighteenth century, encouraged by
Johnson's *Dictionary*, and established by the great Victorian
systematizers and pedagogues. It is a notion against which
liberal spirits, often American, tend to rebel. Here is Aug-
ustine Birrell in *Men, Women and Books*: 'Who cares about
spelling? Milton spelt *dog* with two *g*'s. The American
Milton, when he comes, may spell it with three, while all
the world wonders, if he is so minded.' Hoisting the same
black flag of spell-as-you-like, here is Mark Twain in a
speech in Hartford, Connecticut, in May 1875: 'I don't see
any use in spelling a word right, and never did. I mean I
don't see any use in having a uniform and arbitrary way
of spelling words. We might as well make all our clothes
alike and cook all dishes alike.'

English is a notoriously difficult language to spell, because it is so mongrel and mixed, incorporating ways of
representing sounds by letters taken from many languages.
A Romance language such as Italian or French is far easier
to spell, because it comes from a single source (Latin), and
most of its words follow a regular pattern of phonetic
representation. However, bad spelling is the department
of English that most excites the complaints of the gloomy
folk grammarians who have persuaded themselves that
English is going to the dogs, and that the new generation
is not a patch on theirs in its use of English. It is possible
to exaggerate this supposed Golden Age of Spelling a
generation ago, when the gloomy grammarians were at
school. But, in general, we probably were drilled to spell
better than the new generation. For one thing, we did far
less science and other 'new' subjects. For another, spelling
was drilled into us as a gentlemanly or ladylike shibboleth
that Lord Chesterfield would have recognized and ap-
proved of. It is not a new idea that correct spelling is the
sign of a gent, nor is it confined to the British English.
Here is a President of the United States (Thomas Jefferson)
in a chauvinistic letter to his wife Martha: 'Take care
that you never spell a word wrong. Always before you
write a word, consider how it is spelled, and, if you do not

remember it, turn to a dictionary. It produces great praise to a lady to spell well.'

The twinge from being beaten for spelling things wrong still rankles fundamentally in the memory of the British middle classes in frosty weather. Their education would have been broader and better if they had been able to identify, for example, the flowers, whose names they could spell like little orthographic metrognomes. Until recently *The Times* used to spell Monna Lisa *sic*, with a double *nn*, to demonstrate to the world that we knew its original etymology from Madonna. This was an Anglo-Saxon work of supererogation, since the Italians and everybody except the British call the simpering lady 'La Gioconda' anyway. Until recently *The Times* used to spell *connexion* with an *x*, rather than *connection*, to show that we knew it was derived from a Latin noun, *connexio*, rather than from a past participle ending in *-ectus*. *Connexion* is the etymologically correct spelling, and a signpost to the history of the word. It may be too difficult to preserve it, now that a knowledge of Latin is no longer deemed essential for a Western European, whose language and culture are derived from it.

Bad spelling is sloppy, like wearing a tie with egg stains on it, or tights with holes in them. There are worse sins in writing, such as pomposity, or telling lies, or getting things wrong, or being boring. Some of the best creative writers in the United Kingdom and America cannot spell for meringues, as anybody who has had to edit their raw copy can bear witness. Misspelling is a mark of avoidable carelessness. You can avoid it by using a dictionary. It raises the disobliging implication that, if the writer cannot take the trouble to get so small a thing as spelling right, he or she may not be scrupulous about larger matters such as accuracy and truth.

When cacography, or heterography, or idiography, obscures your meaning, it becomes a more serious fault. When *The Times* leader writer wrote that, 'Menen has an opportunity for a determined effort to *martial* Argentina's feuding interest groups', did he mean to write *marshal*, or was it a sinister invocation to Mars, god of the Falklands and other wars? *Barbecue* is derived from the Spanish and Haiitian *barbacoa*, a framework of sticks set upon posts for cooking. The French *barbe à queue* connexion is an absurd conjecture. American jokesters and advertising sign-writers have changed this to BarBQ. The illiterate now write this out in full as *barbeque*, and it has started to appear spelled like this in British newspapers. What happens next? Pronunciation might in due course follow the new spelling, so that we start to speak of *barbecks*. Or we may work our way towards antiQ, pronounced anticue, like Autocue, furniture. Such a change would be a pity, because it would shift the word farther away from its etymological roots. All words do continually and naturally grow away from their roots, to meet the changing semantic needs of the new world.

There is no divine right in our *anticue* spelling, which has evolved over the centuries. The difficulties and perversities of English spelling preserve the history and meaning of words, like fossils. They are a continual source of complaint and satire:
The Beauties of English Orthography, circa 1850:

> A pretty deer is dear to me,
>   A hare with downy hair,
> A hart I love with all my heart,
>   But barely bear a bear.

Or Evelyn Baring in *The Spectator*:

> When the English tongue we speak
> Why is *break* not rhymed with *freak*?
> Will you tell me why it's true
> We say *sew* but likewise *Jew*?

Dear Lord Cromer, the reason is that pronunciations and spellings of English words have diverged, as both have changed over two thousand years. Our spellings are often miles away from the pronunciation of the words. But they have evolved naturally, and retain fossils of the past. It might well be better if the Norman *qu* had not ousted the Anglo-Saxon *cw*, but it did, and is part of the writing of Shakespeare and all our predecessors. Some of the letters in our alphabet do not really pull their full weight: that q, j, k, and thou whoreson zed, thou unnecessary letter, about which Shakespeare himself had some doubts. But our difficult spelling is better than the perverse tyranny of a new phonetic system, because it has evolved naturally. Whose of the many diverse pronunciations is this new phonetic spelling going to reproduce in symbols anyway? Birmingham, Boston Brahmin, Black West Coast, Bombay, Bejun, Brisbane?

But if you want to spell words creatively, as the spirit moves you, go ahead and do it – provided that you do not mind exposing yourself as somebody who cares for none of these things, and does not mind not getting the little bits of language right; provided that you do not mind being sneered at by contemporary Lord Chesterfields and Thomas Jeffersons as uneducated. Great or even good writers may be able to get away with such negligence. But negligence it is.

7

AMERENGLISH SPLITS

Never the Twain

The American language is in a state of flux based on
the survival of the unfittest.
                          Cyril Connolly, *The Sunday Times*, 1966

S ILENCE AT THE back there. Margaret Thatcher, the Prime
  Minister, speaks in 1988: 'Language, you know, matters
very much. It's so much easier always to be speaking in
your own language when you're negotiating. And we
[Great Britain and the United States] have a similar inheritance, a similar democracy. It [our relationship] *is* very close
and it *will* be, because of history, because of language.'
  Well, up to a point, Lady Iron. You could say, if Oscar
Wilde had not said it first, that we have everything in
common with America nowadays, except, of course,
language. Mark Twain declared: 'When I speak my native
tongue in its utmost purity in England, an Englishman
can't understand me at all.' This was an exaggeration when
Twain wrote it, and it is still an exaggeration, but only just,
for some of the stronger dialects and accents of Black
American and Hispanic American. When the Pilgrim
Fathers set sail, they spoke native British English in their
accents of East Anglia or Wessex. As soon as they set
foot in the New World, the languages began naturally to
diverge. They continue to do so.
  At a superficial level Americans and Britons speak the
same language. It is closest in the written language as

published by university presses and other serious publishers. But if you look closer, we speak separate families
of the English language, known in the trade as registers
or dialects. Misunderstandings are inevitable. Let us take
first a little example of shifting grammar and idiom, too
recent to have been recorded in the latest dictionaries.
Have you taken on board yet (as Americans say, and Brits
have started to copy) what is happening in our separate
languages to what the grammarians tiresomely insist on
describing as the monotransitive prepositional verb, 'look
to'? In British English this is starting to be used to mean
something like expect to, seek to, or hope to. As usual the
trendy phrase spawns first in the sports pages and sporting
broadcasts. You will recognize the sort of thing: 'The home
team will be *looking to* get a result against the visitors next
Saturday.' Here is a characteristic example from a piece
called 'Forever on the Move' by Pat McNeill in *New Statesman & Society* of October 8, 1988: 'The reasons for migration
are many and complex, but most people on the move are
looking to improve their living standards or their safety.'

This idiom is quite new, though I have no difficulty in
understanding what is meant by it. You will find it *passim*,
as a password or shibboleth, in pretentious British journalism and political speeches. But the use is not recorded
in the second edition of *The Oxford English Dictionary*,
published in 1989. This gives nine meanings for *look to*. Of
these the two that are closest to the idiom we are looking
for are, first, *look to*, meaning to direct one's expectations to,
to rely on (a person, etc.), *for* something, as in *Ecclesiasticus*
XXXIV, 15 (Authorized Version, 1611): 'Blessed is the soule
of him that feareth the Lord: *to* whom doeth he *looke*?' Here
is another example of this idiom from *Blackwood's Magazine*,
1892: 'I *look to* you to help us.' This is a familiar English
and American idiom, but it is different from our new *look
to* because it is followed by a person or noun phrase, and
not by an infinitive. The other example in *The Oxford English
Dictionary* that comes closest to what we are looking for is
look to meaning to look forward to, to expect, or count

upon. Here are some examples. William Cowper in *Table Talk*, 1782: 'A terrible sagacity informs/The poet's heart, he *looks to* distant storms,/He hears the thunder ere the tempest lowers.' The Duke of Wellington, 1804: 'The French have never ceased to *look to* the re-establishment of their power.' This *look to* is not the new idiom either. *Look to* is followed by a noun or noun phrase, as in the first example; its *to* is a preposition, not an infinitive marker.

  A Comprehensive Grammar of the English Language, 1985, by Randolph Quirk and his colleagues, our most punctilious record of every nuance and twitch of grammar, knows about *look to* followed by a noun, but has not yet heard of *look to* followed by an infinitive. We can conclude that the idiom is brand new in British English. The evidence for its existence is before our eyes and in our ears every day.

  Contrast this with American usage, where *look to looks to* be developing a different grammar and idiom, apart from the old meanings that are common to both our languages. This is from *The Owl Papers*, by Jonathan Evan Maslow (New York, 1983, pp 26–7 – an owl is being mobbed by crows): 'The owl punched stolidly, the skulking crows surrounding it adding an ominous, professional mood to the proceedings. The owl *looked to be* encircled by six cloaked hitmen, already at work in the early dawn, still groggy and fulfilling a contract without enthusiasm.' There is a *look to* followed by an infinitive, not a noun, with its *to* an infinitive marker rather than a preposition. Fine imaginative writing, if you like that sort of thing. But pure American idiom, where *look to* means what the British would say by 'look as if (or though)'. Americans who care about their grammar have told me that they would not use *look to* in this way. But the only examples I have found of the idiom are American. And American English is so vast that it is not in fact a single language, but an ocean of many languages, grammars, and idiolects. The American *look to* where it is natural in British English to say 'look as though' is idiomatic in Cornwall. It is possible that it was taken across the Atlantic by immigrants from the West Country.

But they left no trace of the idiom in written English before they sailed.

Look to is jargon among bellringers. When the ringers are about to start, the person on the treble (which rings first) calls out '*Look to*, scilicet 'to your ropes'. Presumably it means something like: 'Pay attention to your ropes; be ready to ring.' The next call is: 'Trebles going', meaning that the bell is being pulled up to its point of balance. Then comes, 'She's gone', meaning that the bell is swinging downwards. Tintinnabulary jargon is a rich field of English eccentricity. But this *look to* seems to be the old one followed by a noun (your ropes) rather than an infinitive.

We do in a way speak the same languages, Ma Thatcher. But, by Twain and Wilde, they are different. Here is another example of a small grammatical difference between American English and British English. In this case, as so often, American usage is starting to affect British. There's a lot of American idiom *around*, because of television, radio, pop music, and the general feeling on the British side of the Atlantic that American is smart and modern. American idiom seems to be corrupting the useful British distinction between *round* and *around*. This is a pity, because in some contexts it is no longer clear what is meant.

The history of the words is complex, and the distinction has not always been well maintained. But in British English *round* is the normal word, and conveys the notion of revolving and circuitousness. *Around* can be substituted for euphony in a few contexts: *around* and about; all *around* are signs of decay. But in British English it sounds odd (whereas in American English it sounds normal) to say: 'Drinks all *around*': 'I slept the clock *around*.' In American English *around* has become the master word, and it is now beginning to oust *round* in the United Kingdom, causing confusion.

In British English, if you go *round* the town, you take the bypass and so avoid it. If you walk *around* the town, on the other hand, you are not doing a circuit but a Jan Morris and walking all over it. If a British army camps *round* the town, it encircles it. Whereas, if it camps *around* the town, it makes its camp in the vicinity of it. In British English *round* has connotations of a ring, whereas *around* refers to a general area. 'He made a tour of inspection *round* the house, to see where the burglar got in.' On the other hand: 'The children played hide-and-seek in the bushes *around* the house.' Scilicet, the bushes in the neighbourhood but not necessarily encircling the house. 'I went *round* to Mr Meshach's house to return the lawnmower.' But, 'I saw smoke *around* Mrs Abednego's house.'

I was thinking of getting *round* (not *around*) to working out what was happening to this delicate idiom, when a spate of examples of the rising confusion in *The Times* spurred me on. 'Every citizen has a way *around* the proper channels.' Which language was the writer using? If it was English English, he must have meant that the citizen can roam freely within, or in the vicinity of, the proper channels, in order, presumably, to examine them. If he was using American English, he must have meant that the citizen has a way of dodging the proper channels, of getting past them without becoming involved in them. The context strongly implies that the writer was using the American idiom. But it is tiresome for someone used to the English sense of *around* to have to read the sentence twice to extract its meaning. If as a journalist you make a habit of writing sentences that people have to read twice before they get your drift, you are in the wrong business. By this criterion, quite a lot of journalists are in the wrong business most of the time, and all journalists are in the wrong business some of the time.

Here is another example of the same growing muddle, from *The Times* of the same day: 'The mud oozes up *around* the cable to the surface.' To British ears this sounds as though the mud is oozing in the neighbourhood of the cable. American idiom puts the mud all *round* and touching the cable. The context again implies that the American sense was intended. But it is unsettling for British readers to have to swap languages while crossing the stream. It throws them off the meaning. Anything that obscures or diverts meaning, particularly in a style of writing that is meant to be read as fast and with as little attention as journalism, is a self-imposed handicap.

In American English *around* has always been the dominant word, and is a preferable substitute for nearly all senses of *round* and *about*. Because of American dominance in the language (there are five times as many of them speaking it), the American idiom is creeping into British English, muddying the waters. *Around* to mean approximately (*around* 60 per cent; *around* four o'clock) still sounds an Americanism to me. Each man, and woman's idiolect will be different in such judgements. British speakers still prefer to use *round* for the idea of revolving (they danced *round* the tree), and for the idea of circuitousness, or the other side of something (the shop *round* the corner). But they are willing to use *around* as the Americans do for the idea of surrounding (seated *around* the fire) and for 'here and there' (travelling *around*). American and British speakers alike use *about* informally where *almost* would be better in formal writing (I'm *about* ready); for 'concerning' (a book *about* Procopius); for on one's person (I've no money *about* me – most Brits would say 'on me'); and for 'out of bed' (she's already up and *about*).

These are nice matters of idiom and culture; and idiom and culture are constantly changing. The dominant use of *around* used to be as American as English muffins or French toast. But while they are changing, confusion and misunderstanding abound, and *around* and *about*.

8

SPLIT INFINITIVES

Gawd Knows, and 'E Won't Split on a Pal

I'm going to quietly split, man.

David allowed one eye to minimally fall.
Hotel du Lac, winner of the 1984 Booker Prize,
by Anita Brookner

THE ENGLISH DO not care much for grammar, taking the healthily robust view that their language belongs quite as much to them as it does to grammarians, teachers, journalists, politicians, and the rest of the bossy classes. Almost the only grammatical 'rule' the average English person remembers from school is the one about not splitting infinitives. When he thinks he spots one in his newspaper, he writes in with *Schadenfreude* to register his superiority and outrage. This causes grief to the unfortunate listings clerk or literary editor, who has to reply, defending his paper's usage if defensible, and often explaining what a split infinitive is and is not.

The taboo or fetish against splitting infinitives is deeply engrained in the English psyche. It may go back, as so many things do, to our Latin roots, and to Latin grammar, which was treated for centuries as the model for English grammar. In Latin the infinitive is a single word, *amare*, to love. In English it is often two words: the infinitive marker particle *to* followed by the infinitive, to love.

The argument goes: you cannot split a single-word infinitive; therefore, by analogy, you ought not to split a double-word infinitive. In fact, it is not even true that you cannot split a single word. You can. The rhetorical figure is called tmesis, and the classic example of it comes from Ennius. *Saxo cere comminuit brum*: *saxo* with a rock *comminuit* he shattered *cerebrum* his skull. The *cere–brum* or skull is literally shattered in the verse by the insertion in its middle of the verb 'he shattered'. We do the same thing in English: fan-flaming-tastic; hoo-bloody-ray; and if you are a fanatical non-splitter, you can call it tmesis, I told them to darned well listen.

When a verbal phrase is put into the past, or has a modal that does not take the particle *to*, you can put the adverb immediately before the main verb without being accused of splitting by even the most pedantic purist. 'To really understand' is condemned as a split infinitive. 'To have really understood' and 'to be really understood' are certainly not split infinitives. And 'she should seriously consider her position' is OK. 'For me to have suddenly resigned my job' is also perfectly OK. The cleft would be perceived if 'suddenly' came between 'to' and 'have'. Analogy from these acceptable examples makes people say 'for me to suddenly resign my job' and 'she ought to seriously consider her position', in spite of generations of disapproval from stylists and knowalls.

There are contexts in which the only way to attach the adverb to the right verb is by splitting an infinitive. 'It's difficult to really understand the theory of relativity.' 'Really to understand' sounds clumsy, and does not mean the same thing. 'I want you to clearly understand what I am telling you.' 'Clearly to understand' sounds priggishly prunes and prisms, and kowtows to the tyrannical taboo against splitting. 'Her hardest decision was to not allow the children to go to the cinema.' 'Not to allow' suggests that she had a harder decision, which is quite a different matter. 'The Government wants to better equip successful candidates for careers in the information services.' 'Better to equip' is intolerably ugly, and reeks of primitive fetish worship. 'She has tried to consciously stop worrying about her career.' If we write 'she has tried consciously to stop', we don't indicate whether we are referring to a conscious try or a conscious stop.

Quite often splitting your infinitive is the idiomatic way to say what you want. 'Your task is to *really* understand your students' problems.' 'I do try to understand – to *truly* understand.' 'We tended to rather sit back and wait for developments.' 'To even reprimand a member of the staff, it is important to ensure that the agreed procedure is strictly followed.' A subsequent focus or emphasis in a sentence often invites a split infinitive. 'Well, you ought to at least *try*.' 'As soon as you give the word, I'm going to really *hurry*.' 'She would be the last person to even *think* of cheating.' 'He is reluctant to so much as *speak* to her.'

These examples of split infinitives are idiomatic English, used thousands of times every day by educated and grammatical speakers. For emphasis the air hostess announces: 'For your safety and comfort we do ask you *to please stay* in your seats until the "fasten your seatbelts" sign has been switched off.' I should go ahead and split, if there is no other way to exactly and precisely convey your meaning. Confusion or an unnatural jar in your sentence are worse grammatical sins than a split infinitive, which may on occasions not be a sin at all. But because so many pig-headed fanatics have got it into their little heads that splitting infinitives is wrong, splitting offends their ju-ju; and you had better be prepared to write boring letters of defence and justification. The prudent man recasts his sentence to avoid having to write boring letters. But prudence is not the prime virtue in writing.

The grammar of English is based upon the usage of the vast majority, and their usage is usually based on what is the most convenient and euphonious. Therefore the most famous 'split infinitive' of the twentieth century – *Star Trek*'s 'to boldly go' – is perfectly correct: it forms a pair of iambs in a passage of speech dependent for its effect upon its rhythm. Infinitive-splitting happens all the time in the spoken language, because it feels more comfortable and natural to split. Grammatical effort is often needed to avoid splits. In the flow of speech there simply isn't the time to make the necessary syntactical manœuvres.

In any case, there is the matter of our special relationship with the English language. When the British speak to one another, they are at pains to avoid any suggestion of the theatrical and, most particularly, anything that smacks of foreign excitability, such as (in ascending order of distaste) pointing, fainting, shrugging, gesticulating, embracing (horrors!), weeping (worse), and striking the brow with a clenched fist. Body language, like bad breath, is something that one tries not to notice in *other* people – particularly abroad.

The subtler, less blatant alternative favoured in these islands to achieve the same result as body language is to use special linguistic devices of various kinds. For example, the construction of a sentence may be reversed, word order may be changed, focusing words or phrases may be included at salient points, or the utterance may be interrupted so that an aside can be thrown in. Another common emphatic device in spoken English is exclamation: 'Edith! A cuckoo! Really!' We bung in emphasizers all over the syntax in the place of body language.

'Really' is a handy word we have all used for focus and emphasis since our earliest days. 'Mum, I'm *really* hungry.' 'Dad, I *really* hate school/want a Porsche for my birthday.' In the spoken language 'really' is often used as an alternative for 'very' or 'very much'. It is just as likely to pop up in the middle of an infinitive construction as anywhere else, because, used as a qualifier, 'really' always precedes what it is qualifying. The option of tacking it on after an infinitive is not available.

In the science, as opposed to the art, of composing utterances, whether spoken or written, it is useful to test how words function. Consider these two examples.

1. 'I want you to sing loudly.' 'Loudly' is what grammarians call an adverb of manner, answering the question 'How do you want me to sing?' It qualifies the verb, and must follow it. No one would contemplate saying: 'I want you to loudly sing.'

2. 'I want you to really consider my proposal.' Now to test 'really'. What is it? Can you place it after the verb, like 'loudly'? No. Why not? Because it is not *functioning* as an adverb; it is a lexical addition, an importee introduced for emphasis. 'Really' is not a wicked violator of a virgin infinitive, and has no place amidst the pros and cons of infinitive-splitting. So with 'really' we have a new subject of enquiry: when is a split infinitive *not* a split infinitive? If there is such a thing as technical rape, can there not be also such a thing as a technical split infinitive?

R. W. Burchfield, the editor of *The Oxford English Dictionary Supplement*, and as a New Zealander not influenced by English linguistic snobberies, has traced shifting British attitudes to the split infinitive down the centuries. In Old English the problem did not arise, because *to*-infinitives were rare, and in any case such infinitives were inflected as if they were nouns. Infinitives started to be split, with increasing frequency, from the thirteenth to the fifteenth centuries. The split infinitive was avoided by careful writers between about 1500 and 1800. The Oxford lexicographers have found no examples of split infinitives in the works of Spenser, Pope, Dryden, or (remarkably) Shakespeare. From the time of Byron onwards, the split infinitive has reappeared, and has been used with increasing frequency, in spite of the hostility of prescriptive grammarians.

The first major English grammarian to oppose the use of split infinitives was Henry Alford in his usage manual, *The Queen's English* (1864): 'A correspondent states as his own usage, and defends, the insertion of an adverb between the sign of the infinitive mood and the verb. He gives as an instance, *to scientifically illustrate*. But surely this is a practice entirely unknown to English speakers and writers. It seems to me, that we ever regard the *to* of the infinitive as inseparable from its verb. And when we have a choice between two forms of expression, *scientifically to illustrate*, and *to illustrate scientifically*, there seems no good reason for flying in the face of common usage.'

In his *Modern English Usage* (1926) H. W. Fowler took a more liberal and realistic view of ordinary usage: 'We maintain, however, that a real split infinitive, though not desirable in itself, is preferable to either of two things, to real ambiguity, and to patent artificiality. For the first, we will rather write "our object is to further cement trade relations" than, by correcting into "our object is further to cement trade relations", leave it doubtful whether an additional object or additional cementing is the point. And for the second, we take it that such reminders of a tyrannous convention as "in not combining flatly to forbid hostilities" are far more abnormal than the abnormality they evade. We will split infinitives sooner than be ambiguous or artificial.'

Dr C. T. Onions in *An Advanced English Syntax*: 'The split infinitive is becoming more and more frequent, especially

A WORD IN TIME

in newspapers, but it is generally admitted that a constant and unguarded use of it is not to be encouraged; some, indeed, would refuse altogether to recognize it, as being inelegant and un-English. Instances like "For a time, the Merovingians continued to nominally rule" are particularly ugly. On the other hand, it may be said that its occasional use is of advantage in cases where it is desired to avoid ambiguity by indicating in this manner the close connexion of the adverb with the infinitive, and thus prevent its being taken with some other word.'

In *A Comprehensive Grammar of the English Language* (1985), Randolph Quirk and his fellow authors note the old crux, and avoid being bossy: 'The widespread prejudice against split infinitives must not be underestimated, especially with respect to formal writing, and indeed there is no feature of usage on which critical native reaction more frequently focuses. In consequence, it is by no means unusual to detect awkward and unidiomatic usage that clearly results from conscious avoidance: "She was forced *apologetically* to interpose a question at this point." In this last example, avoidance has produced ambiguity, since one cannot tell whether it was "she" who was apologetic, or those who "forced" her.'

Eric Partridge in *The Concise Usage and Abusage* (1954) wrote: 'Avoid the split infinitive wherever possible; but if it is the clearest or most natural construction, use it boldly.' Good writers continue to boldly go into split infinitives, even when they don't have to, because that is the way that they feel like putting it. Kingsley Amis in *Difficulties With Girls* (1988): 'In face of all this Patrick managed *to quite like* him.' Philip Roth in *The Counterlife* (1987): 'A willingness *to not always, in every circumstance, think* the very best of us.' George Steiner in *The Bulletin of American Academic Arts and Sciences* (1987): 'We want *to really start* our argument with one of the principal attacks on the ancient stabilities.' If you must split, do it. Grammar is our servant, not our master, and it is constantly changing to meet our needs. Thurber got it right: 'Word has somehow got around that

- 55 -

the split infinitive is always wrong. That is a piece with
the outworn notion that it is always wrong to strike a
lady.'

9

PUNCTUATION

Full Points for Commas

Language is a labyrinth of paths. You approach from *one* side and know your way about; you approach the same place from another side and no longer know your way about.
Philosophical Investigations, paragraph 203, 1953, by
Ludwig Wittgenstein

W E WRITE TOO fast in the daily press, and elsewhere. Of course we try hard to get things right: accurate, grammatical, logical, arresting, spelled correctly, easily intelligible, grabbing the attention of the commuter on the blessed Circle Line (running, or more accurately crawling, late as usual because of some indecipherable incident at Farringdon), so that she carries on reading in spite of the fact that she is wedged in so tight between alien bodies that her feet touch ground only when the driver cowboys over points. But inevitably we fail sometimes. Before seizing pen to point out some piffling error to the editor, remember that what you have been looking at in a proper paper such as *The Times* consists of as many words as are in four novels of average length, written, subbed, designed, cut to fit exactly into the jigsaw, headlined, printed, and delivered onto your breakfast table in Shetland or Porthcurno in twelve hours flat. It is a small daily miracle.

Writing fast under pressure produces illogicalities. We

know what we mean. But the way we arrange and punctuate the words produces a different effect. For example,
the best newspaper recently published this remarkable
assertion: 'No Chinese dinner is complete without generous measures of Cognac – usually the pricier grades costing
£50 a bottle.' Come, come, sir. There must surely be some
penurious peasants in the remoter corners of that vast
country who cannot be sure of a regular supply of even
the cheaper and nastier grades of Cognac.

Mind you, illogicalities and punctuation misdirections
can happen in works that take decades rather than hours
to produce. Take Nikolaus Pevsner's *Cambridgeshire*, admirable guide to an endearing if chilly county, on the majestic
topic of King's College Chapel: 'The foundation stone of
the chapel was laid on 25 July 1446. It is 289 ft long, 94 ft
high (interior height 80 ft), and 40 ft wide.' Well, I see
what he means. I am aware that Henry VI left us a better
legacy than most monarchs. But, nevertheless, on first,
casual reading, some foundation stone!

Notice the commas and absence of commas in the
Pevsner quotation. Comma, the shortest stop, is the Latin
transliteration of the Greek *komma*, from *koptein* to cut, and
means a cutting, hence a cutting-off, hence a part cut off,
hence a clause or part of a sentence cut off from the rest.
The punctuation mark comma marks such a brief cutting
off. Heavy punctuators would insert a comma after the
month in the first sentence: 'The foundation stone of the
chapel was laid on 25 July, 1446.' If you reversed the month
and the day, I think you would need a comma: 'The
foundation stone was laid on July 25, 1446.' 'July 25 1446'
is a mess of numbers. But the advantage of the military
order of giving dates, '25 July 1446', is that there is no need
for a comma. If a punctuation mark is not pulling its
weight, and adds no guidance in understanding the sentence, cut it out. Now notice the second comma in the
Pevsner citation, before the 'and'. It comes down on one
side in the teasing question of commas in enumeration.
The teasing question is: when you have a list of things, do

you punctuate A, B and C, with the 'and' standing in for and doing the cutting-off job of a comma, or alternatively do you bung in a comma anyway, and write 'A, B, and C'? This may seem a piffling matter in a world that must have more important things to worry about. But just occasionally that comma in lists can make a difference to the sense. Punctuation was made for man, not man for punctuation. We ought to make our conventions help rather than hinder us.

Old-fashioned punctuators were taught by old-fashioned English teachers (and no doubt whacked when they got it wrong, so deeply is the fetish ingrained in their idiosyncrasies) that an 'and' takes the place of a comma. To put a comma before an 'and' was wrong, and maybe a moral failing, if not a sin. I take the liberal, and no doubt wet, view that if your first clause to be linked by 'and' goes on for so long that you need to draw breath, as there, you might as well insert a comma when the clause ends to show your reader that it is safe to breathe. This convention follows the Renaissance style of punctuation, which naturally followed the style of Latin writers, by using punctuation to mark rhythmical, or rhetorical, or dramatic, or elocutionary pauses, or simply pauses for breath. English, being unlike Latin a largely uninflected language, needs its punctuation marks to show the grammar, logic, and carpentry of a sentence. You can read Latin with no punctuation marks: that was the way it was originally written. Without punctuation English becomes an impenetrable jungle.

Ergo, (comma, I think) when two short clauses are linked by an 'and', the comma is otiose. 'A and B'. When two long clauses are linked by 'and', I incline to putting a comma at the end of the first long clause to let the reader know that she or he has come to the end of a section. When more than two clauses or things are listed, I should always put a comma before the final 'and'. A, B, and C. This is to differentiate the items on your list, to keep them in their own pens, and not let them stray into their neighbour's pen. If all the items on the list are similar, the carpentry sticks together even without the final comma. *The Times, The Guardian,* and *The Independent.* Even without a comma before the 'and', we can see what is going on. But, *The Times, The Guardian,* and *The Morning Post and Advertiser,* with the comma signalling to ignorant but careful readers that the last pen contains one rag, not two. They drank coffee, rum, vodka, vintage port, and tea. We need that final comma to show that the 'vintage' applies to 'port', but not 'tea'. Marks & Spencer, Harrods, Truslove & Hanson, Liberty's, and Truefitt & Hill, to keep the assorted London shops and hairdressers in their proper compartments. (Note how the possessive apostrophe is withering away in shop names, because it is one more damned thing for the public to get wrong. And I suspect that twin names for stores are going out of fashion. Debenham has quietly dropped Freebody. But Dickins & Jones, dear old Chickens and Bones, still hang together.)

That is what I think about the comma in enumerations. But punctuation belongs to all of us. It is impossible to devise a watertight system for such a loose language as English. Whatever punctuation you adopt, there are always going to be illogicalities and loopholes in it. Not to put too fine a point on it, if you can devise a more helpful system for those who have to read what you write, go for it. But then stick to it. Consistency is a major virtue with commas, and with other departments of life.

10

APOSTROPHE

Genitive Gravestone

In such names as Regent's Park, Earl's Court, King's
Road, the apostrophe is gradually disappearing: let it
go, for such is the direction taken by usage, which
seldom (? ever) errs in these matters.
Usage and Abusage: A Guide to Good English, 1947, by
Eric Partridge

T HE APOSTROPHE HAS carried on dwindling, since Partridge noticed that it was on the wane. It has vanished
from its proper place in many trade names, shop fascias,
and the titles of newspapers, magazines, and books. A
walk down any high street will reveal strings of false
plurals: Woolworths, Debenhams, Boots, Currys, Ratners,
Barclays Bank, Lloyds Bank, Pickfords Travel, Dillons,
Dixons, and so on. Correct style and punctuation should
be, as it once was, either F. W. Woolworth, or Woolworth's. De-apostrophized trade names include Mothers
Pride bread, Shippams fish paste, Twinings tea, Batchelors
soup, Diners Club. De-apostrophized magazines include
Farmers Weekly, *Writers News*, and *Harpers and Queen*. Every
rail terminus now has its 'Travellers Friend', every town
its 'Citizens Advice Bureau'. The apostrophe is also being
eroded from place names – Kings Cross, Kings Lynn, Earls
Court, St Albans, St Andrews, Bishops Stortford, Lytham
St Annes are becoming standard. In Cambridge, Fenner's
has become Fenners, Parker's Piece is now Parkers Piece,

King's College (according to a notice affixed to the stalls in its chapel) Kings College. W. Heffer's bookshop is now heffers (*sic*).

It is a cliché that greengrocers and other poor punctuators erroneously use the apostrophe to signal a plural, as in APPLE'S and PEAR'S. The most alarming instance I saw of this was at the time of the marriage of the Prince and Princess of Wales, when in Oxford Street I saw an illegal street trader advertising what looked like ROYAL WEDDING – SOUVENIR PENIS. It turned out to be SOUVENIR PEN'S, but that was bad enough.

Why is there this long decline and confusion with the apostrophe? The Thatcherite reply is to say that it is the fault of the schools for not teaching grammar. A more interesting reply is that it is a silly new stylistic trend, stemming from the takeover of our language by idiot computers and other writing machines. Whatever the reason, the apostrophe continues to disappear, or to be misused when it does appear. Should we just let it go, or even give it a push? Usage seldom (ever?) errs in these matters.

To abolish the apostrophe just because people get it wrong would be wet. If it performs a function by signalling a distinct meaning, we should keep it, even though nine out of ten in the population tend to get it wrong. Small marks can make a big difference. Richard Brinsley Sheridan, who was a witty politician as well as a brilliant comic dramatist, was ordered to apologize for insulting a fellow member of Parliament. 'Mr Speaker,' replied Sheridan, 'I said the honorable member was a liar it is true and I am sorry for it. The honorable member may place the punctuation where he pleases.' Tsarina Maria Fëderovna, the Danish wife of Alexander III, was famous for her soft heart. She saved a prisoner from transportation to Siberia by transposing a comma in a warrant signed by her husband. The Tsar had written: 'Pardon impossible, to be sent to Siberia.' The Tsarina shifted the comma so that the warrant read: 'Pardon, impossible to be sent to Siberia.' The prisoner was released.

For such a silly little mark, the apostrophe has many duties. Its name comes by way of late Latin from the Greek *apostrophē* turning away from. As often happens in our mongrel language, the classical roots have produced two words that look the same but are in fact quite different. The older apostrophe, pronounced with four syllables, means in rhetoric a feigned turning away from one's audience to address someone, usually dead. Sterne in *Tristram Shandy*: ' "Best of honest and gallant servants!" – but I have apostrophiz'd thee Trim, once before.'

Our punctuation apostrophe came into English a century later than the rhetorical apostrophe, and is short for the *apostrophos prosōdia* the turning-away accent, that is, a punctuation mark indicating the omission of a sound or a letter. It should correctly be pronounced as three syllables, 'apostroph', in English as it is in French, but, as *The Oxford English Dictionary* observes sharply, 'it has been ignorantly confused' with the older, rhetorical apostrophe.

The apostrophe floating above the line is a sign that something is missing, for example in a contraction: can't, don't, isn't, we're, she'll, it's (it is or it has), there's (there is or there has), won't, o'clock (of the clock), the '90s (the 1990s), shan't, they've. The omission can be anywhere in the word or words, beginning, middle or end. Beginning: ''Fraid I cannot make it tonight.' Middle: 'The man is a complete ne'er-do-well.' End: 'I'm jus' a bit slosh'.' Without the apostrophe to mark the omission, some of these contractions are liable to be misunderstood, for example, we'll, she'll, and won't.

Another common use of the apostrophe is to mark the plurals of letters, numbers, symbols, or words. Her name contains two l's and her telephone number four 7's. That all happened in the 1960's. Our staff includes two Ph.D.'s, six M.A.'s, two J.P.'s, and, oddly enough, two former M.P.'s. The apostrophe is illogical here, because it marks no omission, but merely links the 's' to symbols that do not have a natural plural.

I should abolish the apostrophe in these odd plurals.

Schools are now emphasizing the three Rs once again. Our staff room includes six DPhils, two PhDs, four MAs, and, oddly enough, five former MPs. Modern punctuation is getting rid of dots and spots where they are not necessary for understanding the meaning. The 1980s were an improvement on the 1970s in some ways. There are too many *if*s and not enough *but*s in that sentence. The word I am thinking of has three ls and two ms.

Unfortunately there are some sentences in which we need the apostrophe to signal that this is a plural and not something different. You must cross all the t's and dot all the i's. The class includes two Louis's and four Lewises: we cannot write Louises, for fear of making a sex change. He walked 500 li's or Chinese miles: here I would settle for 'lis' and work out for myself that a singular Chinese mile is a li. In such exceptional sentences we may need an apostrophe to indicate that this is a plural and not something else. I would go the whole hog, and dot the is. But if you must dot the i's, that is not a good reason for introducing the apostrophe generally to mark plurals. In this use it is illogical, because it marks no omission or turning away. No system of punctuation or grammar can be completely logical. So let us be as logical as we can by writing 1990s, three xs, ifs and buts, BAs and MAs, and reserving the apostrophe signalling a plural for oddities such as i's and t's, Louis's, and folio's, where in fact it is logical, because it marks a missing e from the old plural folioes.

It is when we come to the apostrophe marking genitives or possessives that we find ourselves in overgrown thickets of illogicality and exceptions. English was originally a heavily inflected language, in which the genitive of fox was foxes, and Jameses was the way to say and write 'of James'. The apostrophe was introduced to do its job of marking an omission, fox's, James's. It was gradually extended to all possessives, even those where e had not previously been written for the genitives, as in man's, children's, conscience' sake. According to *The Oxford Eng-*

lish Dictionary this was not yet established in 1725. But memory of the old genitive has faded. The apostrophe was left stranded marking a genitive and an omission that everybody had forgotten.

The genitive causes peculiar trouble in English. At the same time as the old inflected genitive with *e* was being elided and apostrophed away, a new way of expressing the possessive was being introduced in the sixteenth century. The English started to say 'John his book'. This was soon pronounced 'Johns book', and written 'John's book' to mark with apostrophe the elision that had been turned away. This was soon extended to Mary's book, a gender-bending extension to 'Mary his book'. The English cannot bear much logic in their grammar, at least not in the genitive case. What we are left with today, washed up upon this bank and shoal of time after more than ten centuries of grammatical change, is a shipwreck. If we had a linguistic dictator, a Dr Zamenhof to lay down tidy rules for our possessives, he would not start from here. But here is where we are.

An apostrophe followed by s, 's, signals a genitive alias a possessive, originally and strictly referring to people or living creatures, to periods of time (today's paper), and to certain idiomatic phrases (out of harm's way). Loosely and journalistically this has been extended to inanimate objects: London's traffic, the car's exhaust. This applies to all the types of genitive into which careful grammarians subdivide the case. Possessive genitive: Mrs Stevenson's knickers = Mrs Stevenson has some knickers. Subjective genitive: Othello's jealousy = Othello is jealous. Objective genitive: Banquo's murder = somebody murdered Banquo, I wonder who? Genitive of origin: Macbeth's letter = Macbeth wrote a letter. Descriptive genitive: a women's college = a college for women. Genitive of measure: twenty years' absence = his absence lasted for twenty years. Genitive of attribute: the defector's cowardice = the defector was cowardly. Partitive genitive: the baby's eyes = the baby has (brown) eyes. This rule applies even when the word to be put in the genitive ends in an s, making one hiss sibilants like a serpent. The boss's daughter. Morris's prejudices = the prejudices held by Morris.

When we come to plurals, the general rule is that if the plural does not end in s, its genitive is made by adding 's: Women's rights, Frenchmen's accents, children's toys, wolves in sheep's clothing, people's votes, the police's actions, mice's titbits, geese's ganders, the clergy's opinions. If the plural already ends in s, its possessive case is made by adding just an apostrophe on its own, avoiding the double sibilant in speech and writing. Our parents' traditions, the Thatchers' fans. This convention shows in writing that we have in mind more than one parent or Thatcher, rather than our parent's traditions or Thatcher's fans. In the spoken word you may need to recast the sentence if you are determined to indicate that you mean a plural rather than a singular.

And now we come, with a sigh, to the exceptions. As the legendary English headmaster (of Shrewsbury School if he existed) is said to have told his class: 'Boys, this term you are to have the privilege of reading the *Oedipus Coloneus* of Sophocles, a veritable treasure-house of grammatical peculiarities.' Most of the English grammatical pecularities with the genitive are caused by words ending with s or a double s sound, and the natural wish to avoid a sibilance of snakes or genitival cacophony.

There is a growing tendency, for the sake of conformity, to make the genitives of names already ending in s in the same way as other names, by adding 's. Jones's house, Dickens's novels, Keats's poetry. A generation ago these names ending in s made their genitives by the apostrophe on its own and a single iz sound at the end: Jones' house, Keats' poetry. The tide seems to be running strongly for a ziz sound at the end, written with an 's: Burns's poetry, Morris's designs.

There are exceptions with names from the Bible and the classics, which have established themselves in the national idiom with a sole apostrophe to indicate the possessive, as with Achilles' heel and Jesus' parables. It is still idiomatic to say and write Xerxes' army, Moses' basket, Socrates' trial, Euripides' irony, Aristophanes' characters, Thucydides' history, Herodotus' travels, Croesus' wealth. But even here, even with names ending with a double s sound such as Odysseus and Moses, analogy is pulling to make them conform with less ancient names. It has become idiomatic to write princess's and pronounce it with the ugly triple s, which cannot be distinguished from the genitive plural, princesses'. It may become natural to say and write Jesus's disciples, Moses's travels. In the tug-of-war between tradition and analogy, analogy usually wins, as it should in a language that is continually renewing itself.

There is a small class of nouns, not proper names, that make a possessive followed by 'sake': for goodness', conscience', appearance', old times' sake. These phrases have a musty flavour. If we carry on using them, I predict that they will conform to the general pattern by taking an 's, in spite of the rebarbative hiss. For conscience's sake, for appearance's sake. Where this sounds so silly that it is impossible, they will quietly drop the apostrophe: for goodness sake, for old times sake.

There are problems of grammar and logic with compound or noun phrases. We have solved the problem by bunging an 's at the end of the phrase, as though it was a single word. The Duke of York's grin, the University of Newcastle's classics department, my son-in-law's parents, the director of the museum's office, the editor of *The Times*'s opinion, the captain of the team's vote of thanks. This informal 's genitive is starting to appear with less compact modifiers: the girl at the front's smile; the man sitting in the armchair's hat (which is absurd, as soon as you think about it).

With group genitives, only the last member of the group takes the apostrophe. William and Mary's reign; King Charles the First of England's decapitation; Philip, Anne, and Anthony's uncle. Where separate possessions or other attributes are concerned, each noun of the group must be marked in the genitive: rebellion and disorder characterized both William the Conqueror's and Mary Tudor's reigns; Philip's, Anne's, and Anthony's uncles (these were different uncles) all came to the prize-giving.

With pronouns we always use the possessive. Your and my appointment. Your and my appointments (different ones). Isabel's and your appointment (mutual). Your and Isabel's appointments (different). Her, your, and my appointment (one appointment for all three of us). Her, your, and my appointments (different appointments).

Genitives can get in a tangle with strings of nouns in apposition. Here is a crux from *The Times*. 'The Prince of Wales's (later Edward VII) passion for the turf began about 1886.' It is rum to add the 's to the Prince of Wales, but to deny it to Edward VII. But it would be rum to add it to Edward VII's, because it was the Prince of Wales, not his passion, that later became Edward VII. I should recast your way out of the bramble bush: 'The passion for the turf shown by the Prince of Wales (later Edward VII).'

The genitive noun can refer to a place, that is taken as understood. 'We'll see you at Peter's.' 'I'm going to the hairdresser's.' With big business names there is a laudable modern tendency to drop the apostrophe as useless. When the founder was a current celebrity, it was natural to say: 'We are going to shop at Woolworth's,' referring to F. W. Woolworth himself. A stuffy alternative was to say: 'We are going to shop at Woolworth.' It is now becoming idiomatic to write: 'We are going to shop at Woolworths.'

Let us get rid of the apostrophe where it serves no purpose other than to mark the grave of a forgotten genitive. Let us use the little comma in the air only to mark a significant omission, or to make a distinction that cannot be made otherwise. These exhortations are superfluous. The apostrophe is fading away as we speak. We are going to have to invent other ways of distinguishing between cant and can't, is and i's, princess's and princesses'.

11

GASPERS AND SCREECHERS

Off With Their Heads!

Ethelberta breathed a sort of exclamation, not right
out, but stealthily, like a parson's damn.
The Hand of Ethelberta, 1875, chapter 26,
by Thomas Hardy

L ET US SEE if we can get rid of the exclamation mark. It
is a silly looking thing, and misused almost as much as
the apostrophe in greengrocers' shops. It is easily confused
with the single inverted comma and other stops, particularly in fax, print-out, and VDU screen. A prevalence of
gasp-marks is the mark of a naïve or flashy writer, as
anybody who has to read a bundle of children's essays
will discover. If you have to signpost your jokes and
clevernesses with a gasper to draw attention to them, they
can't be very good jokes. A deadpan presentation of such
things, without punctuation to label them, is more effective. Occam's razor should be applied to grammar as well
as to metaphysics. *Puncta non sunt multiplicanda*. If a punctuation mark serves no necessary purpose, commit it then
to the flames, for it can contain nothing but sophistry and
confusion.

Most of our punctuation marks were invented by Aldus
Manutius (1449–1515), the Venetian scholar, printer, and
publisher. He was a founding father of the Renaissance,

and started an academy at Venice for the study of Greek and Latin. He began editing and printing grammars and classical texts (many for the first time) on his Aldine Press, and introduced punctuation marks to help the reader. Before Aldo Manuzio, to give him his Italian name, punctuation had been virtually confined to the period or full stop, and (in some countries) the question mark. Before that, punctuation was unknown, which makes it necessary to keep one's wits about one, and one's foot on the brake for an emergency stop, when reading ancient texts and inscriptions. The invention of printing made possible a standard system of punctuation marks to guide the reader through the text, like road and traffic signs for the driver. The new forms of photocomposition and mechanical writing may make some of the old punctuation marks pointless and confusing, and on the other hand may introduce other and more helpful marks.

The reason for the shape of the exclamation mark, gasper or screecher, is lost in the dawn mists of the Renaissance. The best guess is that it represents the Greek and Latin *Io*, pronounced as in the middle syllables of 'roll me over', a more or less ritual exclamation uttered under the stress of strong emotion, and invoking a god or divine power. '*Io*' is the shout that followers of Bacchus make when whipping themselves up into an alcoholic frenzy. When the villain gets his comeuppance in a Greek tragedy, the heroine may well utter a gloating *Io* or two. The theory is that the first punctuators took the Latin *Io*, set the I over the o, and diminished the o to a dot. It is an apt theory, because *Io* is an exclamation of joy or triumph.

Over the years punctilious grammarians and printers have codified the use of the gasper systematically into its departments. Let us go through the departments and see whether the exclamation mark is necessary. Is it earning its place on the page?

1. Grammarians recommend a gasper after certain interjections, such as Hi! and Oh! It is not necessary there. Hey. See.

2. Words or phrases used in interjections take gaspers.
Good grief! Cripes! The gasper is not essential to understanding the meaning in such words and phrases. Archons
and archimandrites of Athens. Look you.
3. The gasper is recommended by the punctilious for sentences introduced by the exclamatory 'how' or 'what'. How
I love you! What a difference it makes! What a marvellous
performance that was! What big teeth you have, Grandmother! I do not think we are going to stumble over such
sentences without a gasper to signal what is going on.
What a daft idea.
4. Wishes or curses take an exclamation mark. Long live
the Queen! Damn your eyes! Are such exclamation marks
necessary? Heaven help us. Damn the spots. They are not.
5. Urgent warnings or alarm calls. Help! Look out! The
gasper is an emphasizer here. But is it necessary? When
the drowning man shouts 'Help', we do not wait for the
exclamation mark before diving in to the rescue.
6. Peremptory commands, often without a verb. Fire!
Hands up! Attention! Not a word! When passed the slip
of paper with 'Hands up' on it, do you get them up any
slower because the illiterate gangster has forgotten the
exclamation mark?
7. Exclamatory or rhetorical questions. Isn't she fat! Wasn't
that a terrible meal! The exclamation mark here is a signal
that this is not a question expecting a reasoned reply. If you
punctuated such questions with a question mark instead of
a gasper, I suppose real dumbos might misunderstand,
and start giving you an answer. This gives us a clue to the
fact that both the question mark and the exclamation mark
are rhetorical and elocutionary signals rather than front-
line punctuation marks. They indicate a tone of voice as
well as a break in the logic of the grammar.
8. Expressions of surprise, introduced by 'To think that'
or (more formally) merely 'That'. To think that you might
have won a television satellite dish! That I should live to
hear such words from my own daughter! I do not see that
the gaspers add anything essential to such exclamations.

The meaning is just as clear without them. Look. To think that you might have been killed too.

9. Wishes proper take gaspers. Blast your eyes! May we live to see it! Are these gaspers strictly necessary? If they are not, may they cease to clutter my VDU screen.

10. Ellipses and inversions due to strong emotion take gaspers. Not another word! That it should have come to this! Pop goes the weasel! Essential gaspers? Of course not.

11. Apostrophes, when addressing somebody or other. You putrefying rotter! You darling man! Will you misunderstand what is being said if the exclamation marks are removed?

12. Negative expressions of surprise, introduced by 'well, if' or 'why, if'. Well, if it isn't the pirate king himself! Why, if it isn't my old chum Jezebel! Is your gasper essential here?

13. Wishes introduced by 'if'. If only you had told me! If I could just explain! I do not see the necessity for the gaspers here. If they are not necessary, if they are not pulling their weight on the page (or indeed pulling a nanomilliscruple of weight), send for Occam.

14. Wishes or curses introduced by 'may'. May you live in interesting times! May all your troubles be little ones! May all your putts tremble at the lip of the hole and roll on ten feet past it! What do the gaspers add that is not already evident from the semantics?

15. Exclamation marks are used as a signal that there is something (scorn, disgust, sarcasm, a joke, a comment) hidden in the tone of the sentence that is not evident and would not be noticed in the words taken by themselves. You thought it didn't matter! He learnt at last that the murderee was – himself! He eats peas off his knife! This category is the only one out of the categories measureless to man into which modern grammarians divide things in which the gasper seems to be pulling its weight. It is announcing: 'Look out, there is more in these words than meets the eye at first glimpse.'

Such sentences are rare, and almost always report speech. The gasper is performing its one useful role as a rhetorical or elocutionary warning signal. When you are reading aloud to someone, the gasper can do worthy work to warn the reader: 'This is a joke (or a sarcasm, or a bloodcurdling threat), so put on your ogre's voice.' The trouble with this is that, since it comes at the end of the sentence it is marking, it may come too late to warn the reader, who then has to go back to the beginning and start again. Because gaspers are retrospective, one realizes that the thought or voice has to be modulated only when it is too late. The simple Spanish convention of putting an inverted exclamation or question mark at the beginning of the phrase or sentence makes things much easier. ¡Would that the excellent Spanish practice could be adopted here! ¿Surely readers of English would get the hang of things quicker this way? Well, up to a point, Professor Copper. It is yet another nasty little squiggle and dot on the keyboard and the screen. I doubt whether it adds enough to our understanding to make worthwhile the additional mark, and the additional possibility of error.

In private and informal writing some people make dashing use of the gasper. When Aunt Lettice writes from Cape Town: 'I nearly trod on a *boomslang* yesterday in the garden!! I was absolutely petrified!!!!' we can see her mouth as a great O and her eyes popping out with alarm and excitement. The gasper suits Lettice's style and idiolect. But in formal writing, we are well advised to use the exclamation mark sparingly, and never to use repeated exclamation marks or combinations of exclamation and question marks. Abolish the gawky brutes, I say. There are less crude ways of conveying your meaning.

12

HYPHENS AND ACCENTS

Out, Out Damned Dashes

Even where the sense is perfectly clear, a sentence may be deprived of half its force – its spirit – its point – by improper punctuation. For the want of merely a comma, it often occurs that an axiom appears a para-dox, or that a sarcasm is converted into a sermonoid.

Marginalia, 1844–49, by Edgar Allan Poe

THE BRITISH LABOUR Party has accepted that Britain should aim at a 'nuclear weapon-free world' by the year 2000. So it was reported in the first leader of *The Times*, and so it must be true. I just hope that the hyphen belonged to the Labour Party, and not *The Times*. Hyphenated that way, the phrase means (if it means anything at all) a world that is (a) nuclear and (b) free from all weapons. This would be a rum aim. Here is another example of the same hyphen confusion from *The Times* leader columns: 'The anti-property developer fury . . .' This seems to mean the fury of the developers of anti-property, whatever that may be. Something like anti-matter, would you say? A superfluous hair-remover can logically only mean a hair-remover that nobody wants. Where you put the hyphen or hyphens can produce several meanings from a phrase like 'a dirty French novel reading bishop'. Such apparently trivial jots and tittles of punctuation can make a big difference to the sense, as Edgar Allan noticed in the quotation at the head of this chapterette. The British Unitarian Conference was debating whether their ministers should adopt clerical garb, when one member leapt to his feet, and shouted fervently: 'I will wear no clothes to distinguish me from my fellow-men.' Unfortunately the newspaper reports inserted a comma after 'clothes'.

But those damned little dashes cause more trouble than they are worth. Sir Winston Churchill wrote to Sir Edward Marsh, the long-suffering civil servant who corrected the proofs of his literary writings: 'I am in revolt about your hyphens. One must regard the hyphen as a blemish to be avoided wherever possible.' Churchill's instinct with composite words was to run them together (crossword, blackcap) or leave them apart (post office, motor car), except when nature revolts. Nature revolts at different stages for each of us. Americans are happy with coworker. Brits feel nervous about that cow. We write co-op, because of sensitivity for chickens, and in a vain attempt to differentiate between modern pronunciations of 'co-operate' and 'corporate'. We retain a hyphen in de-ice, though there is really no reason why deice should look odder on the page than deist.

As often, Churchill's instinct was sound. Hyphens *non sunt multiplicanda*. We should get rid of the little brutes wherever we can. I would abolish them in many cases, and write, 'anti property developer', 'nuclear weapon free

A WORD IN TIME

world'. But you would run into ambiguity that way too.

Since the hyphen is going to survive for a few years yet, here is a rule to avoid the sort of confusion we have been discussing: watch out for the consequential second hyphen. A first hyphen may necessitate a second hyphen between two words that are not normally hyphenated. For example, ex meaning formerly or *quondam* is normally hyphenated to avoid confusion in some cases with the common prefix ex meaning out of. But if we write, 'Ex-Prime Minister', we suggest subliminally a Minister who is past her prime; which would be tactless. So, if we want to phrase it that way, we should write, 'Ex-Prime-Minister', even though the two legs of even female Prime Ministers are not usually hyphenated. You could avoid the trouble by writing 'former Prime Minister', or even 'ex Prime Minister'. In the same way 'pre-First War' suggests a war even before Cain slugged Abel. It has to be 'pre-First-War'. The first hyphen cries out for a second hyphen even between two words that are not naturally hyphenated. You could avoid the ugliness by recasting the sentence with one of the forgotten soldiers of journalese, a preposition: before the First War.

So, to get its punctuation if not its politics right, the Labour Party should be aiming at 'a nuclear-weapon-free' world. Nuclear weapons are normally unhyphenated. But, because you are sticking on a -free with a hyphen, you must look out for the consequential second hyphen, and link nuclear to weapon with an unaccustomed hyphen, so that the hyphenated -free passes like electricity to both elements of the phrase. Personally, I should evade the nonsense by remembering my prepositions, and writing, 'a world free from/of nuclear weapons'. Unfortunately these strings of nouns and adjectives without prepositions sound more sophisticated and professional to modern idiom. So much the worse for modern idiom. Similarly with 'anti-property developer fury'. If that is the way you are determined to write the phrase, the hyphen after anti- means that you must introduce a second hyphen to tie together both halves of the thing you are anti-: anti-property-developer fury. Why not remember your prepositions, and recast the phrase, 'fury against property developers'? Because to the idiom of some of the chattering and scribbling classes, the latter sounds naïve and un-sophisticated.

In radical or exasperated moments, I am inclined to get rid of those little dashes by treating ex and anti and pre and suchlike as self-sufficient prepositions, and writing, 'anti property developer'. But this is a bit radical for best modern grammar, and it also produces amphibologies and double entendre. An anti property developer could be a developer who was against property. A superfluous hair-remover must become a superfluous-hair-remover if you are going to hyphenate. What's wrong with depila-tory?

Unfortunately, the programme to abolish the hyphen also leads us at once into brambles of confusion. If you remove the hyphens from the following sentences, you alter the sense. We were surprised to come across a man-eating lion. Those are their long-dead relatives. Can I have a light-blue dress? Do you have any cheap baby-food? Near the castle is a large estate reserved for shooting-guests. The author of the style-book (oops) of the Oxford Univer-sity Press of New York declares: 'If you take hyphens seriously you will surely go mad.' You should not take hyphens seriously. A watch's second-hand is not, in fact, its second hand; it is its third hand (though it may also be a minute hand). It is the minute-hand that is the second hand. This information may be used by you at secondhand.

Even in so small a matter as hyphens, modern tech-nology is affecting the language and our pronunciation. Newsreaders on television and radio tend to read from printouts (something like ticket touts?) or Autocues words in block capitals and without hyphens. Consequently when he or she bumps into one of these fashionable strings of words such as FIVE YEAR PLAN or NORTH SEA OIL, he stresses the first word in the chain, e.g. FIVE year plan,

NORTH sea oil, instead of putting a level stress on the attributives and slightly raising the voice on the final noun, as we do in normal speech. A hyphen between FIVE-YEAR and the capitals in North Sea are tiny but helpful signposts to reading.

Computers have introduced a surrealist madness into our hyphenation in where they break words at the end of lines. Although a clever beast, your computer can do only what it is instructed to do by a superior (i.e. human) intelligence. It is at home when it meets a word that it has met before and been programmed to break in the right place. When it meets a new word, it goes berserk, producing this small sample from my menagerie of recently hyphenated *bêtes noires*: the-ories, leg-end, manslaughter, the-rapist, brains-canner, nosep-rint, should-er, bamboo-zle, linger-ie, condom-inium.

There is a superfluity of little hyphens in English, especially when written by a computer; but at least there are no accents, thank Hengist and Horsa. Our rude forefathers managed to write down all the sounds they wanted to make with an alphabet that ended up with twenty-six letters, without any extraneous diacritical marks.

The only diacritic used on English words is the diaeresis, and this occurs on words that look pretty foreign to me, such as Noël and naïve. But how about Brontë? The Reverend Patrick Prunty has much to answer for if he introduced accents into English orthography.

Less efficient languages, such as Arabic, Finnish, Hungarian, and Hebrew, scatter diacritics above and below their words like Christmas decorations. I am alarmed by the proliferation of little circles, some of them blacked out like half moons, that seem necessary in the writing of Burmese. My trusty Atex word processor and computer at the word laboratory can produce more accents than I would care to shake a finger at, including a thing like an inverted circumflex that it calls an upvee – charmingly literal little machine.

I associate the upvee with Czech. It is the mark that

prevents Mr Dvořák being pronounced Dvorak. Accents tend to have names in their country of origin – viz. umlaut, circumflex, and tilde. So I asked a Czech what he called the upvee. *Haček*, he replied. 'Bless you,' I thought. *Haček* means a hook, and is a perfectly good name for the accent. But I suspect that upvee will stick because of the surreally literal mind of the computer.

Accents are one more damned thing to remember. It was an ugly shock, having become proficient at ancient Greek unseens, proses, iambics, and Homeric hexameters, to discover that we still had to learn accents. Greeks of the golden age never used the things. They were introduced by the grammarian, Aristophanes of Byzantium, circa 260 BC, in order to facilitate the correct reading of Homer by people for whom the language had moved on. In the same way, it was a reverse ugly shock when teaching myself Pitman's shorthand, having painstakingly learned the dots and dashes that indicate long and short vowels, to discover that the proficient shorthand-taker only learns the little brutes to leave them out, when he can manage without them. Latin, being a manly language, has no truck with the swine.

Even though English is free from the undergrowth and lianas of accents, that does not mean that we are completely excused them. When we introduce foreign words into English, we may have to retain any accents they have, if we are to make sense. The tabloid newspapers regularly make nonsense by omitting accents from foreign words as though they are unpatriotic and elitist marks. For example, in those exciting yarns about a 'killer bug' in supermarkets, the *Daily Shriek* bellows over half its front page in two lines of about 1000-point, a size undreamed of in the philosophy of a sober Books Page:

DONT EAT
THE PATE

They did not even manage the apostrophe in DON'T; but that was not misleading. DONT EAT THE PATE suggested at first glance that this was a story about cannibalism (along with incest, bonking, and creatures from outer space, a favourite topic in such bog papers), or at any rate about potted heid in darkest Ayrshire. The omission of the accents from pâté, even in English, even in capitals three inches high, was potentially misleading. And that is the sin against the word.

The French themselves tend not to put accents on capital letters; and the more excitable French newspapers certainly leave them off headlines. This too can lead to confusion. When the affair between Princess Margaret and Peter Townsend was finally and unhappily resolved, a Paris newspaper gave the headline in letters three inches high: PRINCESS MARGARET RENONCE PETER. Parisians automatically supplied an accent to make it read: 'Princess Margaret renonce péter'. This translates as: PRINCESS MARGARET GIVES UP FARTING. It did much to seal the *entente cordiale*.

Let us make ourselves some sensible rules about accents in English. We ought to give the accents in German, French, Spanish, Italian, and Ancient Greek words, because the natives do, and because the accents are useful signposts to the pronunciation and history of the words. Swedish and Burmese can look after their accents for themselves. If you find yourself writing such languages in an English publication, it is probably a learned work, and so you will need to put the accents in anyway.

However, foreign words that have taken out English nationality should drop their accents, because there are no accents in English, in the same way that foreigners who have become naturalized citizens of the United Kingdom are expected to conform to British laws. So we write 'depot', 'menage', 'regime', and 'hotel' without their native accents. The original circumflex on hôtel is of no use as a guide to its pronunciation in English, and its indication that the word is descended from 'hostel' and related to 'host', though interesting, is unnecessary in everyday contexts.

However, where the accent makes a difference to the way that the word ought to be pronounced in English, we should keep it, even when the word is naturalized, and even on capital letters. Thus, we should write cliché, soupçon, façade, café, and communiqué. Otherwise roaring John Bulls, led by the lager louts of the tabloid press, will start people pronouncing the words in a Brit way, quite different from their roots. They are already starting so to do, with cayf or caff, and payt, not entirely as a joke, to demonstrate that they are good little Englanders who have no truck with posh foreign ways. And if we put on one of a word's native accents to indicate pronunciation, we might as well put them all on, or we shall produce a deformed monster of a word, a chimera with the head of a lion, the body of a goat, and the tail of a cedilla. So write pâté, mêlée, émigré, and protégé. Put them on capitals and headlines, otherwise you will end up with PATE all over your front page. These few precepts in thy memory look thou charácter. You can then forget about accents in English.

13

PLURAL PUZZLES

Geniuses or Genii?

Our modern grammars have done much more harm than good. The authors have labored to prove what is obviously absurd, viz., that our language is not made right; and in pursuance of this idea, have tried to make it over again, and persuade the English to speak by Latin rules, or by arbitrary rules of their own.

Dissertations on the English Language, preface, 1789, by
Noah Webster

PLURALS IN ENGLISH are easy. You just add an s. Well, up to a point. When irregular plurals meet Latin plurals, then comes the tug-of-war. Greek, Latin, French, and other foreign nouns inflect their plurals in very un-English ways. When they first arrive in English as new immigrants, they may bring their irregular plurals with them, to enable the English speakers using them to show off their polyglot versatility. But once these foreign words have become naturalized, so that they no longer need to be written in italics in English texts, they tend to conform to the English plural by simply adding an s at the end. Alas, not all of them do so. As with all grammar, consensus rules, and the consensus is confused and constantly changing.

The change in English grammar that most gets up the noses of the learned and scholarly classes is the disregard of Latin plurals. One of the baleful effects of dropping classics from the core curriculum of British education is that we are at sixes and sevens with our English plurals. For example, *data* and *media* are in the process of becoming singulars. In Latin *datum* is the singular, 'the having been given thing', and *data* the plural. Until recently *data*, being a comparatively recent naturalized English word, was constructed as in Latin as a plural. 'Many of these *data* are inconclusive.' But it is now often constructed as a singular, especially in scientific writing. 'Much of this *data* is inconclusive.' To complicate matters, the regular English plural *datums* is used as a reference term in surveying. You can explain the change by pointing out that computers, in particular, deal with such uncountable trillions of *data* that the word is becoming an aggregate singular like other uncountable stuff such as sugar and sand. In a similar way *media* (the Latin plural of *medium*), as a holdall word to include newspapers and radio and television and magazines and all the other news *media*, is sometimes treated as an aggregate singular in English, and has even been given a regular English plural, *medias*. 'The *media* is characteristically wrong about this.' 'All the *medias* are wrong about this.' Both these uses are widely condemned, especially the second.

This is not a new process in English. *Stamina* and *agenda* are both Latin plurals, and when they first came into English were treated as plurals. *Stamen* in Latin means the vertical thread or warp in a loom, and there are frequent classical references to the *stamina* or threads spun by the Fates. In English *stamina* meant the congenital vital capacities of a person or an animal, as when Boswell wrote of Johnson: 'He said it was the bad *stamina* of the mind, which, like those of the body, were never rectified.' Similarly *agenda* in Latin is the plural of *agendum*, the gerundive of *agere* to do: the things to be done. It was originally treated as a plural in English: 'Notwithstanding all that has been done, there still remain many *agenda*.' It has now become completely naturalized as an English singular with a regular English plural: 'This Conference protests against the action of the Executive in printing Supplementary *Agendas* for Conference.' *Opera* looks like one of these Latin plurals that have been converted into singulars by English, but the probability is that it is a colloquial feminine singular rather than the Latin plural of *opus* a work. It would sound pedantic and wrong to treat *stamina* and *agenda* as plurals in English today.

English is English, and one of the advantages of its notorious laxity and flexibility is that we can make what we want of our plurals, and we usually do. Often we invent an English plural by bunging an s on the end for popular writing, and keep an alternative 'correct' classical plural for formal or scientific writing. Thus, *formulas* for general writing, but *formulae* if you are dealing with mathematics or linguistics. *Antennas* in general writing or electronics, but *antennae* in biology. *Stigmata* in ecclesiastical, botanical, and medical contexts; but *stigmas* in the figurative sense of imputations or disgraces, a use which is not going to be needed often. 'Children should be allowed to escape the accumulated *stigmas* of their parents.' Here *stigmata* would wrong-foot the reader.

It is a matter of taste and context, not of right or wrong. In general, popular writing I think you do better to write *vortexes, nimbuses, miasmas, narcissuses, indexes,* and *for-*

mulas, though I agree that these are not words that are often called for in the comic press or other popular writing. But in technical or learned writing, use *formulae, indices, narcissi, miasmata, nimbi,* and *vortices*. Some originally foreign words, like *stigma*, use their alternative plurals for a real instead of an optional differentiation. For example, as the plurals of *genius, genii* are spirits, but *geniuses* are humans.

Most Latin nouns ending in -us are what grammarians classify as second declension, and make their Latin plurals with an -i: *stimulus, stimuli*. Other words that retain their Latin plurals in English include *alumni, bacilli,* and *loci*. Other words that have come into English from Latin have made themselves so at home here that they make only English plurals these days: *bonuses, campuses, caucuses, choruses, circuses, viruses*. It would be odd or facetious to say *cauci* or *circi* in English. Some English words have both the Latin and the English plural, for example, *focus* makes both *focuses* and *foci*. Such nouns with both plurals include *fungus, cactus, nucleus, radius,* and *terminus*. Other Latin nouns ending in -us are third declension neuters. So *genus* still makes its old Latin plural *genera* in English. *Corpus* makes *corpora* or *corpuses*. While *minus* makes only *minuses*. Just to complicate matters, Latin fourth declension nouns ending in -us make their Latin plurals by lengthening the vowel in the singular to -ūs. Such words that have been Anglicized are *apparatus, hiatus, impetus, nexus, prospectus,* and *status*. In fact, only Latin fanatics use the old Latin plural for these, except perhaps for *hiatūs*. Prefer the English form, *prospectuses*. Only anti-Latin fanatics say *bacilluses, lacunas,* and *genuses* instead of *bacilli, lacunae,* and *genera*. And not even the most Roundhead, demagogic populist says *specieses, thesises,* or *basises* instead of their retained Latin plurals *species, theses,* and *bases*.

First declension Latin nouns ending in -a make their Latin plurals with -ae. So the plural of *alumna* is *alumnae* in Latin, and is rare enough to retain it still in English. Others that make their Latin plurals still are *algae* and *larvae*. Nouns that have become acclimatized, and use only the idle English plural with -s are *areas*, *arenas*, and *eras*. Nouns that are in transition, and still make both plurals include *antennae* and *antennas*, *formulas*, *nebulas*, and *vertebras*. Other nouns ending in -a are from the Greek and originally made their plurals with -ata, as *dilemma*, *dilemmata*. *Dilemmas*, *diplomas*, *dramas* all now make regular English plurals. Latin neuter nouns ending in -um originally made their plurals with -a, as in *curriculum*, *curricula*. In English those that retain their Latin plurals include *addenda*, *bacteria*, *corrigenda*, *desiderata*, *errata*, and *ova*. Those that have adopted only the English plural include *albums*, *chrysanthemums*, *museums*, and *premiums*. *Forum* usually makes *forums*, and *stadium* makes *stadiums*, though *fora* and *stadia* still crop up in learned writing. English nouns that have not yet made up their minds, and retain both the old plural and the new Anglicized one, include *aquarium*, *candelabrum*, *curriculum*, *maximum*, *medium*, *memorandum*, *millennium*, *minimum*, *moratorium*, *podium*, *referendum*, *spectrum*, *stratum*, *symposium*, and *ultimatum*. With a word like *millennium*, which never occurred in classical Latin because the Romans never got round to the millenniary concept, there is a strong case for using only the English plural, *millenniums*, since the Latin plural never existed.

Third declension Latin nouns ending in -ex and -ix make their Latin plurals with -ices. In English *index* and *appendix* have both their old foreign and their new Anglicized plurals. *Indexes* is used to refer to parts of a book; *indices* is used generally, for example in medical writing, to mean indicators. *Appendixes* is regular for those little bits of the body more honoured in the extraction than the retention; either *appendices* or *appendixes* refer to bits added on at the end of a book. *Codex* makes only the learned Latin plural, *codices*. *Apex*, *vortex*, and *matrix* still make both ancient Latin and modern English plurals.

Nouns from the Greek ending in -is make Greek plurals ending in -es, as *basis* makes *bases*, which is confusingly also the regular plural of *base*. In this way *axes* is both the regular plural of *axe* and the original plural of *axis*. Cf. *ellipses* which is the foreign plural of *ellipsis* and the native English plural of *ellipse*. Greek nouns that keep their irregular plurals in English include *analysis, axis, crisis, diagnosis, ellipsis, hypothesis, oasis, paralysis, parenthesis, synopsis, synthesis,* and *thesis*. *Metropolis* is the only one to have developed a regular English plural, *metropolises*. I guess that most of these Greek words retain their foreign plurals for euphony, to avoid the silly sibilance of a word ending in -ises. Flexibility and convenience are good rules in grammar.

Greek neuter nouns ending in -on make the plural with -a in Greek, and retain it or not, as the case may be, in English. *Criterion* makes *criteria,* and *phenomenon* makes *phenomena*. *Automaton* has both plurals. *Electrons, neutrons, protons,* and usually *ganglions* have Anglicized.

French nouns like *bureau* and *adieu* can make English plurals, *bureaus* and *adieus* in English, or retain their French plurals *bureaux* and *adieux*. Either way, the English pronounce the plurals in an Anglicized way, as though they ended with -z. This applies to *plateau* and *tableau*. French words ending with -s and -x are pronounced without the final sibilant in English when they are singular, and with a final -z in the plural: *chamois, corps, chassis, faux pas, patois, rendezvous*. English dislike of hissing will preserve these foreign plurals, rather than naturalize them to *rendezvouses* or *faux pases*.

Italian nouns ending in -o make Italian plurals ending in -i, *tempo* making *tempi*. *Virtuoso, libretto,* and *tempo* make both foreign and English plurals. Other Italian plurals such as *confetti, macaroni, ravioli,* and *spaghetti* are treated in English as aggregate noncount nouns such as sugar, and honorary singulars. *Graffiti* is usually plural, though you sometimes meet a *graffito*.

Some naturalized Hebrew nouns make their original plurals in -im: *kibbutz* makes *kibbutzim* besides the regular *kibbutzes* in English. *Cherub* and *seraph* are usually naturalized as *cherubs* and *seraphs*, but you can still meet *cherubim* and *seraphim*, especially in the hymn book.

– 87 –

There are still exceptions and oddities that produce such
barbaric plurals for the unwary as *ignorami, octopi, omnibi,
animalculae,* and *Saturnaliae. Ignoramus* is the first person
plural of the present tense of the first conjugation verb
ignoro in Latin, meaning 'we do not know'. In English its
plural must be *ignoramuses. Octopus* means eight-foot in
Greek: its foreign plural is *octopodes,* its Anglicized plural
octopuses. Omnibus is a Latin dative plural meaning 'for
everybody'. Its only possible plural is *omnibuses. Animalcula*
and *Saturnalia* are already Latin plurals. To make them
doubly plural by ending them with -ae is a work of supererogation and solecism. It is all part of the rich compost of
English grammar. Bring back Latin grammar as an essential
basis of the *curriculums* or *curricula,* I say.

14

CUMULATIVE NOS

Be Positive with Negatives

No, nay, never,
Nay never no more.
      Refrain of a traditional English country ballad

W E GET OUR negatives in a twist, and so end up saying the opposite of what we mean. A Disgusted, Tunbridge Wells, writes to the Editor: 'I have seldom experienced anything less insensitive and unwelcome.' Those three negatives and quasi-negatives ended up implying that what he had experienced was exceptionally sensitive and welcome, which, judging from the general tone of letters from dear old Disgusted, I deem not to have been his drift. In standard English grammar today, two negatives are generally regarded as cancelling each other out and producing a positive. 'Nobody didn't enjoy the occasion' means that everybody did. 'Not many people have nowhere to live' means most people have somewhere to live. 'No one has nothing to offer to society' means everyone has something to offer to society. 'Nobody has nothing to eat' means everyone has something to eat.

This is not the case in every language. In Greek, for example, negative symbols are often multiplied to reinforce each other. Jespersen described this form of grammar: 'A speaker spreads as it were a thin layer of negative colouring over the whole of the sentence instead of confining it to one single place.' We used to have the same system of cumulative negatives reinforcing rather than cancelling each other in English. King Claudius, having observed Hamlet telling Ophelia to get her to a nunnery: 'Nor what he spake, though it lack'd form a little,/Was not like madness.' Of course, Claudius was a Dane. And Shakespeare is notorious for writing poetry rather than pedantry. But that and many other such early examples indicate that in the past English used to stack up negatives to support rather than cancel each other. The grammar of negatives varies nicely and bewilderingly between languages. In Hausa, a question expecting the answer no, *num* in Latin, *ara mē* in Greek, 'you didn't really mean that, did you?' in English, is answered by 'yes' rather than 'no', the logic of it being: 'Yes, you are correct in thinking that so-and-so is not the case.' Teacher in northern Nigeria: 'Abubakar, where is your exercise book? You haven't handed it in.' 'I don't know, sir.' 'I don't think you did your prep last night, did you?' 'Yes sir.' 'Well then, where is it?' 'I didn't do it, sir.'

In informal or nonstandard English we still use double or multiple or cumulative negatives to reinforce each other. Television interviewer: 'Are you still a trade union official?' Interviewee, disconsolately: 'I'm not nothing no more.' Plumber, having just replaced a faulty tap washer: 'You don't want to turn it off too hard, not a tap you don't.' The grammarians explain this by saying that in such non-standard contexts, the multiple negatives are being used in place of nonassertive words in standard English. The negatives do not cancel each other out. Mr Dombey's butler hoped that he might 'never hear of no foreigner never boning [nicking, as a dog steals a bone] nothing out of no travelling chariot'; and we get his drift. Dickens meant us to smile at his butlerish, but distinctly un-Jeevesian, grammar. Even in standard English and educated speech, the reinforcing negatives survive vestigially in a few phrases: 'I shouldn't wonder if it didn't rain.' Apart from these rare survivals, in standard English these days double negatives cancel each other out. 'Not all imperatives have no subject' means that some imperatives have a subject. 'Never before had none of the committee members supported the mayor' means that some of the committee members had always supported the mayor before. 'None of us has never told lies' means that all of us have told lies at some time.

One way to sort out your negatives in a multinegative sentence is to switch two of them to positives, and see what meaning comes out. 'I have seldom experienced anything less insensitive and unwelcome.' Perm any two of those negs into positives. I have often experienced something more insensitive and unwelcome. I have often experienced something less sensitive and less welcome. I have seldom experienced anything more sensitive and welcome. None of these gives the meaning required by Disgruntled. Old Tunbridge Wells was indignant, and provoked to take up pen to dash off a fiery letter to the Editor, because he had, in fact, seldom experienced anything *more* insensitive and unwelcome, or so he says. But then, he's always saying that. His view can be expressed in various ways with negatives and positives. I have often experienced something less insensitive and unwelcome. I have often experienced something more sensitive and welcome. I have seldom experienced anything less sensitive and welcome. All these sentences express his alleged experience in different terms, and the last one is the strongest, and the one for which he was fumbling in his fury. Double and triple negatives can convey shades of emotion and emphasis quite beyond those of the positive statement. But they must be used with care, or we stand our intended meaning on its head.

Negatives are dodgy little tools. Here are some recent examples of negative fog. 'No one questioned that the 120 places would not be heavily oversubscribed.' What the writer meant was that he expected all the places to be taken, but that is not what he ended up saying. 'I do not think it is possible that the traditions and doctrines of these two institutions should not fail to create rival schools.' 'Not a whit undeterred by the disaster which overtook them last week.' 'Were it not for its liking for game eggs, the badger could not but be considered other than a harmless animal.' The positive statement is often easier to understand, in the same way that an active verb is often more straightforward than the passive. Here is a bit of Insurancespeak: 'The company shall *not* insure the Policyholder in respect of damage occurring while the vehicle is being driven by the Policyholder *unless* he holds a licence to drive such a vehicle and is *not disqualified* from holding such a licence.' The old head reels as it switches those negatives, as it often does when reading prose from the stylists of the insurance world and the Inland Revenue. Get rid of the negatives, substitute positives, tidy up, and a meaning becomes clear: 'The company will insure you for damage occurring while you are driving the vehicle, provided that you hold a licence to drive the vehicle and are permitted to hold the licence.' Simple, not negative.

Unfortunately, although this is much clearer for Disgusted, it may not be the meaning required by the insurance company. Insurancespeak, like the work of Parliamentary draftsmen and other legal writing, is a highly specialized jargon, based on legal precedents, and intended to be exact, watertight, fool-proof and lawyerproof. By simplifying, or removing the negatives, we may change the precise meaning. The company might not thank me for my rewriting of its policy. This policy sets out the general nature of the cover provided, and then lists a number of limitations to the generality of the insurance company's liability under the policy. To be effective, such limitations *must* be expressed negatively; they should not be expressed positively. If under the general policy wording the insurance company has already undertaken to insure the policyholder in respect of damage occurring while he is driving the vehicle, a positive statement that the insurance company will do so 'provided that you hold a licence . . .' does not clearly limit the insurance company's liability. If damage occurred while the policyholder was driving without holding a licence, he could argue that he was covered by the general wording of the policy, and that nothing in the policy expressly limited that cover. The positive sentence with its proviso does not expressly limit the extent of the cover provided by the general wording, and therefore does not clearly express the meaning that is intended. With the insurance company otherwise liable under the general wording of the policy, that meaning can be clearly expressed, in a legally ship-shape and Bristol fashion, only by the negative statement that the insurance company shall nevertheless *not* be liable *unless* . . . Note that it may be necessary to express either of the limiting circumstances negatively. The drafting of legal documents is, no doubt, all too frequently obscure and long-winded, and can be improved. But anyone who is drafting a legal document has to have firmly in mind that the aim is to produce a document that can not only be understood, but also cannot be misunderstood. This inevitably means that immediate comprehensibility by Disgusted, Tunbridge Wells, and elegance sometimes have to be sacrificed.

Outside legal jargon, reversing the negatives does not always mechanically give the same meaning. 'The test does not show that John is not the father of your child' is not the same as saying 'the test shows that John is the father of your child'. Negatives allow us a vast range of emphasis and finely shaded meanings in English.

A particularly fashionable form of double negative emphasis is the rhetorical trick of litotes, which substitutes for a positive notion its opposite with a negative. Glasgow as 'no mean city'. In 1 *Corinthians* XI, 17 and 22, 'I praise you not' is an emphatic and sly way of saying 'I blame you'. And that rhetorical old scribbler Paul again, in *Acts* XXI, 39, giving Glasgow its epithet twenty centuries later: 'But Paul said, I am a man which am a Jew of Tarsus, a city in Cilicia, a citizen of no mean city.' Litotes is the Greek word for frugality, derived from *lītos* which means single, simple, meagre. It is a very English form of indirectness, much overused by politicians, lawyers, and the pompous and self-satisfied classes generally. Judges are apt to spatter their comments and judgements and *obiter dicta* with litotes and other sorts of multiple negatives. They even use the trick in their summings-up to juries, who may find cumulative negatives difficult to untangle. This is partly, no doubt, because of the lawyer's dislike of ever committing himself positively. But litotes flourishes mostly, I believe, because it sounds clever, and proclaims a silly kind of professionalism, spilling over into ordinary conversation with phrases such as 'not unimportant' and 'not so much that it is not'. You can imagine the prats who say that sort of thing. The negative is an essential tool of English grammar. But it is a small, sharp, pointed and precise tool, which needs to be used with delicate exactness. Sloppy profusion of negatives produces either nonsense, or the impression that you are a pedantic ass.

15

ARTICLES

A Brief History from A to An

Aitches don't make artists – there ain't no H in Art.
'The Cockney Tragedian', a music-hall song,
by Albert Chevalier

THERE IS A display ad in the papers that shows a
Giacometti stick man shouting at another in huge black
type: 'AN UNO FOR 0% FINANCE.' Presumably Fiat, the
manufacturers of Uno motor cars, employ experienced
advertising agents. But their grammar and pronunciation
sound rum to me. My instinct is to say, 'A UNO', if I ever
had to say anything so silly. For such a little word, the
indefinite article A causes a lot of grief. Its explanation and
illustration occupy six vast pages of the 1989 edition of *The
Oxford English Dictionary*, and I do not suppose that this
mountain of close scholarship is ever looked at by anybody
other than professional grammarians. Ordinary people do
not consult the dictionary about the indefinite article. Like
the rest of English, the use of A is in a state of constant
flux, as pronunciations and other fashions change. Let us
see whether we can agree on the state of the art of A as it
runs at present.

The rule and practice are that A goes before words
beginning with a consonant sound: a bicycle, a yuppie, a
horse, a eulogy; and AN goes before words beginning with
a vowel sound: an onion, an hors d'œuvre, an omelette,
an heirloom. The trouble arises because not all words

beginning with consonants begin with a consonant sound, and not all words beginning with vowels begin with a vowel sound; and in any case pronunciations vary widely, and are stubbornly defended by their owners as the right way to do it. In particular, words starting with H cause trouble over whether to aspirate (sc. pronounce) the H or not. Many of these words beginning with H come into English from French. The usual pattern is that when they first arrive they are pronounced in a Frenchified way with an unaspirated or inaudible H, and accordingly take AN. But after these immigrant words have been around for a time and become acclimatized, we Anglicize them, and start pronouncing them in a robust, Anglo-Saxon style, sounding the H. Such words then sound funny and pretentious if you persist in keeping an AN in front of them.

The complexity is compounded by the modern trend to pronounce foreign words in their native way, to proclaim that we have been on a package tour to Alicante, and know that this is how the Spaniards say it. So travelled Brits are starting to say 'Paree' not entirely jocularly, but to demonstrate that they are men of the world. (Have you noticed how some British are going around saying 'Good Moaning', imitating the popular BBC telly programme '*Allo 'Allo*? – a rare example of television changing idiom and pronunciation before our very ears.)

Accordingly A goes even before words that start with a vowel, if that vowel is pronounced like a consonant, and before aspirated H. For example: A eulogy, euphony, European, ewe, ewer, Ukranian, unanimous, unicorn, uniform, union, unison, unit, universe, university, Uno for that matter, useful, usurper, one, hope, herb, herbal, horse, hospital, hospitable, humble, history, hero, herald, harmony, horizontal, hostage. Never mind how the word is spelled, if it is pronounced with an initial consonant sound, it sounds better with an A before it. On the other hand, AN is always used before words starting with a vowel sound, and these include words starting with unaspirated H. Thus, AN heir, honour, honest, hour. AN humble sounds to me like Uriah Heep; but it all depends on how you pronounce 'humble'.

However, pronunciation is constantly changing, not least in the dodgy matter of whether or not to aspirate H. AN was formerly used even before a lightly aspirated H when the syllable introduced by the H was unaccented. Thus pronouncers of the previous generation used to say AN historian, hotel, hysterical scene, hereditary title, habitual offender. Some purists still use AN in these cases, as well as AN horizon (yet A horizontal), AN heroic (yet A hero), AN heraldic (yet A herald), AN hereditary, AN hotel, AN hotel-keeper, AN hiatus, AN historian, AN hyena. It all depends on how heavily you aspirate your Hs. AN hotel and AN historian sound a touch pretentious to me. But speakers who prefer to keep the AN before such words should not try to have it both ways, having their H and eating it, by saying AN and aspirating the H. They should say: AN 'otel, AN 'istorian. But that is their affair. Pronunciation is a very personal register of language, part of our idiolect, in which we have been brought up. We choose it to suit our image of ourselves which we present to the listening world.

Laying down the law about how other people ought to pronounce English is the act of a (an?) hero or an (a?) idiot. The rule applies to abbreviations, acronyms, and other symbols for words that can be pronounced. What decides whether to A or AN is not the letter at the beginning of the word, but the sound you make as you pronounce it. For example AN MP, AN RA. Even though these funny little abbreviations standing in for words start with consonants, we pronounce them as though they began with vowels: AN Em Pee, AN Are Ay. AN UNO still sounds funny to me. But perhaps UNO is being pronounced in an Italianate way, OONO, in which case an introductory AN would be OK. But I am ignorant about cars, regarding them as a jam on the face of our civilization.

The other argument raging around A at present is whether to pronounce it A as in 'hat', or Ay as in 'mate'.

The Ay pronunciation is being adopted by Conservative politicians and pretentious creeps from all parties because it sounds posh. (Incidentally, is that posh as in 'gosh', or POESH roughly as in 'coach'? A lot of the British are saying the latter, not always jocularly.) Fashions in pronunciation of simple little words change faster than any other branch of language. We shall sound quite as funny (we already do) to the next generation as previous generations sound to us.

The pronunciation of the definite article follows a similar pattern, with divergences before diphthongs and Hs. The general pattern is to pronounce THI before a vowel sound or unaspirated H, and THER (or sounds to that effect) before a word starting with a consonant sound. Thus, THI onion, omelette, hour, honest, heir, honour; but THER eulogy, ewe, horse, hospital. Very few of the purists of pronunciation who persist in saying AN historian carry their convictions to saying THI historian. They tend to say THER historian, like the rest of us. Pretentious creeps in the House of Commons who are introducing Ay for the indefinite article are doing the same thing to the definite article by pronouncing it, with portentous emphasis, THEEE.

16

I AND ME

Pronoun Slippage

Ego sum rex Romanus, et supra grammaticam. (I am the King of Rome, and above grammar.)

> The Emperor Sigismund, at the
> Council of Constance, 1414

W HO'S THERE? 'I.' No, you really can't say 'I' in reply to the question. The natural reply is 'me'. It is idiomatic even if it is not grammatical. This illustrates how usage is constantly changing our grammar, which is no more than an attempt (doomed inevitably to failure) to describe the established practice of the best speakers and writers of a language. The attempt is doomed because there is no agreement about who are the best speakers and writers; their practice is not established; and even when it is established, usage changes it. The grammar of our personal pronouns is in confusion. It always has been, dear boy.

The fashionable British theory is that our children are no longer taught grammar in permissive modern schools, and so panic between 'I' and 'me', and go for the one that sounds more formal, and so end up saying things like: 'It's down to you and I now.' The academic American legend is that the I–me solecism is a hypercorrection forced into American English when generations of schoolmarms pounded into the heads of generations of schoolchildren that they mustn't say 'me' in such combinations as 'me and Johnny done it'. As the Kansas farmer, reacting against his schoolmarm, said to Nelson Antrim Crawford, the student of American country ways and language in about 1915: 'That sure is a great school. It's practical. They don't teach no goddam grammar there.'

The fashionable theories are rubbish, as fashionable theories often are. The confusion about the cases of our personal pronouns is older and more interesting than the populist cry that grammar is going to the dogs, and that our children are not a patch on our generation, which is, it goes without saying, perfect. Uncertainty about pronouns has been inherent in English grammar for ages. I think it came in with the Normans, mixing in their French pronoun practice with the Old English ways.

For example, the I–me solecism is very old. There always has been a tendency to use the nominative form, especially 'I', as an objective after a verb or preposition, especially when it is separated from the governing word by other words, or when it is part of a compound object, as in, 'This is strictly between you and I.' Here are some examples of this 'bad grammar' from good writers. Shakespeare, *Merchant of Venice*: 'All debts are cleared betweene you and I.' *As You Like It*: 'My father hath no childe but I.' *Sonnet 72*: 'And hang more praise upon deceased I.' *The Oxford English Dictionary* gives copious examples of I being used instead of me from Ben Jonson, Vanbrugh, Thomas Hughes, *The Guardian*, and other masters of sound grammar. Even if their usage is as painful as a broken head to purist grammarians like Priscian, do we dare to say that they all simply got it wrong? Samuel Pepys is particularly strong (or weak?) with his Is and mes. Open the diary anywhere, and the fellow is at it. November 22, 1660: '. . . did take my wife and I to the Queenes presence-Chamber.' December 27, 1660: '. . . who pleased my wife and I.' October 20, 1663: 'Mrs Sarah talking with my wife and I.' May 8, 1667: '. . . if God send my wife and I to live.' November 20, 1668: 'This morning up, with mighty kind words between my poor wife and I.' I suppose you could try saying that Pepys was bad at grammar, or had a flaw with pronouns in his idiolect; but that seems to me an impertinent and hoity-toity line to take. A more persuasive argument would be that using 'I' for 'me' was very frequent in the sixteenth and seventeenth centuries, but is now considered ungrammatical by tidy-minded purists following in the footsteps of the systematizing Victorian pedagogues.

But it won't do. Here are some recent examples of this so-called bad grammar from winners of the Booker Prize, and other professionals of English grammar. Thomas Kenneally: 'Their arrival made Genia and I realise we were very nearly imprisoned in our own house.' Penelope Lively in *Moon Tiger*, which won the Booker in 1988: 'Let's talk about each other, that's all I'm interested in at the moment.' 'Me too,' says Tom. Brian Moore in *The Colour of Blood*, which nearly won the Booker in 1988: 'We? Who's we?' 'Myself and another priest.' Of course, characters speaking in novels are not upon oath to observe the rules of English grammar to the last pedantic apostil. But there is a considerable body of evidence that our best writers and speakers find it natural and easy to say 'I' where 'me' is strictly correct, and vice versa. Professor Marilyn Butler of Cambridge: 'The men are more formal and authoritarian in tone than she.' Evelyn Waugh: 'He was five years older than me.'

That is a formidable team of solecists and bad grammarians. You can say that they don't know their Is from their elbows, but I am not man enough to say so. It is more sensible to observe that the idiom of personal pronouns has fluctuated from an early date, and that our present confusion is just a new wave from an old sea. In particular, the answer to the question 'Who is it?' is 'It's me.' 'Who's there?' 'Me,' not 'I'. After 'than' and 'as' there is great diversity of usage. 'Jim would have run the farm as good as me.' 'He started to encounter kids as gifted as he.' 'Me too' and 'me neither' are ungrammatical but idiomatic. 'Silly me' and 'Me, I prefer to go to bed with a good book' are ungrammatical but idiomatic. We change our grammar all the time to suit ourselves and our purposes. Us too. Grammar is our servant, not our master, even though it breaks Priscian's head.

Me, I blame the Normans. The French use *moi* as an emphatic pronoun even when it is a subject. Louis XIV was obviously right to say: *'L'état, c'est moi.'* *'Je suis l'état'* does not produce the same effect at all. 'Me too' in English is similar to *'moi aussi'* in French, not *'je aussi'*. 'As good as me' is the same idiom as *'aussi bon/bien que moi.'* 'Me, I prefer to go to bed' compares with *'moi, je préfère me coucher.'* 'It's me' cf. *'c'est moi.'* In all these examples *'moi'* is being used for emphasis, which seems to be the case in the English examples also. Notice that this confusion about pronoun cases does not occur in any of the other Germanic languages. I suggest that our English confusion (or, to be positive about it, our opportunity to make more distinctions with our pronouns) goes back to 1066 and all that.

As in *The Jackdaw of Rheims*, heedless of grammar, they all cried, 'That's him!', for emphasis. And apart from emphasis for educated speakers, the use of pronouns varies widely in regional dialects from Kansas to the West of England. For example, from Dorset:

Oh where, oh where be that black blackbird,
  Oh where, oh where be she?
Oh her be under wurzel bush,
  And us be after she.

Later in the folk verse:

Oh us be under wurzel bush,
  And her be after we.

In the Somerset folksong, 'There were three sailors of Bristol City', recorded by Thackeray, the shipwrecked sailors end up saying, 'There's nothing left – us must eat we.' In Gloucestershire the local dialect for 'Your gosling bit my leg' is 'Your goose-chick bit I's leg', an unusual use of I as a genitive. In Devonshire pronouns become even more complicated, so that 'we are' becomes 'we'm', but 'we will' becomes 'us'll'. The use of personal pronouns in English has a rich and varied history, affected by influences from Norman invaders to Kansas farmers. It would be mad to try to impose a single grammatical uniformity on such varied little words.

17

PREPOSITIONS

Ever Onward and Upward

A preposition is a very bad word to end a sentence
with.
Ascribed to an unnamed English school inspector

SOME WORDS CHANGE their meanings to meet changing
social conditions. You can read the social history of
England in miniature in the wonderfully meandering
meanings down the centuries of such words as 'nice', and
'silly', and 'liberal'. Other words change their meanings
for no good reason other than fashion, and the innate
human tendency to parrot and copy-cat each other. The
use of the smallest words in the language, its prepositions,
can identify in which century (sometimes in which decade)
a piece of English was written.

Have you noticed the ongoing, onward rush of 'on'?
It is becoming everyone's preferred preposition, and is
ousting other formerly idiomatic prepositions in its push
for *Lebensraum*. In a few centuries from now its ubiquity in
a piece of writing or recorded speech will identify the piece
unerringly to the linguistic experts as having originated at
the end of the twentieth century. Here are some 'on's that
are current, and sound wrong, or rather novel, to me: a
cinema *on* Leicester Square; a shop *on* Regent Street; a one
on one relationship; the implications of X *on* Y; children's
learning ought to be evaluated *on* its own terms; he rode
on taxis (rather than buses). I should have used in, in,

to, for, in, and in respectively. Residents of Hampstead Garden Suburb say that they live *on* the Suburb, perhaps to distinguish themselves from lesser breeds who live commonly in the suburbs. Television commentators speak quaintly of some participant in a quiz show being *on* his or her score. Sports chatterers say that a player or team is *on* 20. I guess that this is not a serious oncome or onding, but just an ephemeral *on-dit*. Something is happening *on*/in the restless tides of English idiom.

The American idiom of having a committee *on* rather than for something is coming in. The British now seem to do something *on* weekends, rather than at them; (there is an idiom that seems slightly different, and more traditional, to speak of, '*on* weekends in the country'). 'Black *on* black violence' is a common phrase, no doubt shortened from 'against' in the first instance for headline brevity; but it has become the idiom.

For its size, *on* is a tiresome little word, being both a preposition (*on* the table), and an adverb (now read *on*). It is further complicated by *onto*, which stern purists used to condemn as a useless innovation. In fact, *onto* is now well established, and has the same relation to *on* as *into* has to *in*. It conveys the idea of motion more vividly than *on* on its own. The cat jumped *onto* the table, in my contemporary idiom, gives, by a whisker, a more lively image than the cat jumped *on* the table. She drove *onto* the pavement is, of course, different from she drove *on* the pavement. When there is a notion of motion, *onto* is your preposition.

Possibility of confusion and egg on VDU screen arises when *on* is used as an adverb, and accordingly *on to* as two separate little words is right, and *onto* is wrong. Let us walk *on to* Wapping. Pass it *on to* the editor. Let us struggle *on to* victory or defeat. Keep right *on to* the end of the road.

When it is a preposition, *onto* (purists would say *on* or *to on* its own) is your man. It is even pronounced differently. *Ón tó* (adverb and preposition) is a spondee (two longs, equally stressed, dum-dum). *Ónto* (articulated preposition) is a trochee (long short, stress on the first, dum-di).

The cat has jumped up *on(to)* the bookcase. Give me a hand up *on(to)* the stage. The audience leapt *on(to)* its feet in a sycophantic standing ovation. My sardine sandwich has fallen *on(to)* my computer keyboard, sardine downwards as usual. Come *on(to)* these yellow sands. Yes, I know that Ariel sang *unto*, but the principle is there. I must get *on(to)* that committee. She's simply climbing *on(to)* her usual populist bandwagon.

As usual, the grammar of cricket is tricky. (American readers are excused this paragraph.) He played the ball *on to* (or *onto*) his wicket? Is the *on* adverb or preposition here? 'He played *on*' is idiomatic on its own in peculiar cricket jargon. The distinction between *on* and *upon* is equally nice, depending on rhythm, idiolect, emphasis, or simple accident. *Upon* my soul, but *on* no account. Burton-*upon*-Trent and Kingston-*upon*-Thames, but Henley-*on*-Thames. Newcastle *upon* Tyne, but Newcastle *under* Lyme. Prepositions and place-names are two of the most erratic elements in the English vocabulary: if you try to find logic in them when they are combined, you will surely go mad.

The modern craze for *on* is turning it into a miniature cuckoo word, pushing out the proper and precise fledglings from the nest. She reassured me *about* (better than *on*) my promotion prospects. He was persuasive *with* or *about* (better than *on*) his Homeric theory. His complete apathy *towards* or *for* (better than *on*) grammar.

Quite why we are going *on* about *on* is a mystery, as change in idioms often is. Perhaps we are obsessed with the silly little word because a lot of fashionable contemporary phrases include *on*: for example, to go *on* about something. *On-going* is another very fashionable modern weasel phrase, suggesting continuity where no continuity is logically possible, as in the *on-going* climax or crisis. *On* plays an important part in our new world of instant communications. There really is no alternative to *on* in the slogan of our times: 'Please 'phone [fax/buzz/bleep] me soonest *on* 782 5168.'

Up and *down* are two other little prepositions/adverbs

that are changing their idioms under our noses. The country bumpkin, recruited into the French army, could not march in step because he could not tell his *droit* from his *gauche*. The sergeant solved the problem by putting a piece of hay in his left boot and a piece of straw in his right, and shouting *foin, paille, foin, paille*. (A similar fable is told in many languages.) The stage directions we can cope with in getting through the army (or life) need to be simple. This may explain why we are increasingly coming to talk of the north as *up*, and the south as *down*. That is the way that they are shown on most maps and atlases. Idiot weather forecasters grin and gabble about cloud coming *down* (they mean south) through England. We talk of driving *up* to Scotland, or *down* to the New Forest. The announcer, speaking from Broadcasting House (the umbilicus of the civilized world) talks of a Test Match *up* at Trent Bridge in Nottingham.

This is a significant change in idiom in the past few years. In more hierarchical days, journeys to the metropolis or most important centre in a district were *up*, irrespective of their direction along or across a meridian to the North Pole, and journeys away from the centre were *down*, whatever their direction. Until quite recently London was generally accepted as the most important centre in the United Kingdom, and all journeys were described as *up* to London. Journeys away from London were *down*, even if they went north. In 1846 Lord Chancellor Campbell wrote: 'At Christmas I went *down* (from London) into Scotland and, crossing the Cheviots, was nearly lost in a snowstorm.' Miss La Creevey, miniature painter and London landlady in *Nicholas Nickleby*: 'You don't mean to say that you are really going all the way *down* into Yorkshire this cold winter's weather, Mr Nickleby?' British trawlermen used to speak of making a trip *down* north, even when they were heading to the Kara Sea or somewhere else within a few degrees of latitude of the North Pole, very rightly regarding Grimsby or Aberdeen as the centre of the world, and all voyages from there as by definition *down*.

The Oxford English Dictionary explains this metropolitan use of *down* as being to some place that is conventionally viewed as lower in position, e.g. from the capital to distant parts of a country. The fledgling Victorian railways conformed to this convention, making the *up*-line the one by which trains arrived at their London terminus, and the *down*-line the one by which they left for the sticks. A passenger leaving Glasgow by train for Edinburgh is first of all on the *up*-line, because it leads to Edinburgh, the capital of Scotland, which is deemed the more important terminus in the infinite wisdom of British Rail. But as soon as he comes to a junction where there is a connection southwards, his line becomes a *down*-line, because on it there are now trains running from London to Edinburgh, i.e. *down*. There are no examples in the second edition of *The Oxford English Dictionary* (1989) of our new prepositional idiom of *down* meaning to the south, and *up* meaning to the north. The idiom is new.

The apparent exception to the rule is the use of *up* and *down* in relation to British universities, particularly the older two. To go *up* to Oxford means to take up residence at the beginning of term, until you come *down* at the end of term, unless you have had the bad luck to be sent *down* (expelled) earlier. But if your parents come to visit you, they will come *down* to Oxford from London, and you will take a trip *up* to London for the day. This is merely an extension of the hierarchical system of *up* and *down*. As a member of the university, you go *up* to the centre of your universe. As an ordinary citizen, you go *up* to London from Oxford or Cambridge.

We are changing this idiom because the north tends to be shown at the top of the page in most maps. Some imaginative maps, which print the world upside down or aslant, can give you a new perspective on history, in which Western Europe is not the centre of the world. Britons speak of Australia as *Down* Under; but, of course, Britons would be *Down* Under not *Up* Over to the Australians.

It is not just the Brits who have this simplistic, *foin-paille*, *up-down* pattern of geography. In reports of the Korean and Vietnamese Wars, you come across such expressions as 'below the seventeenth parallel'. A US Air Force report speaks of an aircraft flying *'under* Bermuda' – a hazardous journey, if you stop to think about it. Our modern *up-down* view is not a completely new idiom. In *The History of the Decline and Fall of the Roman Empire*, Gibbon writes of, 'the Black nations that might dwell *beneath* the torrid zone', and, 'as *high* as the sixty-eighth degree of latitude'. It is one way, but not the only way, of looking at the world. If *up* and *down* go on like this, perhaps we shall start saying left for west and right for east – and then we really shall be in the *foin*, or do I mean the *paille*?

18

SANDBOY

Sandboys' Sadder Side

We will smoke together and be as merry as sandboys.
Edward FitzGerald, letter, 1889

ENGLISH PROVERBS ABOUT happiness are cynical and
hard-nosed. Proverbs tend to be. Nothing like a bit of
pessimistic folklore to cheer up the English. Take the
idiomatic proverb or phrase 'happy as a sandboy', or, as
it might be, a sandgirl. We still say it all the time, without
sounding obsolete. You might well think that these sandboys and sandgirls who are proverbially happy as children
are on summer holiday on the beach, larking about in the
sand, building sandcastles and walls to keep the tide back
where Canute failed, burying father in the sand while he
is asleep, and engaging in the other sandy activities that
have made the English seaside holiday a terrifying national
institution. The truth is stranger and darker.

The flaw in happy sandboys as children at the seaside
is anachronism. The seaside holiday is a comparatively
modern innovation. It was started by the Prince Regent,
who hoped that sea water and ozone and bracing Brighton
air might cure the swellings of the glands in his neck. He
was followed by the smart, silly set who 'rush'd coastward
to be cur'd like tongues by dipping into brine'. The contemporary satirical verse shows that this was considered
a novel activity. Before that the seaside and sandy beach
had been regarded by the English as marginal and

impoverished places, to be avoided by all except fishermen, mariners, travellers, and others who had business there. The fashionable classes used big hats and parasols to avoid suntan, which was a mark of poverty and the working class. Lying on the beach trying to become brown did not become a mass enthusiasm and folly until after half way through the nineteenth century.

However, sandboys had become a byword for happiness long before that, well back into the eighteenth century. The sandboy, also known as a sand urchin, was partly responsible for the passing of the Hawkers Act of 1888: he was one of the persons therein defined who 'travelled with a horse or other beast bearing or drawing burden, and went from door to door, selling goods, wares or merchandise'. The 'boy' did not necessarily imply that he was of tender years: it was the patronizing put-down still used in some cultures by the employing classes to keep their servants in their place. What the sandboy was selling was sand, originally shovelled up from a seaside beach, later on, after the railways had arrived, from a station goods yard. There was a good market for sand in the cities. Builders' merchants needed it for mixing cement, publicans spread it on their floors, and householders bought it for their gardens. Various other manufacturing industries used sand. There were no motor vehicles. Decent money could be earned if you owned a horse and cart, or even a donkey, by hawking sand around the cities.

Here are some contemporary examples of the sandboy's trade. Peter Egan in *Life in London*, 1821: 'Logic appeared to be as happy as a sandboy, who had unexpectedly met with good luck in disposing of his hampers full of the above-mentioned household commodity.' The pseudonymous 'John Bee' defined them in his *Dictionary of the Turf*, 1812: 'Sandboy, all rags and all happiness; the urchins who drive the sand-laden neddies through our streets, are envied by the capon-eating turtle-loving epicures of these cities. "As jolly as a sandboy" designates a merry fellow who has tasted a drop.'

What your sandboy was doing was loading sand in sandbags onto the back of a poor old donkey with sagging knees, and hawking it around the streets. Sandboys, some of whom were old men, acquired their proverbial reputation for happiness not because they enjoyed their work, but because they spent their money as fast as they earned it on getting drunk. The happiness of a sandboy is derived from the unkind imputation that he is as hooted as a foghorn, as lit-up as Oxford Street with the Christmas lights, and as plastered as an Adam ceiling. Here is clinching evidence for this assertion from *The Old Curiosity Shop*, which Dickens published in 1840: 'The Jolly Sandboys was a small road-side inn, with a sign representing three Sandboys increasing their jollity.' Sandboys are older and sadder than might be supposed on first acquaintance. Proverbs have deeper roots than many plants in the garden of language.

An eighteenth-century folksong in praise of humble trades begins:

Who liveth so merry in all this land
As does the poor widow who sells the sand?
& ever she sings as I can guess –
Will you buy any sand, any sand, Mistress?

The song ends:

Who liveth so merry and be of such sport
As those that be of the poorest sort?

Note that here we have a sandwidow rather than a sandboy. Note also that it is not merely drunkenness that brings happiness in folksong. The song is, of course, of the cheerer-upper sort. But people have always sung best when they have had least to sing about.

Our other proverbial sayings about happiness are equally depressing. The oldest is 'Call no man happy till he dies', which was first said in Greek by Sophocles in *Oedipus Tyrannus*, first performed some year shortly after 430 BC: 'Deem no man happy, until he passes the end of his life without suffering grief.' Ovid translated the saying into Latin in *Metamorphoses* iii, 135: *'Dicique beatus/Ante obitum nemo debet.'* The pessimistic prophecy about happiness came into English in 1545 in Teverner's translation of *Erasmus' Adages*: 'Salon aunsered kynge Cresus, that no man coulde be named happy, tyl he had happely and prosperouslye passed the course of his lyfe.' It was versified with typical ingenuity by John Florio in his version of *Montaigne's Essays* in 1603: 'We must expect of man the latest day,/Nor e'er he die, he's happie, can we say.' The saying is still current. Here it is popping up again, after twenty-five centuries of life, in one of C. S. Forester's nautical swashbucklers in his Hornblower series: 'Call no man happy until he is dead . . . He was seventy-two, and yet there was still time for this dream to change to a nightmare.'

The other English proverb about happiness consists of variations on the theme: 'If you would be happy for a week take a wife; if you would be happy for a month kill a pig; but if you would be happy all your life plant a garden.' In spite of the fashionably green spirit of the third leg of the tripod, the other two legs are unfashionably anti-feminist and carnivorous, and the proverb is not much heard these days. It was first recorded in English by Thomas Fuller in his *Worthies* in 1661 in the following form: 'I say the Italian-humour, who have a merry Proverb, Let him that would be happy for a Day, go to the Barber; for a Week, marry a Wife; for a Month, buy him a New-horse; for a Year, build him New-house; for all his Life-time, be an Honest man.' Here is a variant of 1809, recorded by a plodding S. Pegge in *Anonymania*: 'If you would live well for a week, kill a hog; if you would live well for a month, marry; if you would live well all your life, turn priest . . . Turning priest alludes to the celibacy of the Romish Clergy, and has a pungent sense, as much as to say, do not marry at all.' There is not a lot for our comfort in other current happiness sayings. 'Happy is the country which has no history.' 'A deaf husband and a blind wife are always a

happy couple.' Joyce Grenfell: 'Happiness is the sublime
moment when you get out of your corsets at night.' Kingsley Amis: 'As happy as a man interrupted at his investiture
with the Order of Merit to be told that a six-figure cheque
from a football pool awaits him in the lobby.' Paul Theroux:
'As happy as a louse on a dirty head.' Dylan Thomas: 'I
believe with all my heart that we'll live together one day
as happily as two lobsters in a saucepan, two bugs on a
muscle, one smile, though never to vanish, on the Cheshire
face.' Robert Frost, in the title of a poem: 'Happiness makes
up in height for what it lacks in length.' Charles Schultz,
in the title of a *Peanuts* book: 'Happiness is a Warm Puppy.'
Arthur Marshall: 'I have to tell you something. I cannot
help being happy. I've struggled against it but no good.
Apart from an odd five minutes here and there, I have
been happy all my life. There is, I am well aware, no virtue
whatever in this. It results from a combination of heredity,
health, good fortune and shallow intellect.' Aldous Hux-
ley: 'Happiness is like coke – something you get as a
by-product in the process of making something else.'
Bernard Shaw, in *Man and Superman*: 'A lifetime of happiness! No man alive could bear it: it would be hell on earth.'
Edith Wharton: 'If only we'd stop trying to be happy we
could have a pretty good time.' Alan Bennett, in *The Old
Country*, 1978: VERONICA: 'Are you happy?' HILARY:
'Why does everybody keep asking me that? No. I'm not
happy. But I'm not unhappy about it.'

The English take their happiness gloomily, at any rate in
their customary sayings and saws, confirming foreigners'
views of us as cold fish. The most sensible observation
on the topic was made by A. Edward Newton in *This
Book-collecting Game*: 'Gilbert White discovered the formula
for complete happiness but he died before making the
announcement, leaving it for me to do so. It is to be very
busy with the unimportant.' And if you cannot manage
that, I suppose you can try the melancholy road of being
as happy as a sandboy.

19

WOODEN SPOONS AND OLD BLUES

Still Causing a Stir

Sure my invention must be down at zero,
   And I grown one of many wooden spoons
Of verse (the name with which we Cantabs please
   To dub the last of honours in degrees).
             Don Juan, III, cx, 1820, by Lord Byron

S OME SLANG IS as evanescent as a family spectre at dawn.
But other slang endures long after we have lost its
original meaning. It becomes a respectable member of the
English lexicon, even though we have long forgotten its
racy or shady origin, and its metaphor has become dormant
or dead. For example, the wooden spoon is still much in
use, particularly on the sporting pages of the newspapers,
where there is continual speculation about wooden-
spooners, wooden-spoonists, and who is going to win the
wooden spoon. Here is an old bit of slang that survives as
mysteriously as Dick Whittington's cat.

It is reasonably well known that an actual wooden
spoon, looking a bit like an oar, and decorated with collegi-
ate heraldry, used to be presented to the last of the Junior
Optimes, that is the man (no women allowed in those dim
days, Best Beloved) who came bottom of those taking
honours in the Mathematical Tripos at Cambridge
University. In plainer words, it was the booby prize. It

was a wet English public-school joke of the kind you would expect from the junior, cloth-cap-and-earnest-conversations-about-the-meaning-of-life university. There is a reference in a Cambridge guide book published in 1803 to 'Wooden Spoon for wooden heads: the lowest of the Junior Optimes'. English evidently needed a jovial slang term for somebody who came last; and wooden spoon caught on, and extended its meaning beyond Cambridge. By 1858 a retired statesman could write in his memoirs, without explanatory gloss: 'The wooden spoon which is given to the Minister in the House of Commons who has been in the fewest divisions.' The phrase crossed the Atlantic. At Yale the wooden spoon was formerly the student who took the last appointment in the Junior Exhibition. It then dropped its sense of coming bottom, and was used to describe the most popular student in a class. In Britain it retained its original meaning of something given to a loser, and is now widely used particularly in sporting contexts, filling a hole in the national vocabulary that is evidently not filled by booby prize or consolation prize.

In another example of Cantab humour, those who got firsts in the Mathematical Tripos were called wranglers, sc. disputers or arguers, and the undergraduate who came top was called the Senior Wrangler. This slang is even older than the wooden spoon. As early as 1750 we find: 'The Wranglers have usually expected that all the young Ladies of their Acquaintance should wish them Joy of their Honours.' But English is rich in metaphors for those who come first, and wranglers are obsolescent, even in Cambridge.

In 1824, T. H. Wedgwood, destined to become a famous etymologist, came bottom in the Classical Tripos list. By analogy Cambridge introduced the wooden wedge, or the wedge on its own, as the classical variant for the wooden spoon. Not surprisingly it did not catch on generally, and lasted at Cambridge only for the generation who remembered Wedgwood.

The last occasion on which an actual wooden spoon was awarded was in 1909: the recipient was C. L. Holthouse of St John's College. Years later he presented the peculiar object to his old college, and there it still hangs in the Combination Room. After 1909 the names of the men in the three classes of the tripos were no longer arranged in order of merit, but alphabetically, as they still are today. So it is no longer possible to tell who gets the wooden spoon or who is the Senior Wrangler.

It used to be a cheerful Cambridge custom to hang an actual wooden spoon from the gallery in the Senate House on Degree Day. On November 17, 1877, Charles Darwin appeared in the Senate House to receive an honorary Doctorate of Law. According to a chronicler of the occasion: 'The undergraduates who filled the galleries and cheered heartily suspended (in place of the wooden spoon on the day of admission of Honour candidates) a monkey – quite to Darwin's satisfaction.'

In spite of its obscure and exclusive origin, the wooden spoon has become an essential term in English for the booby prize, or the person or team who comes last in a contest. The old slang flourishes, and sends out new roots and suckers, long after the schoolboy custom and memory of it have died. You cannot open your mouth or punch your VDU in English (or any ancient, complex language, for that matter) without writing history of a sort.

Wooden spoon is the oldest and most demotic piece of slang with which our two oldest universities have enriched the language. Blue is generally used for an athlete who represents Oxford or Cambridge, but its origin is boring. In the first University Boat Race, rowed at Henley in 1829, Oxford had worn dark blue striped jerseys and black straw hats, for reasons that are forgotten. When they came to row the second race, not until 1836 on the Thames tideway, at the last minute somebody pointed out that Cambridge had no colour on their bow. So an undergraduate ran to a shop by the river at Westminster, where the race started that year, and bought a piece of light blue Eton ribbon.

This has persisted as the Cambridge colour. Dark blue signifies Oxford and Harrow. Light blue signifies Cambridge and Eton. For those outside the magic circle, the slang is not much use.

Oxbridge is a portmanteau abbreviation for Oxford and Cambridge, and for the type of the historic British university. Some find it convenient shorthand; others find it snobbish and tendentious, implying that redbrick and concrete and plate glass universities are not quite in the first division. Oxbridge has been around in the language for a long time. Thackeray was the first to popularize it, in *Pendennis* in 1849: 'Repeated differences with the university authorities caused Mr Foker to quit Oxbridge in an untimely manner.' '"Rough and ready, your chum seems," the Major said. "Somewhat different from your dandy friends at Oxbridge."' Thackeray also introduced the reverse portmanteau word in *Pendennis*: 'He was a Camford man and very nearly got the English Prize Poem.' H. G. Wells also used Camford in *Holy Terror*: 'Camford had never made the slightest attempt to give any coherent picture of the universe to the new generation that came to it for instruction.' But whether for reasons of euphony or seniority, Camford never caught on.

Cambridge has been less prolific than Oxford in spin-offs into the English language. Apart from Cambridge blue, Cambridge calf is used in bookbinding, a fine and dark sprinkled calf of two tints, a square panel being left in the centre of the sides. Cambridge chimes were the composition of Joseph Jowett and William Crotch, first rung in 1793 at the Church of St Mary the Great, Cambridge. Cambridge coprolite is greensand; a Cambridge roller is an agricultural implement made up of loosely mounted ring segments; and a Cambridge sausage is a choice variety.

For some reason Oxford has been more fertile with nomenclature, as with Prime Ministers. Pages of *The Oxford English Dictionary* are taken up with Oxford derivatives, from Oxford bags, those absurd grey flannels wide at the ankles that were favoured by the Brideshead generation, to the Oxford Movement and the Oxford Group. The most influential and controversial Oxford derivatives are Oxford English and the Oxford accent. The English is that popularly supposed to be spoken by a member of the university, which has always been an ignorant assumption. The terms are rich with snobbery and the class war. 'It might be said perhaps that the Oxford accent conveys an impression of a precise and rather foppish elegance, and of deliberate artificiality.' And here is John Braine exercising the chip on his shoulder: 'Dick assumed an Oxford accent. "It's *naht* old-fashioned, dear brethren, to think of Hell in the language of fire and brimstone."' Winston Churchill was commended: 'Lacking the Oxford accent, he spoke as a Briton to Britons.' No doubt there have always been snobbish and silly undergraduates and dons at Oxford who have spoken with an affected drawl, and dropped the gs off the ends of their present participles, as in huntin', sootin', and fissin'. It is more realistic and less socially divisive to speak of the received accent to describe the educated pronunciation of south-east England with no regional accent.

20

PARROT

Picking on Poor Polly

My name is Parrot, a byrd of paradyse . . .
Speke, Parrot, I pray you, full curtesly they say;
Parrot is a goodly byrd, a prety popagye.
    Speke Parrot, circa. 1525, by John Skelton

T HE PARROT HAS a hard time in our vocabulary, as well as in our kitchens. Stewed parrots' tongues were a delicacy for the nuttier Roman emperors, partly because they were extravagant and accordingly exclusive, and partly because it was believed that the parrot's trick of imitating human speech, and so speaking foreign languages, would be transferred to those who ate it by sympathetic magic. You would think that the parrot would be a metaphor and proverb for prettiness or cleverness. Instead the poor popinjay has become a byword for death and disease, although the parrot is in fact remarkably long-lived. The latest example of this unfairness to parrots is the new British slang phrase 'dead parrot'. This is used by the trendy to mean something completely and irrevocably moribund. The vogue came in in 1988 when the joint policy statement, called *Voices and Choices for All*, was issued by David Steel and Robert McLennan, as the basis for a merged Liberal and Social Democratic party. This was widely condemned by all factions of both sides as a 'dead parrot' document, representative of few of the views of either side, too right-wing and Thatcherite, and offering no hope of joint action. So the two party leaders at the time were told to go away and try again. *The Observer* wrote: 'At that point Mr Steel's future – like his document – was widely regarded as a dead parrot. Surely this was the end of his twelve-year reign as Liberal leader?' *The Observer* was right. Thereafter David Steel was politically dead parrot.

The origin of our slang is often as elusive as what song the Sirens sang. But with dead parrot we know. Dead parrot as an image of stone dead and no hope of recovery derives from the famous BBC television series *Monty Python's Flying Circus* of the Seventies. A notable sketch showed a disgruntled customer returning to a pet shop with a parrot he had bought there which turned out to be dead, and the shopkeeper trying to convince him that it was not. From such trivial beginnings language grows. If dead parrot sticks in the language, at least we shall know how it got there.

'Sick as a parrot', the traditional phrase to express extreme chagrin by footballers and football managers when they have lost, is another recent disobliging parrot phrase.

It came into British English slang in the Seventies, created by the remorseless demands of television for instant and snappy analysis and comment after a game of football. You can date it. After Liverpool's defeat in the 1978 Cup Final, Liverpool's player Phil Thompson, pressed to comment while still bleeding from defeat, declared to the watching nation that he felt 'sick as a parrot'. Within a week other sportsmen, and sports writers, were copying him. The satirical magazine, *Private Eye*, encourages the cliché by constant mockery. By 1980 an instant BBC radio play about the European Cup Final, written on the spot and developed according to the result, was entitled *Over the Moon/Sick as a Parrot*.

'Over the Moon', the alternative cliché to express delight at winning, is older than 'sick as a parrot'. This probably comes from the children's nursery rhyme 'Hey diddle diddle/The cat and the fiddle,/The cow jumped *over the moon* . . .', which first appeared in print *circa* 1765. But there is a quotation that may refer to it in *A lamentable tragedy mixed ful of pleasant mirth, conteyning the life of Cambises King of Percia*, by Thomas Preston, printed in 1569:

> They be at hand Sir with stick and fidle;
> They can play a new dance called hey-diddle-diddle.

Commentators have offered diverse and increasingly implausible explanations of the 'over the moon' rhyme: that it refers to the worship of Hathor; that it is about various constellations such as Taurus and Canis Minor; that it describes the flight from the rising of the waters in Egypt; that it portrays Queen Elizabeth I, Lady Katherine Grey, and the Earls of Hertford and Leicester; that it is about Papist priests urging the workers to work harder; that the expression 'the cat and the fiddle' comes from (a) Katherine of Aragon (Katherine la Fidèle), or (b) Catherine, wife of Peter the Great, or (c) Caton, a supposed governor of Calais. The best guess is that the rhyme comes from the game of cat (trap-ball) and the fiddle (i.e. music) provided by some inns in the sixteenth and seventeenth centuries.

In this jungle of insane antiquarian scholarship, the only safe line is to say that the rhyme commemorates the athletic lunacy to which the strange conspiracy of the cat and the fiddle incited the cow. But 'over the moon' as an expression of great joy was in English before the footballers of the late twentieth century picked it up. It is said to have been originated by the family of Catherine Gladstone (née Gwynne), the wife of the Victorian Prime Minister. The diary of May, Lady Cavendish, for February 7, 1857, records how she broke the news of her youngest brother's birth to the rest of her siblings: 'I had told the little ones who were first utterly incredulous and then over the moon.'

We can date 'sick as a parrot' even more precisely. In the Seventies there were a number of heavily publicized cases of travellers from West Africa dying of psittacosis or parrot fever (a viral disease of parrots and other birds that can be transmitted to man, in whom it produces inflammation of the lungs, pneumonia, and often death). After the sensational tabloid papers had been full of such alarming stories, laid on with a shovel and 72-point headlines, footballers, who read such papers, introduced 'sick as a parrot' into their gladiatorial post-game vocabulary.

At least that is my theory. But you can, if you want, note that the phrase 'as melancholy as a sick parrot' was current in the seventeenth and eighteenth centuries, for example in the plays of Aphra Behn. To speak or prate like a parrot is a proverbial simile for talking much rubbish, almost certainly dating from Skelton's Pythonesque poem *Speke Parrot* of about 1525. This has little on dead parrots, but at least observes: 'When Parrot is dead she doth not putrefy.' And it goes on:

And remember among how Parrot and ye
Shall leap from this life, as merry as we be:
Pomp, pride, honour, riches, and worldly lust,
Parrot saith plainly, shall turn all to dust.

Skelton's parrot was enormously influential. We can trace it echoing down the centuries in English literature and proverbs. George Gascoigne's *The Glass of Government*, 1575: 'Yong men of quicke capacitie, do (Parrotte like) very quickly learne the rules without booke.' 1587: 'Shee had not such credite as I gate,/Although a King would heare the parret prate.' John Lyly's *Endimion*, 1591: 'Speakes the Parrat? shee shall nod heere-after with signes.' Shakespeare's *Othello*, 1604: 'Drunk! And speak parrot! And squabble, swagger, swear!' Ben Jonson's *New Inn*, 1630: 'He prates Latine,/And 'twere a parrat, or a play-boy.' A dictionary of sayings, 1639: 'He prates like a parrot.' Another dictionary of Spanish and English idioms, 1706: 'Papagayo – To talk like a Parrot, That is, Either to talk very much, or to talk nothing to the purpose.'

The other parrot proverb derived directly from Skelton's parrot poem is the now obsolescent phrase 'an almond for a parrot'. Skelton: 'An almon now for Parrot, dilycatly drest.' An almond for a parrot was used to mean either a reward for speaking, or a reward for keeping silent. As usual, there is some confusion in our parrot phrases. For example, in Buttes' *Dyets Dry Dinner* of 1599: 'Phillis was turned into an Almond-tree, for telling tales out schoole: euer sithence, it hath bene a by-word: an Almond for the Parrat.' Shakespeare's *Troilus and Cressida*, 1602: 'The parrot will not do more for an almond than he for a commodious drab.' Ben Jonson's *The Magnetic Lady*, 1631: 'Almond for Parrat; Parrat's a brave bird.'

Skelton introduced, or at any rate popularized our name for parrot. Before his influential poem, our name for the gaudy bird was popinjay, which has cognates in most European languages, the earliest being the twelfth-century French *papegai*. This probably came from medieval Greek and Arabic imitations of the cry of the bird in some African or other non-European language, assimilated to the name of the European chattering bird, the jay. The origin of the name parrot is also peculiar. There is no cognate of parrot in any other language. Etymologists guess that it comes from Perrot, said to be a French man's proper name, a diminutive of Pierre, like Pierrot, which is a French nickname for the house-sparrow. The difficulty with this is that there is no record of the name Perrot being used for the parrot in French; though Littré gives pérot as a nineteenth-century familiar name for the parrot. In addition, Perrot is not recorded as a man's name in sixteenth-century England. So points of contact are missing in the Perrot derivation.

Our parrot names and metaphors are inapt. But they are nothing like as rude as what parrots say about humans behind their backs:

A parrot next, but dead and stuff'd with art;
(For Poll, when living, lost the lady's heart,
And then his life; for he was heard to speak
Such frightful words as tinged his lady's cheek:)
Unhappy bird! Who had no power to prove,
Save by such speech, his gratitude and love.

21

BC–AD

Just a Minute

Some pleasures live a month and some a year,
But short the date of all we gather here.
                    'Retirement', 1782, by William Cowper

JEWS DO IT from the date of the Creation, which is taken
to be October 7, 3761 BC, in the Christian calendar.
Muslims begin their Year One with the *Hegira*, the day
on which Mohammed fled from Mecca, *aka* by the Julian
date as July 16, AD 622. Ancient Greeks measured time by
the Olympian Games, held every four years, and founded
in 776 BC; or by the Archons of Athens, whose register
went back as far and as unpersuasively as the register of
vicars in small parish churches. Romans did their chronology by their eponymous consuls, and from the date of
the legendary foundation of Rome (*Ab Urbe Condita*, AUC,
from the City having been founded) put at 814, 753, 751,
748, or 729 BC. I should settle for 753. We could go into the
Chinese, Egyptian, Babylonian, and Mayan chronologies,
but I doubt whether it would be prudent. Life is too short.

But at least, after millenniums (*sic*, just, I think, rather
than millennia, because it is a modern, sc. Anglo-Latin
word, unknown to the Ancient Romans, and therefore
uninflected) of mathematical muddle about our dance to
the music of time, we have got our dates sorted out and
running smoothly now. Well, up to a point, Lady Copper.
We are about to have interminable articles and argument

in the newspapers about whether the next millennium actually starts on January 1, 2000 or 2001. The latter is correct, but it hasn't got a hope of winning. All those irresistible zeroes have a fatal attraction for giddy journalists. We seem to have established the terms 'two thousand and one' and 'two thousand and ten' and so on to refer to the years of the next century. 'Twenty one' and 'twenty ten' and so on are less clumsy, and follow the traditional form. Why do we not adopt them?

And here is another teasing little chronological puzzle that vexes me. When did we start counting dates backwards from the birth of Christ, and when did we introduce the typographical abbreviation BC? They seem simple little questions. But nobody knows. Go to the prime source for the history of the English language and usage. *The Oxford English Dictionary*, which is understandably terse and impatient with abbreviations, having enough untruncated words on its plate, gives no dates or quotations for BC in either of its editions or any of its supplements. As a last resort they have scanned the *OED*, that vast pyramid of English, using their latest technological toy, the *OED* on a compact disc with a read-only memory. But this will not accept a query for a lemma consisting solely of initial letters. So we are left with the question. The Oxford lexicographers will try to repair the omission and find a date for the introduction of BC in a future revision of the dictionary. This is not a question on which the fate of nations hangs; but it is interesting because it is odd. You would have thought that somebody would have noticed the introduction of such a useful and momentous change in our system of measuring the passage of time.

Early antiquaries and others who needed to think about the past worked from the date of Creation, *anno mundi*, the year of the world. For example, William Stukeley, writing between 1724 and 1743, uses AM for his dates. This date was originally computed in Greek by Eusebius, Bishop of Caesarea, in the third century AD, and amended in Latin by St Jerome in the fourth. Joseph Scaliger, the greatest scholar of the Renaissance, in his *De Emendatione Temporum* revolutionized ancient chronology by insisting on the recognition of the historical material relating to the Jews, the Persians, the Babylonians, and the Egyptians. But he did so without negative counting backwards from the birth of Christ or any other such fixed date.

The notion of counting backwards had come in by the time of James Ussher (1581–1656), scholar of the new Trinity College, Dublin, and later Archbishop of Armagh. His chief work is the *Annales Veteris et Novi Testamenti*, a chronological summary in Latin of the history of the world from the Creation to the dispersion of the Jews under Vespasian. He fixed the date of the Creation at October 23, 4004 BC, and his tables are said to be the source of the dates later inserted in the margins of the Authorized Version of the Bible. In Ussher's chronological tables, one column is headed 'Years Before Christ', and is the first instance I can find of backwards dating. By an oversight this heading is actually retained even when the table passes AM 4004 (=Julian Period 4714) and enters the Christian Era.

The earliest use of the abbreviation BC that I can find is in John Blair's *Chronology and History of the Ancient World* (1756). Blair's chronological table, like Ussher's, has a column of running figures headed 'Years Before Christ', but in the sections headed 'Men of learning and genius', 'Remarkable events', and 'Statesmen &c' he employs the abbreviations BC and AC (*sic*, After Christ) on Table 20. The expedient is required because Table 20 covers events either side of the birth of Christ, and confusion would have resulted had he stuck to the practice adopted elsewhere of dating events by a figure giving the year before/after Christ without any identifying phrase or abbreviation. The preface draws special attention to this use of AC and BC, suggesting that it was something novel (and in the case of AC, of course, not destined to become standard). It is significant that BC makes its first known appearance in circumstances where special constraints of space within a tabular layout came into play. BC took time to catch on. Given the generous conditions of eighteenth-century publishing, there was nothing working in favour of abbreviating, for example, 'the year before Christ 480' when it appeared in continuous text rather than a column or table, or even in the marginal dating of the Authorized Version. You can find 'before Christ' written in full *passim*, for example, in John Jackson's *Chronological Antiquities* of 1752. By the time we get to *History of Greece* by W. Motford, although marginal annotations use the abbreviation BC, the main text retains the full form. John Lemprière prefixed to the second edition of his *Classical Dictionary*, published in 1792, a chronological table in which the dates are shown as BC or AD. That he was pioneering may be deduced from his footnote, which both explains the abbreviation and labours the obvious, namely that the Julian year, the era from the foundation of Rome or the Olympiads, 'will easily be discovered by the application of the rules of subtraction or addition'.

The full acceptance of BC as something respectable enough to be incorporated into a historical narrative may therefore be a nineteenth-century development. And, to revert to the substantial rather than the typographical issue, the actual use of Olympiad and AUC dating by Classical scholars (especially when writing on Roman history and Greek literature) persisted long after reliable tables existed to provide BC equivalents.

There is no problem about AD. It was introduced by Dionysius Exiguus, 'the titch', a Scythian monk who lived at Rome *circa* AD 500–550. He called himself Exiguus out of 'humility' according to his hagiographer, and he is famous for his contributions to ecclesiastical chronology. When called upon to construct a new Easter cycle, he abandoned the era of Diocletian, and (wrongly) accepting 753 AUC as the Year of the Incarnation, introduced AD, and the system we still use. This 'Christian Era' was adopted in England at the Synod of Whitby, AD 664, and later became widespread on the Continent. Except in

Russia. The former Byzantine dating was introduced in Russia in 988, when Prince Vladimir Svyatoslavovich converted to Christianity, and it was determined that the Creation of the world had occurred 5508 years before the birth of Christ. The year 988 was thus 6496, according to this Russian reckoning. This system lasted until 1700 (7208 Byzantine style), when Peter the Great introduced the Christian AD calendar. The only further change to the Russian calendar was made in 1918, when the country changed from the Julian calendar to the Gregorian, as England already had in 1752.

Too many dates can drive men mad. There is less problem about our established usage. Orthodox Jews, and perhaps followers of other non-Christian religions, prefer to use CE for Common Era instead of AD. Grammatically and logically the AD should come before the date, and the BC after. Item: 'The Roman conquest of Britain began in AD 43.' AD is now usually printed in small capitals, without points after each capital. But by analogy with the placing of BC, AD is sometimes slipping after the date, even in historical works: 'The Roman Emperor Claudius I lived from 10BC to 54AD.' Analogy is a sore decayer of your whoreson dead idiom. We should avoid this for as long as we can. In spite of its meaning, AD is illogically but usefully used to designate centuries, being placed after the specified century: e.g. the second century AD.

22

GENTLEMAN

Where's the Gent?

I do hope I shall enjoy myself with you . . . I am parshial to ladies if they are nice I suppose it is my nature. I am not quite a gentleman but you would hardly notice it.

        The Young Visiters, 1919, by Daisy Ashford

F RENCH AND ENGLISH are separated by only a narrow channel, and are being joined by a tunnel. But our languages and attitudes are oceans apart. You can translate them, often with ludicrous results. Hamlet's 'thrift, Horatio, thrift' comes out as *'de l'économie, Horace, de l'économie'*, which makes me giggle. In 1989 Chanel, the scent-makers of Paris, changed the name of the men's after-shaves and other pongs that they sell in the United Kingdom from 'A Gentleman's Range' to *Pour Monsieur*, which is what they are called in the rest of the world. The English, gents or not, affect to be a bit shy of the non-U overtones of perfume (which gentlemen call scent), and go in for deodorants with powerful smells and unthreatening macho names such as 'Old Jockstrap'. Gentleman is a translation of *monsieur*, but they are not the same thing at all.

I suspect that one reason for Chanel's volte-face is that 'gentleman' is becoming an embarrassing concept and an obsolete word in our progress towards a classless society. It has been in English since the thirteenth century, originally as an epithet of rank to describe a man of gentle birth, which was in the beginning used synonymously with 'noble', but afterwards distinguished from it, either as a wider term, or as designating a lower degree of rank. The English, and I dare say most races, are keen on such fine class discriminations, especially if they personally end up on the right side of the line. The College of Arms, and other such specialists in class, decree that a gentleman is properly somebody who is entitled to bear arms, although not ranking among the nobility. At this stage in English history, almost anybody who is prepared to pay researchers to dig deep enough into his pedigree can find an entitlement to bear arms lurking there somewhere. Almost anyone can claim to be a gentleman; as a consequence the term is falling out of use.

Esquire as a label on envelopes to address a gentleman is travelling in the same direction into history and obsolescence. The esquire was originally a young man of gentle birth, who was an aspirant to knighthood, and as a kind of gentle apprentice attended upon a knight, carried his shield, and acted as his fag or caddy. The College of Arms rule that an esquire is a man belonging to the higher order of English gentry, ranking immediately below a knight. But after so many centuries of class rise and fall, and such pettifogging rules about who is an esquire (a barrister is, but a solicitor is not), it is impossible to know who is to be addressed as Esq., and who as plain Mr. So we either address everybody as Esq., or forget the title for everybody. We are all esquires now, but none of us owns up to being a gentleman. Public lavatories are labelled 'Men', or embarrassing whimsies such as 'Divers' or 'Cowboys', rather than 'Gentlemen'. In sport those who used to be described as Gentlemen are now more aptly called amateurs, and there are not many of them left. The annual cricket match called 'Gentlemen versus Players' was an anachronism in its title, even when it was still played. Lord's has abolished the different gates from the pavilion onto the pitch for gentlemen and players. Why, as a vocative to a mixed audience, do we say 'Ladies and Gentlemen' but reverse the order for 'Men and Women'? Is it a true shibboleth to say that today it is only ladies and gentlemen who do not think it rude to refer to each other as men and women? It sounds like old English snobbery under a new guise to me.

A girl today might say: 'He's ever such a nice man, or fellow, or bloke.' But not 'ever such a nice gentleman', as she might easily have said a generation ago. She might just still say: 'He's ever such a nice *old* gentleman.' But there would be a touch of conscious archaism and a vanished age in the description. In addressing a male audience, one would probably still say, 'Gentlemen'; and I think 'Ladies and Gentlemen' is a safer way to start a formal address than 'Men and Women' or jocular variants such as 'Chaps and Chapesses'. The threatened species of gentleman survives in the nature reserve that snuggles around the Court, with such designations as Gentlemen-at-Arms, the Gentleman Usher of the Black Rod, and Gentlemen-in-Waiting. But the titles are something musty, and part of the show business rather than the efficient side of the constitution. Apart from these fossilized uses, the old specific sense of a gentleman as someone entitled to bear arms, though not ranking among the nobility, is dead: 'There are no men of quality but the Duke of Monmouth, all the rest are gentlemen.' This is a dark saying today. People still use the abbreviation gent. in a tongue-in-cheek and not particularly friendly way.

Chanel is right that the gentleman is out of fashion in modern English. I hope that the scent-makers are right that 'Monsieur' will give their smells a trendy label with a whiff of Parisian chic. But I am not sure. The English have tended, in their chauvinist or rather John Bull way, to find the word funny, and to shorten and distort it to 'mounseer' and 'mossoo'. The word is almost always satirical or jocular in Shakespeare: 'Monsieur, are you not lettred?' Affecting not to be able or bothered to pronounce French words is a boring old English 'foreigners are funny' put-down.

Monsieur itself has ancient and odd connotations, not

all of them positive. *Un joli monsieur* is ironic for a thoroughly nasty piece of work. *Jouer au monsieur* is to put on airs, and act the squire. A *monsieur-dame* is idiomatic slang for a pouf or pansy. Monsieur was the title given to French bishops, the public executioner, and the French king's brother. One can say 'Bonjour monsieur', but it is difficult to think of a context in which one could say 'Good morning, gentleman'. One can say a great monsieur, a real monsieur, and a nice monsieur, just as one could say (though it sounds dated) that somebody is a great gentleman, a real gentleman, and a nice gentleman. But whereas the French can speak idiomatically of a nasty monsieur, or a foul monsieur, it sounds odd to say a nasty gentleman, or a foul gentleman. The words are not interchangeable. One day Gide called on Proust. Proust, as usual, was ill and laid up in bed. Céleste, Proust's devoted servant, apologized for not letting Gide in, and explained: 'Monsieur cannot receive Monsieur but Monsieur begs Monsieur to believe that Monsieur is constantly in Monsieur's thoughts.' You really could not make that sentence substituting Gentleman for Monsieur.

Gentlewoman is the feminine of gentleman, and even more obsolescent. It means the same as lady, but the latter has several specialized meanings that do not go with gentlewoman, for example, the Virgin Mary, the plural of 'madam', a titled woman, beloved, wife (?), and just a generally polite way of describing a woman. Lady would be the naturally polite way in modern English to describe an unknown woman: 'Pick up that umbrella, Johnny, and give it to the lady.' Cleaning or tea lady are better contemporary idiom than charwoman or scrubber. Fowler thought that in the sense common to both gentlewoman and lady (as feminine of gentleman, i.e. a woman of good birth and breeding, or a woman of honourable instincts) gentlewoman was sometimes preferred as free of ambiguity or as more significant. The English class caravan has moved on in the generation since Fowler laid down the law. There are no contexts except historical ones in which it would be natural to use 'gentlewoman' today.

I hope for Chanel's sake, and for the improvement of the body smell on the Northern Line, that a scent by any other name will sell as sweet, even when the names are as widely opposed as French and English. Gentleman is dead; Monsieur rules, OK?

23

LIBERAL

Taking Liberties with the Liberal

You know what they say; if God had been a liberal,
we wouldn't have had the ten commandments. We'd
have had ten suggestions.
The After Dinner Game, BBC TV, 1975, by Malcolm
Bradbury and Christopher Bigsby

'LIBERAL' SEEMS TO have become a term of abuse. In
the United States 'liberal' is now used to mean an
unpatriotic, wimpish, Commie bastard. In the United
Kingdom the Liberal Party decided in 1988 that they preferred to call themselves Democrats. All men (and women)
of good sense (or at any rate of fashionable views) agree
that liberals are variously and suitably described as wet,
professional, bleeding-heart, pinko, parlour, screaming,
double-domed, limousine, champagne, knee-jerk, and
hypocritical. Let us have nothing to do with the creeps.
But let us see what is happening to the word. Words
pejorate as fast as leaves fall from the trees in November.
Liberal is a strongly political word, and therefore naturally
a Janus word, facing in two directions, and meaning different things for those who stand in different places in the
political spectrum. It is a classic example of an antilogy or
phrop, a word that comprises opposing meanings.

The roots of liberal are classical. In Latin the original
meaning of *liber* was somebody with the legal and social
status of a free man, as opposed to a slave (the vital

distinction in the ancient world). The roots and cognate branches go back to the old Paelignian and Faliscan languages in Italy, and to the ancient Greek word for 'free'. From it came *lībertas*, liberty, the state of being free. Līber was the name of the Italian god of vegetation and growth, later identified with the Greek Dionysus or Bacchus. For social and snobbish reasons, *liber* in Latin and liberal in English came to mean the sort of behaviour you could expect (or a liberal would expect) from a free man: i.e. gentlemanly, ladylike, noble, handsome, generous, magnanimous, decent, easy-going, and so on. In a significant development, liberal arts very early came to mean the useless studies fit for a gent, i.e. philosophy, the humanities generally, and other such élitist rubbish that cannot pay its way in monetarist terms, as opposed to banausic pursuits that make money, such as stockbroking, running wine bars, and brick-laying. You can find 'liberal arts' used in this way *passim* in Cicero.

It is one of the paradoxes of the ancient world that we think of it as the mother of democracy, and the birthplace of the artistic and intellectual fecundity that is the foundation of western civilization; but at the same time it ran on slavery and the preservation of the status quo for the ruling class. For under a century Athens practised democracy, but it was a very partial kind of democracy, reserved exclusively for free-born male citizens. If you were a slave, a woman, or a foreigner, you had no rights. And even there, it was not what we should call a liberal democracy, but deeply structured by class, and élitist. For instance, in Aristotle's *Politics* you can read that learning to play a musical instrument is considered a banausic manual occupation, not a liberal art suitable for gentlemen. Some of Aristophanes' nastiest jokes seem distinctly illiberal to us, sneering at Euripides because his mother is a greengrocer, or at Strepsiades in *The Clouds* for marrying above his station.

This old distinction between liberal and slavish came into English in the bones of the word. As early as 1422 we find 'liberal' used in English to describe such independent, worthless activities: 'Liberal Sciencis, fre sciencis, as gramer, arte, fisike, astronomye, and otheris.' The word has always been a Janus, with the freedom and generosity ('in giffynge liberal' 1387) fighting against the sense of unrestrained licence. Freedom can look like anarchy. It depends on where you are standing. At times liberal came close to meaning licentious. For instance, here is Shakespeare, that liberal old Proteus, but when it came to politics a status-quo conservative, in *Much Ado About Nothing*:

Who hath indeed most like a *liberal* villain
Confessed the vile encounters they have had.

Or Gertrude in *Hamlet* describing Ophelia's fantastic funeral garlands:

Of crow-flowers, nettles, daisies, and long purples,
That *liberal* shepherds give a grosser name.

From its beginning there has been a conflict between freedom and licence in the word. From the eighteenth century onwards an offshoot of the licentious sense of liberal was the meaning 'not rigorous', which could be taken as either 'not harsh' or 'not disciplined'. It was this ambivalent sense of liberal that enabled Adlai Stevenson, a liberal hero, to define a liberal as somebody who has both feet firmly planted in the air.

With the ending of monarchies and slavery in Europe, liberal shifted its context. Gibbon used liberal to mean 'open-minded', and thence 'unorthodox', as in 'liberal opinions', which could be a pro-word or a boo-word, depending on who was speaking. The word became party-politicized as early as 1801: 'The extinction of every vestige of freedom, and of every liberal idea with which they are associated.' A periodical proudly, and even defiantly, named *The Liberal* was founded in 1822. The shellback British reactionaries and chauvinists disparaged it by trying to give it a nasty foreign flavour (as they still do), by referring in their writings to the Ultras and Liberals of

Paris, and even spelling the word in a sinister foreign way, as *Liberales* (Southey, 1816), or *Liberaux* (Scott, 1826). The label was used as a nickname, intended to be offensive, for advanced Whigs and Radicals by their opponents. As the nineteenth century went on, advocates of reform and changing the status quo consciously adopted liberal, in its generous pro-sense, and within a generation, the word had become orthodox. The two opposing parties in British politics started to call themselves Liberals and Conservatives instead of Whigs and Tories.

In the United States the word is pulled in a tug-of-war between right and left, as it has been in Europe. George Washington used liberal to describe somebody who would not deprive Jews and Roman Catholics of their rights in the brave new democracy. Franklin D. Roosevelt defined the liberal: 'Say that civilization is a tree which, as it grows, continually produces rot and dead wood. The radical says: "Cut it down." The conservative says: "Don't touch it." The liberal compromises: "Let's prune, so that we lose neither the old trunk nor the new branches."' The liberal is attacked from the right. Herbert Hoover: 'Fuzzy-minded totalitarian liberals who believe that their creeping collectivism can be adopted without destroying personal liberty and representative government.' Barry Goldwater, addressing a US Chamber of Commerce conference: 'If you think President Johnson is going to give you any better attention than you have got, you're very, very mistaken. If he's a conservative, I'm a screaming liberal.' From the right liberals are attacked for telling other people what to do with their money. From the left they are attacked for not having the courage to change the status quo. 'A liberal is a man who leaves the room when a fight begins.' Stokely Carmichael, the illiberal Black activist: 'What the liberal really wants is to bring about change which will not in any way endanger his position.' In the United States a 'white liberal' is used as a term of contempt to describe whites who talk about racial equality, but are not prepared to fight for it in what militants deem a sufficiently dedicated manner.

Marxist historians criticize liberals for being sentimental, ineffectual, and lacking rigour in their logic. Conservatives hate liberals for purporting to be unselfish and generous, while underneath they stick to the law of the jungle and the market, like everybody else. Robert Frost, the crusty old American poet, defined a liberal as 'a man too broad-minded to take his own side in a quarrel'. With enemies such as these, liberals must have something going for them. There is life in the old liberality yet. Freedom is a fine old ideal; and a great deal better than the alternative.

24

PERSONAL NAMES

What's in a Name?

Names?
Alpha and Omega.

GED.

O be some other name!
What's in a name? That which we call a rose
By any other word would smell as sweet.
  Romeo and Juliet, II, 1595, by William Shakespeare

I AM NEVER entirely persuaded that a rose *would* smell quite as sweet if I had to call it 'onion' or 'popadum'. But let it pass, Juliet. We have it on high authority that no good can come from association with anything labelled Gwladys or Ysobel or Ethyl or Nancye or Mabelle or Kathryn. But particularly Gwladys. We are sensitive about our names. Lord Emsworth's favourite (only) reading after *Whiffle on the Pig* was *Debrett's*, which through much practice always fell open at the right place, half way through the Es. I note that correspondents out of the blue to newspapers are livid if the respondent gets their names wrong by so little as an umlaut or a tittle, and that their rage increases in proportion to the illegibility of their signatures. Our names are our precious private labels. Get them wrong, and you assault us.

Margot Asquith, second wife of the British Liberal Prime Minister, was proud of her name and everything else belonging to her. It was her autobiography that Dorothy Parker reviewed in *The New Yorker*, and described the affair between Margot Asquith and Margot Asquith as one of the prettiest love stories in all literature. When Jean Harlow, the platinum-blonde American movie star of the Thirties, met Lady Asquith for the first time, she addressed her by her Christian name. She dropped a second brick by pronouncing Margot as though it rhymed with 'rot'. Lady Asquith corrected her, sweetly: 'My dear, the *t* is silent, as in *Harlow*.'

Names are also linguistic and onomastic archaeology. Our surnames, hereditary names borne by members of a single family and handed down from father to son, are comparatively recent. In most of central and western Europe they started to become fixed from the twelfth century onwards, and developed and changed over the centuries thereafter. The normal pattern is that in the eleventh century people did not have surnames; by the fifteenth century they did. The richer and more powerful classes tended to acquire surnames earlier than the working classes and the poor, while surnames were quicker to catch on in urban areas than in sparsely populated rural areas. The greater the number of Johns and Marys living in a congested community, the greater the need of surnames to distinguish between them. As society became more complex and organized, a more reliable and complex system of nomenclature became necessary for such gloomy matters as the collection of taxes.

Our surnames come from divers and diverse sources. Some are polygenetic, that is, they are coined independently in many different places, for example, Smith, Brown, and Newton. A few look as though they are monogenetic, that is, all the bearers of the name are descended from a single nomenclator. For example, Asquith and Auty, the one a local topographic or habitation name, and the other from a Norse personal name, are both so strongly identified with West Yorkshire that the chances of their being monogenetic must be rated very high. The same is true of the rare name Aske, as in Haberdashers' Aske's, the famous public schools that have now moved out to the fringes of north London. The charitable Aske came from Yorkshire, and almost certainly had a habitation name. There is a place called Aiskew in North Yorkshire, made up from the Old Norse elements *eiki* an oak and *skógr* a wood.

In Europe, and therefore in the United States and other places colonized from Europe, we have patronymic surnames and (fewer) metronymic ones. Other names illustrate a relationship between the first bearer of the surname and the given name incorporated in the surname: for example Bateman was originally Bate's man, the servant of Bate; Watmough was connected by marriage (mough in Middle English) to a man called Wat. Many names come from habitations (Bradford, Redhill), topography (hills, castles, trees), or from regions or races, for example French and Welsh, scilicet Celtic.

A few names come from the distinctive signs attached to houses as identification before the days of numbered streets, and addresses, and postal codes; for example, the family of Rothschilds take their famous name from the 'Red Sign' outside their old house in the Jewish quarter of Frankfurt-am-Main. Names come from occupations (Baker); from nicknames (Blake means swarthy or dark-haired – Tolstoi means fat); anecdotes lost in the shredding-machine of time (Death, Leggatt, which originally meant a deputy or ambassador in Middle English); imperatives commemorating either a characteristic action (Shakespeare) or a particular incident (Tiplady); status (Franklin, Bishop); seasons (May, Lenz); and from ornamental and arbitrary and every other imaginable peg under the sun.

The bible of names is the Oxford University Press's *A Dictionary of Surnames*, 1989, a vast history of the origins and meanings of 70,000 surnames of European origin that are in use in the English-speaking world. Turning to the most interesting entry on the Emsworth principle, I find that I have been wrong about the Howards. In order to prick the snobbish pretensions of the family to Norman blood, I have been saying for years that Howard means nothing grander than the hog-ward, or the man who looks after the pigs. In fact that *how* element was more likely a ewe than a pig. But I regret to say that in its Germanic roots the name can stand for strong spirit, and in its Old Norse elements, high guardian. For heaven's sake keep quiet about it, or the Howards will become even more pleased with themselves than they are by nature.

Most European names have long roots, of varying interest. To take a straw poll of English politicians of the Nineties, no mystery about Thatcher, though note the interesting Norfolk variant of Thaxter. Ashdown is a regional geographical name, either from Ashdown Forest in East Sussex, or from the Ashdown that was the name of the Berkshire Downs until the nineteenth century. I am sorry to report that Kinnock does not feature in the great Oxford *Dictionary of Surnames* at all; but then neither does Emsworth. Why did you name your baby 'John', as Sam Goldwyn is said to have asked: 'Every Tom, Dick and

Harry is named "John".' Or, as Dame Edna Everage defi-
nitely said: 'Marie-Joseph? It's a *lovely* name. It just sounds
silly, that's all.'

It is a wise parent whose children are satisfied with their
Christian or first names. Most of us have rueful fantasies
that our lives would be improved if we were called something less plain if we are called Jane, or something more
plain if we are called Aphrodite or Ebenezer.

Sam Goldwyn arrived as an immigrant to the United
States with a surname that was deemed un-American, or
at any rate unpronounceable, by the immigration officers.
So he adopted the name Goldfish. Goldwyn evolved as
the name of his movie company and then his personal
name from an amalgamation of Goldfish with the name of
an early partner, Edgar Selwyn. A lawsuit was brought,
challenging Sam's right to use this invented name. In
the course of the hearing the judge, a Solomon come to
judgement who eventually ruled in Goldwyn's favour,
observed: 'A self-made man may prefer a self-made name.'

There is a lot of self-made naming going on these days.
Pamella Bordes, a notable bimbo of 1989, put the second
l into Pamela because it was different, and perhaps because
it suggests the fashionable double-barrelled first name,
getting two names for the price of one, as in Sue Ellen or
Pam Ella. Pamela itself was first used by Sir Philip Sidney
in his *Arcadia* (1590). If he invented it rather than picked it
up, it is not clear what he meant by it, though a derivation
from the two Greek words meaning 'all honey' is possible.
Samuel Richardson brought it into general use with Pamela
Andrews, the heroine of his best-selling novel *Pamela* in
1740. In the eighteenth century the name's pronunciation
varied between Pameela and our modern Pamella. The
peak popularity of Pamela for naming little girls in
English-speaking countries was in the Fifties. The name
has faded now.

Marilyn is another of these invented names, getting the
best of both names, Mary and Ellen. One of its earliest
users was Marilyn Miller, the American musical star of

the Twenties, originally named Mary Ellen Miller. In the Forties Marilyn Maxwell (christened Marvel Maxwell, poor kid) began to appear regularly on cinema screens. By now the name had reached Britain, and became popular in the Fifties. Then came Marilyn Monroe (originally Norma Jean Baker or Mortenson), who was renamed by a casting agent with Marilyn Miller in mind. Since then it seems to me that the name has faded in popularity in Britain. Teachers are the people who are best placed to keep closely in touch with changes of fashion in popular nomenclature. This fashion tends to follow the celebrities of screen, stage, television screen, and royal soap opera. Fifteen years ago it was all Gary, Darren, Lee, Wayne (pronounced Way-ern in the British Midlands), Jason (J. E. Sern), Trac(e)y (Tracée), and Julie (Julée).

Australian soaps that are beginning to lather our television screens are a rich source of brave new names, such as Cheradyth, which I take to be another two-pronged, best-of-both-worlds name, combining the delights of Cherry and Edith. On balance, I am quite relieved that my parents and godparents did not choose it for me. And what strange new name for girls is this Kylie, also from *Neighbours*, but this time the real name of the celeb star, Kylie Minogue, rather than a fictional character? Jolly interesting, as it happens. It comes from *karli*, a name for a kind of boomerang in Nyungar and related languages of the Aborigines of Western Australia. It is recorded as early as 1835 in Australian English: 'I am sorry that nasty word boomerang has been suffered to supercede [*sic*, that's Oz for you] the proper name. Boomerang is a corruption used at Sydney by the white people, but not the native word, which is tur-ra-ma; but kiley is the name here.'

Kiley was adapted in transferred use to mean a small piece of board upon which two pennies are rested for spinning in an Australian game: 'The game is played with two pennies, a mattress, a thin piece of wood called a kip (sometimes a stick or a kiley), and amazing dexterity and ardour.' Kylie's use as a girl's first name has been confined

to Australia, at any rate until the arrival of the soap opera
Neighbours on the astonished television screens of the rest
of the world. It has interacted with Kelly, the Irish surname
used as a Christian name for both boys and girls in Australia. And it was influenced by Grace Kelly, who played
a leading role in *High Society* (1956), a film that had a strong
influence on fashion in names and other things. The names
of the character Grace Kelly portrayed in the film, Tracy
Samantha, were also taken up by the impressionable
classes from that time.

Because there is no gender in English grammar, the
English tend to muddle the genders of Celtic names, as
the Australians have with Kelly. In Welsh the endings
-wyn (masculine) and '-wen (feminine), meaning fair,
white, and blessed, find expression in the Christian names
Gwyn (male) and Gwen (female). The English mind sometimes perceives the ending -yn to look feminine. Perhaps
the matter is confused by the fact that Gwyneth is feminine,
but Gwynedd masculine. The former is never reduced to
a diminutive Gwyn in Welsh-speaking families, because
to do so would render the name masculine. But Gwyn
is found as a girl's name in English and Anglo-Welsh
households. Perhaps this is why Wyn is creeping in as a
girl's name in English. The wyn element seems to have an
erroneous female sound to the Anglo-Saxon ear. There are
several instances of English girls being given as name not
the feminine Olwen, but the masculine Olwyn, which
means a wheel. Logic and exactitude have as little to do
with names as they have with the other departments of
language.

We are continually making up new names. In the popular BBC radio farming soap opera, *The Archers*, Shula
Hebden *née* Archer, an interminable female character, was
named by a throw of lettered cubes by her parents Phil
and Jill Archer, who made up her name from the five
letters revealed. Presumably they did not care for the
alternative, Lusha. Interestingly, Shula has not caught on.
J. M. Barrie invented the girl's name Wendy for *Peter Pan*

in 1904, after a child had used the phrase 'friendy-wendy' to him. In fact it was already a Cambridgeshire surname taken from the village of Wendy; and there are several Germanic first names in existence, such as Wendelburg and Wendelgard, which might have produced such a pet name. The name has been helped along by three second-division British actresses: Wendy Hiller, Wendy Barrie, and Wendy Craig.

Lorna was made famous and popular by R. D. Blackmore's novel *Lorna Doone* (1869). He based his girl's name on the Scottish place-name Lorn, a district in Strathclyde. It also had a suitable sound of being forsaken. The Mac-Dougalls of Lorn were a famous family, and Lorna Doone eventually turns out to be Lady Lorna Dugal. As a girl's name, it has caught on, especially in Scotland. It is a common pattern for emigrants to create first names from surnames and place-names in the old country, for example, Bruce, Gordon, Fraser, Lindsay, Stewart, Murray, Elliot, Graham, and, most spectacularly, Clyde. Americans tend to go overboard on this, although first names beginning with Mac are not unknown on this side of the Atlantic. This is different from the practice in the Celtic and Norse fringes of the use of first names and patronyms almost as alternatives: for example, Pritchard, O'Brien, MacDonald, Anderso(e)n.

Thelma was invented by Marie Corelli for the heroine of her novel *Thelma* (1887), presumably based on the Greek *thelēma*, will. Thelma Ritter, the comedienne with the funny face, gave it a boost, but the name has faded. It is now quietly used, mostly by black American parents. Fiona was invented as the first part of his pseudonym, Fiona Macleod, by William Sharp (1855–1905). It is derived from the Gaelic *fionn* fair or white, became very popular in Scotland, reached a peak in England in the Seventies, but is not used in the United States.

There are tides in the names of men, and particularly of women, and they are shifting, pulled by the moon of fashion, all the time.

25

PUBLIC NAMES

Trade Names in a Fertile Field

Somewhere, what with all these clouds, and all this air,
There must be a rare name, somewhere . . .
How do you like Cloud-Cuckoo-Land?
                    The Birds, line 223, 414 BC, by Aristophanes

NAMES ARE POWERFUL and sometimes valuable spells. I hope that Woolworth know what they are up to in the Nineties in trying to move up-market by changing the name of their headquarters to Kingfisher. Changing the name does not necessarily improve the image. It was a fiasco in 1978 when Chrysler changed the name of their European cars to Talbot, after the original French firm, Automobiles Talbot, of Suresnes, a suburb of Paris. The French took the name from the old Norman family, especially John Talbot, the first Earl of Shrewsbury, who covered himself with gore and glory in the French wars from 1420 onwards. The large white hound called a talbot, formerly used for hunting and tracking, now extant only in heraldry, is said to have got its name from the family. The immediate source of the modern French Talbot motorcar was the contemporary Earl of Shrewsbury, a descendant of the original John Talbot. He was one of the financial backers of the French Talbot, when it was called in full the Clement-Talbot, that is, the French Clement car made to be exported to Britain.

As car *qua* car, I have no views on the Talbot's merits.

Driving in cities in the late twentieth century is for wimps and Hooray Henrys and owners of Rottweilers. Even with the decay of the London Underground system, driving a car in London is one of the silliest activities known to man in the Nineties. But as name of car, the proud and curious old name of Talbot was something less than a Rolls-Royce success. Indeed in the names of cricket sides and other such frivolities, Talbotian is still used to mean an amiable no-hoper.

Companies and persons try to hang on to their names, and restrict their use to a particular meaning, for example as a trade mark. A proprietary name or proprietary term is a word or phrase over which a person or company has some legal rights, by having registered it in the Patent Offices of the United States or the United Kingdom, or for other languages elsewhere.

Lexicographers, who are bound by their calling to go where the wind of usage blows them, have to record words that are registered or claimed as proprietary names or trade marks. In the same way that novelists put at the front of their books the assertion that the characters in the book are imaginary and bear no relation to any real person (to avoid libel), lexicographers print at the front of their dictionaries the assertion that their inclusion of words that are claimed as proprietary names does not imply that they have acquired for legal purposes a non-proprietary or general significance, nor any other judgement concerning their legal status. But of course the general public is continually using proprietary names as general words. There is no stopping them. The tradesmen should be flattered that their name is so popular.

Their disclaimer has not prevented poor lexicographers being hauled into court for merely recording the way in which we users of language have adopted and adapted proprietary names for wider uses than their proper trade mark. The fizz industry is notably litigious to restrict the name champagne to the sparkling wines grown in the flinty province of Champagne in eastern France. But names are slippery things. You cannot cage them. Champagne is an old nineteenth-century metaphor in English, and the fizz-makers should be gratified: 'It was of the two Lyttel-tons, Alfred and Edward, that the phrase the champagne of cricket was first used.' Babycham, the fizzy pear juice in twee bottles designed for the female drinker, formally takes its name from its device of a cute baby chamois, and its slogan, 'I'd love a Babycham'. The intimations of champagne in its name are a coincidence, no doubt, and a bonus for sales to the impressionable. But they sorely vex the champagne-makers of Rheims.

Biro is the proprietary name of a particular brand of ballpoint pen, named for its inventor, the Hungarian László Biró. Prudent public writers try to write ballpoint pen rather than biro, unless they are referring to that particular brand. But it is a biro nuisance. Ballpoint pen is longer and clumsier, and does not turn into a verb so well. The general public writing privately uses biro all the time to mean any old ballpoint pen. Biro is a very successful name, with the echo of giro, and the final o reinforcing the image of a pen whose nib is a miniature ball-bearing. Here are examples of the generalized use from good writers. Margaret Drabble in *Jerusalem the Golden*: 'Even the sight of a broken biro on his windowsill was of interest to her.' And here is Len Deighton, defying the biro lawyers in *The Ipcress File*: 'The biro'd message – Inquiries third floor.' 'Ballpointed message' would be intolerably clumsy.

Hoover is another contentious proprietary name. The machine that took the backache out of housework was invented by J. Murray Spangler, a caretaker in an Ohio department store; but his invention was marketed and named by the businessman, William Henry Hoover. It is a pity that Spangler's name was not attached to the sucking cleaner, because it has apt echoes of sparkle and spangle. But hoover turns into a verb quite well. It is widely and loosely used as a general term. How many housewives or househusbands hoover the carpet with an Electrolux, which does not make anything like so good a verb? *Pace* the lawyers, we have made 'to hoover' a general verb.

British journalists must always write the clumsy vacuum flask, unless they actually mean the one with the proprietary name Thermos. This is a good name, a straight transliteration of the Greek adjective meaning hot. The name was registered as a trade mark in 1907, and is still a proprietary term in Great Britain. You risk a writ, or at least a pompous letter from a lawyer, if you bandy thermos about in public in a generalized sense to mean any old vacuum flask. In 1963, however, the name became legally generic in the United States as the result of an application made against King-Seeley Thermos Co. by the comparatively small company of Aladdin Industries. Names, like the rest of language, cannot be controlled by lawyers. They go where the tides of usage take them. Corinth long ago lost its battle to restrict the name 'currants' to its own native dried grapes, and Genoa is no longer the sole manufacturer of jeans. Denim comes from other places besides de Nîmes.

If trade names are the newest names in the language, place names are the oldest. But they too have their controversies and their lawyers. In English, names like Kent and the Thames go back at least twenty-five centuries, and maybe even farther than that, into the shadows before the Celts. Place names, particularly river names, continue to be used long after their original meanings have been forgotten. Such words from a much older and preliterate language are preserved by oral tradition, and are then eventually recorded in writing centuries, maybe millenniums, after that original language has been forgotten. The most interesting academic debate going on at present concerns the ancient roots of linguistics and archaeology. Who are we Europeans, and where do the languages that we speak come from? Were the Indo-European languages and culture spread across the face of the world by conquest, mass tribal migration, or peaceful osmosis outwards with the spread of agriculture? Let us not go into that tangled question here. But put your money on the last suggestion.

Even house names can be linguistic archaeology. I met a man from Woking who had been puzzled for sixteen years by the name of his early Thirties house, 'Bullbeggars'. Even an enthusiastic fantasist has trouble in seeing a linguistic connection between a bull and a beggar. Bullbeggar is in fact a word for a bogy or spook going back at least to the sixteenth century. That bull is nothing to do with a male cow. Popular etymology has altered it from bogle, or from the Dutch *bulleman*, a ghost. That beggar has nothing to do with a mendicant. Popular etymology has altered it from boggart. Bullbeggar came into its own as a word at the Reformation, because of the rude punning allusion to papal bulls. Bullbeggars Lane in Woking is not far from my acquaintance's house, and presumably gave the house its name. Dark streets, particularly those near graveyards, are commonly named after ghoulies and ghosties and long-leggety beasties, and thing that go bullbeggar in the night.

The country is older than the town. The names of rivers and fields sometimes come from times before the Romans built the first street in Britain. Nobody bothered to study field names until John Field's pioneering study of 1972, *English Field Names*. But field names are relevant to such fashionable new studies as local history, landscape archaeology, genealogy, linguistics, and agricultural history. They come from owners' names or crop varieties, topographical and archaeological features, famous battles and forgotten jokes. Some of them go back a very long way indeed, preserving language that is otherwise dead. Many of them are distorted over the years, like Bullbeggar, by folk etymology. All language is a democracy, but place names are particularly demotic.

For example, we do not need experts to tell us why Galley Hill is called Galley Hill. Well, as a matter of fact, we do. As a boy near Lavenham in Suffolk, I was told and potently believed that it was so called because a ship had been found there, maybe a Viking long ship, or one of those men-of-war whose beams are erroneously supposed by folklore to support the timbered houses of Suffolk. Silly, really, if I had thought about it. Lavenham is thirty miles from the sea. And any builder stupid enough to want to use ship's timbers would have had to go to a port like Harwich or Yarmouth to collect them. Fields called Galley are named after the gallows. It was not unusual for a manor to have its own gallows for the execution of thieves, strangers, and others the lord found undesirable. The word comes straight from the Old English *galga* for the hanging-tree. In less savage times, over the centuries, folk euphemism softened the name to Galley. Fields called Gibbet are not quite the same. A gibbet, from the Middle English *gibet*, was a single post with a jib from which the bodies of certain criminals were hung in chains as a warning and an advertisement.

Fields called Slaughter, however, found all over England, have a less bloody history. All that they mean is that this is land on or near which a sloe tree (Old English *slāh*), valuable in the days before the supermarket, used to grow. The field called Danes Blood in Hertfordshire you can do for yourselves. The plant called Danewort, *Sambucus ebulus*, named from the same forgotten battle, is now very rare in Hertfordshire, the effect of the slaughter of the marauding Scandinavians having evidently worn off. Many fields with Damas in their names may come from damask, because the ridge and furrow of medieval cultivation looked like the patterned material that originally came from and took its name from Damascus. But you need to examine the other evidence. Damas and its cognates may preserve a reference to the Dame's House, referring either to an endowment to the Virgin Mary, or to a noble lady's property, or to a convent. There are older and stranger roots than turnips in the land you tread, and odder ink than messy blue in your biro.

26

ARGY-BARGY

Racialist Insults

> British Xenophobia takes the form of Insularism, and
> the Limeys all moved to an island some time ago to
> 'keep themselves to themselves', which as far as the
> rest of the world is concerned is a good thing.
> *The National Lampoon Encyclopaedia of Humor*, 1973

THE BRITISH REALLY ought to stop calling the Argentini-
ans 'Argies'. They don't like it. The word exemplifies
the bulldog British chauvinism and xenophobia that abroad
is unutterably bloody and foreigners are fiends; and the
British are brave, super, and noble, cheers, cheers, cheers.

The Argies, and their adjective Argie or Argy, came into
the English vocabulary in 1982 during the Falklands affair.
Here are some recent examples from the Press. 'It is my
proud privilege to loan the ship to the British Government
for use in our heroic crusade against the Argie hordes.'
'British actress Julie Christie has been signed to play the
lead in an Argentinian film which has now been retitled
Miss Mary. The original title gave both Julie and the Argies
the heebie-jeebies. It was called *Miss Maggie*.' 'Now there
are two they make distinguished twins; clockwise and
anticlockwise chronicles of Thatcher's newly tumescent,
patriotic, Argy-bashing Britain.' 'Mrs Thatcher's "lesson"
for them does not have to do with the Argie-bashing affair.'
'The programme rages at the Arts Council, Fergie, the
"Tory propaganda machine in White City" and zapping

Argies (*still?*).' 'Small boys still play at Argies and Commandos.'

The word is the latest example of a universal tendency to put down foreigners and one's enemies with dismissive nursery nicknames. Frog is the oldest in English, going back at least to 1330: 'Formest was sire Gogmagog, He was most fat foule froge.' And here is Fanny Burney in *Evelina*: 'Hark you, Mrs Frog, you may lie in the mud till some of your Monsieurs come to help you out of it.' The Indo-European roots of the word are connected either with 'slimy' or 'the hopper', and the idea that the insult is derived from the un-British French cuisine of frogs' legs is etymological folklore attached five centuries after the word first became an insult.

Jerry is a much later example. It replaced the original Fritz(y) during the First World War, and was used half affectionately: 'Poor old Jerry's copping it hot from our heavies.' This popular slang is almost always impossible to derive precisely. But apart from sounding like German, Jerry may come from the similarity between the German steel helmet and a chamber-pot, which has been called a jerry (from the large bottle, jeroboam) since 1825.

Compare the racialist diminution of Nip (as in 'There's a nasty Nip in the air') and Jap, both of which are far older than any war the British fought with the Japanese. Here is a Victorian example from *The Literary World*: 'The fearlessness of death, which makes a Jap submit to the loss of his own life rather than to permit the death of a father to go unavenged.' The Japanese find Jap more offensive than Nip. During the Second World War Allied prisoners were advised not to use the word 'Jap', which was a red rag to their guards. The most common Japanese term of abuse is *baka*, which means roughly 'idiot'. POWs remember being beaten up for saying to their working party words to the effect of 'This little bugger's not a bad chap' about their sentry, because to Japanese ears it sounded like '*baka Jap*'.

We reduce the terror of our enemy by giving him a

A WORD IN TIME

nursery diminutive, as in Boney for Napoleon Bonaparte. Hitler was referred to familiarly as Adolf and Mussolini as Musso throughout the Second World War. But the wars are over. Nevertheless, Argy seems to be establishing itself in colloquial and populist newspaper jargon, the tabloid English that nobody actually speaks. Apart from its use as a patronizing little nickname to insult foreigners, it has the merit of brevity.

Headline English in the tabloid blats is influential. Headings in huge type on a small page need short, sharp, rambo words, which is why in the tabloid screamers every argument becomes a storm or row, rivalry becomes war, development becomes move, difficulty becomes snag, to cancel becomes to axe, and to criticize is better as to slam or blast. The words are punchier than their exact replacements, but above all they are shorter. You try fitting ARGENTINIAN into a tabloid headline in screaming 160-point type. Headlines sell the story with short, sharp words. G. K. Chesterton understood the inky art: 'If I choose to head an article "An inquiry into the conditions of Mycenean civilization, with special reference to the economic and domestic functions of women before and after the conjectural date of the Argive expedition against Troy", I really have no right to complain if (when I send it to the *Chicago Daily Scoop*) they alter the title to HOW HELEN DID THE HOUSE-KEEPING.' Such brevity tends to be the soul of misunderstanding and amphibology rather than wit, as in RAMBO GUNS CLAMPDOWN (on a proposal to restrict the availability of the kind of repeater shot gun used in various mad and sensational massacres in the Eighties), or WILSON TAKES OUT HIS CHOPPER (about a Cabinet 'reshuffle'), or the classic FIFTH ARMY PUSH BOTTLES UP GERMANS (about the last German offensive in the West in December 1944).

With the newcomer Argie, a contributing etymon (the original ancestor of a word, as for example the Indo-European *owi* is the etymon of the English 'ewe') may be argy-bargy, which is Scottish, originally argle-bargle, and

means a silly and noisy dispute, quite a good description
of the Falklands campaign. Patronizing racialism and xenophobia are deplorable but universal human vices. Argie/
Argy seems to be establishing itself. You should hear what
the Argies call the British.

In fact, British racialism and racial superiority are slowly
diminishing. We have advanced some way since the wogs
began at Calais. Britons are becoming marginally less insular and xenophobic, because of our multiracial society,
our membership of the European Community, and mass
package tourism that lets us go abroad to meet the wogs,
and discover that they are in many ways just like us. The
use of such vulgarly offensive racialist insults as wog
has declined, is declining, and will probably continue to
decline. One does not abuse one's friends who live next
door; at least not if one has any sense or sensibility. Wog
always was a lager lout's word, even in its heyday before
the Second World War:

King Zog
Was always considered a bit of a wog,
Until Mussolini
Quite recently
Behaved so indecently.

Wog encapsulates in a three-letter headline word all that
is nasty about British imagined superiority. The agreeable
irony is that people from any other nation under the
sun would be embarrassed to be seen reading the British
tabloids in which words like WOG and FROG and ARGY
appear in headlines.

WOG is foul and childish and peculiarly English. But its
linguistic history is interesting. The folk etymology is that
WOG is an acronym for some such phrase as Westernized
Oriental Gentleman, or Worthy Oriental Gentleman, or
Wily Oriental Gentleman. Another theory is that it is a
flawed acronym for Workers in Government Service,
which was the phrase used to describe Egyptians employed by the British Services during the Twenties and

Thirties. Balderdash. None of these many suggested folk etymologies is satisfactorily supported by evidence. They are ingenious, contrived explanations invented after the word came into use. The most likely derivation is from a nursery curtailment of 'gollywog'.

The insult came into the lexicon from the Indian Army and Navy and Civil Service earlier this century, when the movement for Indian independence was growing, and the British felt their position threatened. The earliest printed example of Wog is in a dictionary of *Sea Slang* published in 1929. This defines Wogs as: 'Lower class Babu shipping clerks on the Indian coast.' The fact that a definition was felt to be needed indicates that the word was new. The terse insult was extended from Indians to Arabs, to anybody from the Middle East, to anybody with a tan, and, for true, barking xenophobes, to any foreigner; or, in extreme cases of egomania, anybody except the speaker. White Wogs were British and Continental European residents in Near and Middle Eastern countries. Here is Evelyn Waugh in *Officers and Gentlemen*: 'He turned up in Western Australia leading a group of Wogs.'

Down Under in Oz, wog has a different history and different connotations. A wog means a germ, or any other small organism or virus causing infection, particularly the trots or 'flu. 'I've got the wog' means 'I'm feeling a bit crook'. As with most slang, the etymology is uncertain. But it seems probable that the Australian wog comes from pollywog, the common English and hence Australian dialect word for a tadpole. In the Australian nursery a baby is sometimes called a wog, as it might be called diddums, or similar inane and increasingly old-fashioned endearments. Australians also use wog to describe immigrants from Greece and others from the Mediterranean. The situation is further confused by the Australian use of 'to wog', meaning to spit. 'Wog gut' is diarrhoea. Down Under or Up Over, wog is an ugly little word that is dying. Let it die. Good riddance to it.

27

BIMBO

How to Handle a Woman

Bimbos who went about the place making passes at innocent girls after discarding their wives.
Full Moon, chapter v, 1947, by P. G. Wodehouse

T HIS IS THE decade of the bimbo, linguistically if not socially. It started, like much new English, in the United States, with the sexual misadventures of a number of fringe American politicians, and a greater freedom by the gutter Press and Peeping Tom television in hounding them down in the Eighties. Bimbo has come to mean a pretty young woman considered as a sex object, who may be, in the stern old Yorkshire and New England euphemism, no better than she ought to be, or, in the more recent Californian euphemism, fun-loving. Bimbo in its new sense was picked up almost immediately by the Peeping Tom Press and gutter television in Britain and the rest of the English-speaking world. In one sense at least the world has indeed become a global village, viz. in the tendency of the media to copycat each other instantaneously.

Bimbo is older and more interesting than it seems on the surface. It came into New York streetwise slang from the Italian-American *bambino* in the early 1900s to mean a man, especially a mean and menacing one. It was New York gangster street talk, cf. bozo and baby. This was classic euphemism, calling something nasty by a nice name in order to make it less dangerous. As the ancient Greeks called the terrifying Furies the Eumenides, literally 'the kindly ones', to appease them, and the shipwrecking Black Sea the Euxine, 'the friendly to strangers', as a sop to fortune, so New Yorkers felt safer calling an ugly great killer 'little baby' in Italian. For example, that tough crime writer Dashiell Hammett: 'The bimbos once helped pluck a bank.' And again: 'One of them bimbos which hurls a mean hammer.'

Almost as early bimbo started to mean a fellow, chap, or guy, with no implication that the bimbo was a hoodlum, but with intimation that he was insignificant. Bimbo was always male, and usually contemptuous, as in the Wodehouse epigraph at the head of this chapter. Raymond Chandler: 'There's a thousand berries on that bimbo [sc. possible victim]. A bank stick-up, ain't he?' Young P. G.

Wodehouse, who was charmed by New York slang and had a good ear for it, used bimbo *passim* in the Twenties to describe the Gussy Finknottles of the world. *Bill the Conqueror* (1924): 'The bimbo Pyke arrived.' The nearest slang synonym to this is the Yiddish *nebbish*, from the Czech *neboky*: 'Nobody listened to the poor bimbo.'

With new slang, and new language generally, it is quite usual for several meanings to develop simultaneously, as people try out the new words, get them wrong, adopt them, adapt them, and change them to suit their various purposes. It took nearly a century for the terms of Newtonian physics to settle down in their final form. In the Twenties, in addition to its New York meanings of thug and wimp, bimbo was also being used to mean child or kid, as it still was in Italian. And also in the Twenties bimbo started to be used as a slang name for a woman, especially a young woman, especially a good-looker. 'What kind of bimbo did he think I am?' From an American detective magazine of 1937: 'We found Durken and Frenchy LaSeur seated at a table with a pair of blonde bimboes [*sic*, the original plural] beside them.' Pretty soon, language being male-dominated, or at any rate most pulp crime fiction of the tough-guy genre being written by men, bimbo had come to be used to mean a prostitute. In this sense, the nearest American equivalent was hooker. Bimbo as hooker is found from the Twenties on. 'Not that you were just a bimbo to me. I've discovered that I'm a little in love with you, too.' 'Some escort agencies are just fronts for prostitution. Men call up and the service just sends out some bimbo in blue jeans from Brooklyn.'

This latest sense of bimbo as prostitute is probably connected with the common New York use of bimbo as the name for a monkey or monkey-doll, especially the one that held the collecting bag for street organ-grinders, who were in the New York of the Twenties and Thirties typically desperately poor Italian immigrants from the Mezzogiorno and Sicily. The only other use of bimbo in slang, recorded since the Fifties, is to mean the posterior, especially the female posterior. This must be derived not from the American-Italian *bambino*, but from the Scottish public-school thinning of the vowel in bum to mean the buttocks. Since the Twenties to bim as verb has been prep school slang for to cane, properly on the bottom.

Bimbo is a complex little word, with quite a long and muddled history. Until quite recently the sense of bimbo as hooker (or in the United Kingdom tart) was the dominant one, as explained by that notable etymologist James Bond in *The Spy Who Loved Me* from the early Sixties: 'Bimbo . . . it's gangster language for a whore.' Language moves on continually. In bimbo's new word of the decade role, she doesn't have to be a whore, just a young woman content with the role of brainless, pretty-pretty ego-masseuse. Tabloid journalists whip themselves up into a frenzy of lascivious self-righteousness 'exposing' them. Bimbo is still pretty derogatory. If called a bimbo, you should belt the speaker on his snoot with your handbag.

Male names for pretty woman are usually rude and unkind, in a reverse euphemism, a dysphemism, making something desirable but dangerous safer by putting it down. Two Glasgow hairies are walking along Sauchiehall Street. (Hairy is Glasgow slang for a hatless slum girl conscious of her station in life. In Glasgow, as in Rome, the hat is still the badge of feminine quality, and a shibboleth of the class system. Without a hat, you are a hairy or a harridan.) Two American sailors on leave from the base at Holy Loch meet them, and one of the sailors says to one of the hairies: 'Come with me, doll, and I'll give you something you've never had before.' She turns to her friend, and says: 'Look, Jeanie, here's a fella whae's got leprosy.'

It is a melancholy reflection on the male bias of language, or the fact that until recently men have dominated the publication of language, that disagreeable names for women outnumber disagreeable names for men by a hundred to one. If you look in any thesaurus of slang, you will find hundreds of coarse, sexist, and cruel words to describe a woman, and only a handful of slang words to describe a man, most of them flattering, or at any rate nudge-nudge admiring: sport, stud, rooster, swordsman, and so on. The reasons for this are that until recently men were the only sex allowed out into the big world to make and spread slang, and that historically (and unfairly) female promiscuity has been deemed more serious than male, because of its effect on legitimacy and inheritance.

The prevalence of slang names for women, usually but not necessarily derogatory, is common to all languages and cultures. And the roots go deep. Australian hearties call a young woman a sheila or shelah, probably in a generic use of the Christian name transported Down Under by involuntary Irish immigrants. At any rate, here is what is thought to be the seminal use of the sobriquet as a generic, from the Sydney *Monitor* of as early as 1822: 'Many a piteous sheila stood wiping the gory locks of her Paddy, until released from that duty by the officious interference of the knight of the baton.'

The latest trendy terms for young women in London in the Nineties are fresh and fit. The young say things like: 'My, she's fresh.' They mean: 'My I fancy her, she's a bit of all right, a good-looker, a dish, but not exactly a bimbo.' The fashion is, as usual, far older than the young suppose. Slang recurs, and crops up again after lying fallow for a century, as the teasels did when they dug the North Sea oil pipelines in the Eighties. Fresh has been used in the jargon of amorous venery since about 1840. A fresh bit in the nineteenth century was a beginner, or a new mistress; a bit of fresh was slang for the sexual favour, as the etymologists stuffily put it. Fit has been used to mean good-looking, especially of bimbos, since at least 1870.

Male chauvinism in nomenclature extends to plants as well as humans. Before the recognition and proof of sexuality in plants during the seventeenth century, the use of the terms 'male' (*arren, mascula, mas*) and 'female' (*thelus, femina, foemina*) for them from the Ancient Greeks onwards was metaphorical, not biological. Accordingly the useful fibre- and seed-producing female individuals of hemp (*Cannabis sativa*) were called 'male', and the seemingly useless and disposable male individuals were called 'female' by Rabelais and sixteenth-century herbalists. Similarly, the hop-producing female individuals of the hop (*Humulus lupulus*) were called 'male', and the unproductive, seemingly useless male individuals were called 'female'. This unchivalrous usage persisted in the Rhône basin of France until late in the nineteenth century. The botanists at least have now removed this absurd male bias from their science.

Fit and fresh, the latest London words for young woman, are less coarse and hostile than most. Perhaps male attitudes are improving, under pressure from the feminist revolution, which has made even the most rampant male chauvinist self-conscious. But you will never take the sexual bias out of language; at least, not until you take sex out of life, which would be a pity.

28

WORD CHANGES

Substituting a Fresh Ilk

Chaucer, Henry James and, very humbly, myself are practising the same art. Miss Stein is not. She is outside the world-order in which words have a precise and ascertainable meaning and sentences a logical structure.
Letters of Evelyn Waugh, December 27, 1945, edited by
Mark Amory, 1980

USE, NOT HISTORY, determines the meaning of our words. We change our meanings continually to suit our new uses. Purists have been crying in the wilderness for years that *prestigious* really means 'practising juggling or legerdemain'. So it used to. You can see in the word the old Latin roots for dazzling the eyes of the audience with the speed of one's hand. But *prestigious* is no longer much used to mean good at conjuring tricks. We have other words to do that job, which in any case is not so popular in an age when magicians are old-hat on television. *Prestigious* is commonly used today as the adjective of *prestige*, which lacked an adjective. It means conferring *prestige* or endowed with *prestige*. It is all right: do not panic. Nobody is going to force you to use *prestigious* in this way if you dislike the tinsel quality of popular *prestige*, or the shady origin of its adjective. But, if you use *prestigious* in its original, 'etymologically correct' sense, you are liable to be misunderstood.

The time has come to recognize that the same vulgar pejoration (or change) has happened to that funny little word *ilk*. Purists and other busybodies have been grumbling for years that it really doesn't mean what most people suppose when they use it. And the world has not paid a blind bit of attention to the purists. 'The Walkers are a numerous race. One of the *ilk* has suggested that an ancestor probably walked to the Crusades.' And here is a theatre critic sounding off: 'It was because Oskar could play the part of brother to Amon and his *ilk* . . .' Here is a popular novel: 'One doesn't like or dislike a fellow of that *ilk*. He was a kind of barrow boy in a shop.' The authorities are unanimous in proclaiming that *ilk* is a Scots word meaning 'the same'. *Ilk* does not mean family, or kind, or set, or name, or sort, or 'of that kidney'. But that is the way that it is commonly used, and so that is what *ilk* is coming to mean. The funny little word has an irresistible attraction for joky journalists who want to liven up their pieces. Fowler condemns the slipshod new use as a popularized technicality. Sir Bruce Fraser declared that the schoolmaster who wrote to *The Times* about the damage done to the BBC by 'Mrs Whitehouse and her *ilk*' should write out fifty times: 'I must not use words I do not understand.' The second edition of *The Oxford English Dictionary* condemns the new meaning of *ilk* as erroneous. By the third edition, it looks as though *ilk* will have become established.

Ilk comes from the Old English word *ilca* meaning 'the same'. It is related distantly to the Latin *is, ea, id* 'that', and to *idem* 'the same'. Since the sixteenth century *ilk* has survived only in Scottish in two principal uses. The first is as a territorial label. 'Hamish Haggis of that *Ilk*' means Hamish Haggis of Haggis. It indicates that Hamish lives on the family estate from which he takes his name, and it distinguishes him from the Haggises of Bearsden, and his more distant cousins, the Haggises of Highgate. The second principal surviving use of *ilk* is as an adjective *ilka* (two words, *ilk* and *a*, joined together) meaning 'each' or 'every', as in 'ilka lassie has her laddie' – a consummation devoutly to be wished, but seldom achieved. Here is Sir Walter Scott (who else?) with the first correct use of *ilk*: 'Then they were Knockwinnocks of that *Ilk*.' And here is the old historiographer royal of tartan feudalism again with an example of the adjective used correctly: 'That will be just five-and-threepence to *ilka* ane o' us.' *The Oxford English Dictionary* still condemns as wrong such uses as: 'This publication was undertaken by John Murray, the first of that *ilk*'; 'Mr Hume, or Mr Roebuck, or any member of that *ilk*'; '*Robert Elsmere*, the forerunner of so many books of that *ilk*.' Fowler suggests that our common maltreatment of the little word is partly unconscious and due to ignorance of the meaning of *ilk*, and partly facetious: 'Indulgence in such worn-out humour is much less forgivable than for an Englishman not to know what a Scotch word means.'

In its strict sense there is very little use for the word inside the United Kingdom, and none outside. My use of *ilk* has declined to nil since the lamented death of Iain Moncrieffe of that *Ilk*, valued and unpredictable reviewer for *The Times*. Journalists seem to need the funny little word in its erroneous senses, perhaps simply because it is an odd little word, and fancier than kind or sort or 'of that kidney'. (Does anybody write 'of that kidney', itself an old piece of physiological facetiousness, any more? Shakespeare did in *The Merry Wives of Windsor*: 'Thinke of that, a man of my Kidney; that am as subject to heate as butter.') If you use *ilk* in its new sense, you are going to annoy purists and Scots. Nothing necessarily wrong with that. But you are also proclaiming that you either don't know or don't care about the word's original meaning. Nothing wrong with that, so long as you don't mind been seen as caring for none of these things. It is going too far to use it repetitiously as in, 'politicians of all stripes and *ilks*'. You can have stripes or *ilks*, if you must, but not tautologously together. Iain Moncrieffe would have snorted and laughed at that redundancy of *ilk*.

Ilk is shifting its meaning by accident and ignorance.

Other words get changed deliberately, and such changes are more dangerous, because they are intended to pull the wool over our eyes. The language of advertising is discourse of emotion and persuasion, not of description. Its purpose is to make the reader buy, or at any rate feel good about the product. 'Sensational': well, we all have sensations, but how do I know that the sensation I am going to feel about this product is not going to turn out to be nausea? 'Fortified with': possibly something not at all fortifying. 'New, improved Wizzo in the larger package': the old Wizzo was so disgusting that any change will be an improvement; and the package may well be larger, but what about the contents? 'Bestselling': better than what? What was the print-run, and how many copies were returned unsold from the booksellers? You don't expect us to believe bestseller lists, do you?

Fresh is at present one of the most popular words in the deceptive lexicon of advertisers' weasel-word rhetoric. In our ecologically concerned age it carries connotations of lush green newness and health, of tiny blonde tots with good breath trotting barefoot through spring meadows, with never reality like a cowpat or an adder in sight. So we are bullied by advertisements for 'doorstep *fresh*' milk, suggesting that it has come steaming from the udder of a Jersey cow just milked by a roguish milkmaid looking like Marie Antoinette, when the truth is quite different. What is so *fresh* about doorsteps anyway? There is an advertisement for 'aroma *fresh*' coffee at a kiosk at Liverpool Street Station beside an urn of Stygian black mud that has been stewing there as long as the tyrants in Phlegethon, the river of blood, in the seventh circle of the *Inferno*. We are urged to buy *fresh* milk and *freshly* made sandwiches. Does anybody actually sell *sour* milk and *stale* sandwiches? Well, since you ask, lots of people do, including British Rail's absurdly named Travellers Fare, but even they don't boast about it. What are we to make of '*freshly* squeezed' orange juice, especially when it comes in a carton labelled that it is 'best used' before a date two years from now? *Freshly* squeezed ought to mean squeezed on the spot, in front of my very eyes, on the doorstep, or in the supermarket aisle. That would be *fresh* in the accurate acceptance of the word. You could argue that *fresh* is the most abused word in the English language at present, and that its use must constantly contravene the Trade Descriptions Act.

There is occasions and causes why and wherefore in all things, including the wrong number of this sentence. Before banning the word *fresh* from the English language, let us examine its roots and linguistics, look you. The word is first recorded by Orm, the Augustinian monk from the east of England, in the twelfth century, and by it he seems to mean something like 'eager' or 'ardent'. In the thirteenth century we find *fresh* being used to mean brisk or vigorous. Robert of Gloucester (*floruit* 1260–1300) in his metrical chronicle, which gives the first account of a town-and-gown riot at Oxford, uses *fresh* to mean not salty when applied to water. In the fourteenth century the sense of *fresh* meaning new or novel came in to fill a contemporary need. This is the sense in *fresh*'s most famous appearance on the stage of Eng Lit: 'Tomorrow to *fresh* woods and pastures new'.

But such an old word as *fresh* in its eight centuries of life acquires many overlapping meanings. *Fresh* can be used to mean 'not faded', as in *The Tempest*: 'Our garments are now as *fresh* as when we put them on.' It can mean blooming and fair, as in *A Midsummer Night's Dream*: 'Hoary-headed frosts/Fall in the *fresh* lap of the blooming rose.' It can mean healthy-looking, as in *Innocents Abroad*: 'If you've got a nice *fresh* corpse, fetch him out.' *Fresh* has been used to mean anything from drunk to sober, and from strong (of the wind) to open (not frosty) of the weather. It is a word with strong positive connotations, a pro-word, and therefore a useful word for advertisers. The fault, dear Brutus, is not in the language itself, but in mistaking advertising slogans as statements of fact, when they are a quite distinct register. The correct response to a word that is becoming fashionable in advertisements is: 'Why are these *fresh* bastards lying to me?' In this context *fresh* means impertinent.

29

PICKING THE RIGHT WORD

Why You May Never Tell Lays

The flame which had before laid in embryo now burst forth.

Tom Jones, I, vi, 1749, by Henry Fielding

No two words are exactly the same, just as no two humans are exactly the same, not even identical twins. Part of writing well is picking exactly the right word for what you want to say instead of one that is nearly right. One of the causes of writing badly is scoring a near hit, and picking a word that is not quite right. When *The Times* headline-writer wrote BRITONS LAY LOW AFTER TERRORIST ORDEAL IN SPAIN, he or she fell into an old-fashioned word-pit, and chose the word that was quite wrong. The confusion between *lie* and *lay* is an old chestnut. To mix them up is a sign of carelessness as significant as nicotine stains or two-day stubble.

Lie and *lay* offer traps of pen
That have bothered most excellent men.
  You may say that you *lay*
  In your bed yesterday:
If you do it today, you're a hen.

The two little verbs are *lay*, *laid*, *laid*, and *lie*, *lay*, *lain*. *Lay* is the transitive, to make to *lie*, and their old English forms are different in only one letter, *lec̵gan* and *lic̵gan*. Today *lay* is only transitive, except for specialized nautical uses such as to *lay* at anchor, to *lay* by the wind, and to *lay* on the oars. Sailors will have their funny little ways, in language as in life. *Lay* is one of the more complicated words in English, having well over sixty main meanings in the biggest dictionaries. Originally it could be used intransitively, as a reflexive or passive like *lie*, and was so used by writers as exact as Bacon ('Nature will lay buried a great Time, and yet revive') and as dashing as Byron (*Childe Harold's Pilgrimage*, IV, clxxx: 'Thou dashest him again to earth: there let him *lay*'). But during the nineteenth century the useful distinction between the two words was introduced, and is now firmly established. You must have a burden or some other object to *lay* down. *Lie* is the intransitive verb that you use for lying down without an object: 'Brer Fox, he *lay* low.' To use *lay* intransitively to mean *lie* is now only dialectal or illiterate.

Because the words are so similar in their tenses and their senses, there is considerable scope for confusion, and *lay* for *lie* is one of our most popular solecisms. In particular, we use *laid* (which belongs to *lay* only) instead of *lay* the past tense and *lain* the past participle of *lie*: 'We *laid* out on the grass and could have *laid* there all day.' We also get our compounds in a twist. To overlay is to superimpose. To overlie is to lie on or over something. To underlay is to put under. To underlie is to lie under. You overlay a coat of paint with another coat of paint; and you underlay a carpet with felt or old copies of *The Times*. But a layer of coal may underlie or overlie a layer of sandstone. If you confuse your lays and your lies, you suggest that your English grammar, or at any rate your ear for language, is unsound. The distinction is a useful one, and we should do our best to preserve it from the inexact users of language.

Here is another useful distinction between a pair of linked verbs that is in danger of being eroded by illiteracy. We recently printed a letter in *The Times* that advised '*substituting* junk food with fresh fruit'. This confirmed my suspicion that the confusion between *substitute* and *replace* has spread even to *The Times* letter-writing classes, and has become a menace to meaning. I blame football and other sports, where you have a *substitute* waiting on the bench or warming up, and then being *substituted* for some muddied hacker already on the field, who shakes hands resentfully with him as he comes off, and is then said to have been *substituted* (that is replaced, or better displaced or superseded).

Over the centuries the two words have developed different meanings and different constructions, as have *lay* and *lie*. If I wish to poison my wife, I will *substitute* strychnine or weed-killer for her sugar; but I will have to *replace* her sugar with (or perhaps by) strychnine or paraquat. *Substitute* has now developed the dominant meaning of putting something in the place of something else. And the only preposition that it can take is 'for'. If you find yourself *substituting* 'by', or with any other preposition, you are wrong, or at any rate misleading.

It took time for this nice distinction to be established. Good, idiomatic writers in the past used *substitute* to mean *replace* or 'take the place of', followed by every preposition in the book. 'I hear Don Emanuel de Lyra is like to be one of the Plenipotentiaries, and come in as *substituted* by the Duke of Villa Hermosa.' 'Good brandy being *substituted* by vile whiskey.' Since the Victorian ordering of grammar (as of so much else), such uses were regarded as incorrect. Not any more, they ain't, because of the influence of popular sport. When saccharin is used instead of sugar, it is idiomatic to say that saccharin is *substituted* for or *replaces* sugar, and that sugar is *replaced* by or with saccharin. We seem to have decided to substitute *substitute* for *replace*, or, as we say now, to substitute *replace* by *substitute*. 'The Minister said she hoped to *substitute* coarse grain with home-grown barley.' The Minister ought either to have used the forgotten word *replace*, or, if she was determined to use the fashionable word *substitute*, she should have said, 'to *substitute* home-grown barley for coarse grain'.

Does the erosion of these fine distinctions really matter? Or are we pedantically pettifogging? Idioms and the prepositions that go with verbs change as ceaselessly as the pebbles on Chesil Beach. The history of any old word is a story of continual change of meaning, connotation, and idiom. Yes, it jolly well does matter, partly because we are eroding a useful established distinction, and partly because the resultant confusion is potentially dangerous. The current use of *substitute* instead of *replace*, particularly in the passive, and particularly in scientific and technical contexts, means that the writer and the reader may understand a specification in opposite senses. Can any reader confidently obey the instruction to '*substitute* a 3A fuse with a 15A one'? Electricity is frightening enough without imposing grammatical ambiguity on it. Those who have to deal with specifications in industry should be aware of this potentially lethal shift in grammar; and those who write the specifications could help by *substituting replace* for *substitute* throughout – or, if they prefer, *replacing substitute* with *replace*. Those of us who have to *replace* fuses or read other men's English should always read *substitute* with narrowed eyes, until the idiom has settled down again.

We must teach our children such English grammar. But it is not as easy as it used to be. We have recognized that English grammar does not run on railway lines, like the grammars of Latin, Ancient Greek, and other dead languages. These seem to run on railway lines only because they are finite. We possess all the Golden Latin that has survived, except for small accretions from newly discovered papyri and inscriptions. So we can say confidently that such-and-such a construction 'always' takes the subjunctive, because there is no example in our corpus of it taking anything else. If Cicero and Virgil were still writing, they might one day use something other than the subjunctive, because it sounded right, or for effect, or to be difficult, or because idiom was changing.

English grammar is the general consensus of the way we say and write things at present. So it changes constantly, more like a park with many paths across the lawns and through the bushes than a railway line. Alfred Austin, the poet laureate remembered for his lines about the illness of the Prince of Wales (which he probably did not write) 'Across the wires the electric message came:/"He is no better, he is much the same"', was once reproached for the grammatical errors in his verses. I dare say he had used *substitute* instead of *replace*. Alfred replied majestically: 'I dare not alter these things: they come from above.' We may excuse errors in our grammar by claiming that they were dictated from on high, or sound right to us. We must be prepared for others to disagree, and claim that our English sounds wrong to them. In the long run grammar drifts in the direction of its most influential users.

As well as *lay* and *lie*, and *substitute* and *replace*, one of the ways it is drifting at present, perhaps because of guidance from above of the kind that influenced Alfred Austin, is towards confusion between *may* and *might*. Particularly on the sports pages and in sporting broadcasts, those maternity hospitals of illiteracy and new slang, the sports hacks and commentators continually say *may* where until recently correct grammar demanded *might*. 'Botham *may* have caught him in the slips.' This sounds to me as though the great wally elephant actually caught the ball, but the umpire gave it Not Out for reasons that seemed good to him at the time. In the new sporting use what is meant by that *may* is: 'Botham *might* have caught him in the slips (if he hadn't been talking to his neighbour at the time, and as it happened the ball flew past him for four).' *May* indicates a higher degree of probability than *might*, and I suspect that it is considered more genteel or 'correct'. This *may/might* seem a small matter of grammar. But it can make as big a difference to the meaning as our current confusion between *lay* and *lie*, and *substitute* and *replace*.

The grammar was easier a generation ago, when it was taught on the railway-line principle, as though English were an inferior kind of Latin. *Might* was described in the old grammars as the unsatisfactory English equivalent of the Latin pluperfect subjunctive, representing a past contingency, which is not realized and so is contrary to fact. *May* was described as a wet English substitute for the Latin present subjunctive, indicating a possibility that *may* or *may* not be contrary to fact. If you muddled your *mays* and your *mights*, Old Chalky roared with rage and hurled the blackboard cleaner at you.

These days we have a different, more accurate model of English grammar. *May* and *might*, *can* and *could*, *will* and *would*, *shall* and *should*, *must* and *ought to* are known as 'modal auxiliary verbs', because they help the main verb distinguish between moods, such as that between possibility and actuality. In their primary function *may/might* relate mainly to permission: 'You *may* look at the kittens, but don't touch.' *Can/could* relate to ability. *Will/should* relate to prediction. *Should/ought* relate to escapable obligation. *Must* relates mainly to inescapable obligation. These are the modern grammatical categories. In their secondary function most of these modal auxiliaries can be used to express the degree of certainty or uncertainty that a speaker feels about a possibility. They range in a rough and variable scale from the greatest uncertainty (*might*) to the greatest certainty (*must*): 'He *must* have caught him: that umpire should see an oculist.'

What seems to have happened is that the Lunch-Time O'Balls sporting journos have let *might* drop out of their vocabulary, and *replaced* or *substituted* it with *may* as the modal of greatest uncertainty. This sounds wrong to those of us whose ears still tingle on frosty mornings from Old Chalky's ruler. It is also wasteful, because we are losing one of the very fine distinctions of probability provided by our modal auxiliaries. But if it goes on for long enough, *may may* become *might*, and *might might* become dead. But until that happens, we *must* resist the confusion between *lay* and *lie*, *replace* and *substitute*, and *may* and *might*.

30

WICKED, BLOODY, DEVILISH

Bad Language from the Playground

There the wicked cease from troubling, and there the
weary be at rest.

Job, Authorized Version, iii, 17

INSTEIN WAS A late talker, and his parents were worried
about him. At last at supper one night he broke his
silence and spoke his first words: 'The soup is too hot.'
His parents were greatly relieved, congratulated him, and
then asked him why he had never said a word before.
Little Albert replied: 'Because up to now everything was
in order.'

Unlike Einstein, most children chatter before they can
think. Children's slang and school playground talk have
opposing tendencies. On the one hand, they show deep
continuity, going back an astonishing number of generations, as demonstrated by the work of Peter and Iona
Opie; on the other hand, and on the surface, they are as
changeable as any other register of language, probably
more so. Each new peer group wants its own slang and
codes, to distinguish it from the ones that went before.
Last term's slang is dated and dating and boring. At an
age when they are learning faster and experimenting with
language more rashly than they ever will again, they coin
their side-splitting new private language, as children have

done since Romulus and Remus first howled at the moon. They think it is brand new. It is usually old slang recycled.

The latest in word of supreme commendation in London primary schools is 'wick', replacing the long line of fab, terrif, wizzo, smashing, and all their predecessors. You must wear your wizzo with a difference from the sixth form and the staff room, to declare your independence. Wick is short for 'wicked', and it is widely used in playing grounds of my acquaintance, with a slight spice that it is somehow naughty, or at any rate that it is not a word that any grown-up would use in that sense. This represents the novelty factor in playground slang.

Representing the 'nothing new under the sun' factor, wicked as commendation is neither as new nor as daring as the little bleeders suppose. Since the early 1900s wicked has been American slang for impressive or prodigious, cf. 'mean'. 'He can shake a wicked spatula.' 'Look at that wicked bat he swings.' From impressive it came to be used to mean excellent, splendid, remarkable, wizzo. For example, Scott Fitzgerald in *This Side of Paradise*, published in 1920: '"Tell 'em to play Admiration!" shouted Sloane. "Phoebe and I are going to shake a wicked calf."' Or, to bring the idiom across the Atlantic, the *Western Mail* of 1977: 'He could, as I say, sidestep off either foot, but what sped him on was a wicked acceleration over twenty yards.' Wick is quite old.

Here is a fascinating example of this idiom in Ulster dialect of 1867–8, taken from *Primate Alexander, Archbishop of Armagh*, edited by Eleanor Alexander, 1913: 'I was particular that those to be confirmed should not be brought before they could sufficiently understand the solemn rite, and I said so to her. "O! your Reverence Lordship," she cried, "he's well able for it. He's wee, but he's right and wicked!" It seemed to be the strangest testimony a candidate for confirmation ever received from a loving mother. But "wicked" in our Northern dialect means not morally bad, but intellectually alive and keen. Something in the sense of Newman's epithet for strong vegetable life and force, "Quick in sap and *fierce* with life". It may be the latest word of commendation in London playgrounds, but a century and a half ago wicked was being used in County Donegal to mean intellectually alive and keen, and so fit for confirmation.

This represents the common tendency in slang of standing the meaning of a word on its head, as a private code that the beaks, or Nanny, or Old Chalky won't understand. The children underestimate the memory and imagination of Old Chalky. Another glaring current example of this tendency of slang to stand value words on their heads is the use of the most general word of disapproval in English, 'bad', to mean good, admirable, excellent, or terrif. Since the Fifties this use of 'bad' as a hurray-word has been common among Blacks, teenagers, jazz musicians, and the trendy who pick up their slang from them. But this use of bad to mean good is far older than the Fifties, in accordance with the immutability principle of slang. Its use can be attested from the time of slavery in the Southern States, when this sense of bad as pro-word was marked by a lengthened vowel and a falling tone in pronunciation.

The same process can be seen at work with 'devilish'. This word came into the language in the fifteenth century to mean like a devil, and accordingly execrable. Within two centuries the word had been stood on its head in slang to mean no more than 'very', and then 'very good' in an enthusiastic and commendatory sense. For example, Samuel Rowlands, the satirical rogue, in *The Knave of Hearts*, 1612: 'Because we finde/Mony makes fooles most divellish proud in mind.' And here is Byron in a letter to Miss Pigot in 1807: 'I should be devilish glad to see him.' Here is a folklorish anecdote that illustrates the upside-down use. Some people were looking at the tombstone of a man named Strange, at the foot of which was engraved the epitaph: 'An honest lawyer.' Somebody said: 'Strange – an honest lawyer; very strange.' Everybody laughed. Somebody else who was present recounted the story later, getting it a bit wrong, saying: 'A funny thing happened the other day. We were looking at the tombstone of a man called Smith, described as "an honest lawyer", and one of us remarked: "Peculiar – an honest lawyer – devilish peculiar."' Here is a regional variation of the use. Two Glaswegians visited Arran and climbed Goat Fell. At the top they admired the stunning view with amazement, and one of them said: 'Man, Tam, the works o' Goad's deevilish.'

Here is an example of a slang word that has been stood on its head in the opposite direction, from an originally commendatory meaning to a rude intensifier: bloody. This, *pace* Bernard Shaw, has no profane associations such as 'By Our Lady' or 'God's Blood'. The word has been in English for a millennium meaning of the nature of, composed of, or like blood. It came in as an intensifier meaning 'very . . . and no mistake, exceedingly, abominably, desperately' with the Restoration, and has since evolved into a cottonwool qualifier. James Murray, when he was dealing with B in *The Oxford English Dictionary* more than a century ago, noted with Lowland respectability: 'Now constantly in the mouths of the lowest classes, but by respectable people considered "a horrid word", on a par with obscene or profane language, and usually printed in the newspapers (in police reports, etc.) "b----y".' The best view is that 'bloody' at first referred to 'bloods' or aristocratic lager louts and yahoos at the end of the seventeenth century. The phrase 'bloody drunk' (Dryden, 1684: 'The doughty Bullies enter bloody drunk') evidently meant 'as drunk as a blood', cf. 'as drunk as a lord'. Thence it spread into the lexicon of slang, helped on its way by popular notions about the drama and violence of blood. The topsy-turvy principle of slang has turned a theoretically commendatory word, 'like a rich Hooray Henry', into a Low Life intensifier.

I think you can see this tendency of slang to stand words on their heads, giving them the opposite sense to their natural one, in languages other than English. In the *Georgics*, i, 146, Virgil wrote: '*Labor omnia vicit, improbus.*' 'Work conquered everything, *improbus* work.' The Latin lexicographers translate this *improbus* as 'unrelenting, persistently and without regard for others claiming more than one's due, unconscionable, shameless, greedy, presumptuous, relentless'. I think it means no more than 'bloody work' or even 'wicked work'.

Another piece of ragingly popular British school slang is 'to waste', meaning no more than to clobber or trounce rather than to devastate. Fettes boy: 'Loretto wasted us last week', that is, on enquiry, bowled them out for 15. This too is old-hat, from the States this time, where it dates from at least the Vietnam War: 'The intention to waste My Lai.' It has been American teenagers' slang since the Fifties. *Gorky Park*: 'You want to go chasing after the guy who wasted your detective.' It's wick, and bāāād, and wicked, and a wicked waste, but most slang has been spoken before, and much of it makes its effect by reversing or at any rate changing the conventional meaning of the word.

31

WORD GAMES

2GUD to be True

GED.

An average English word is four letters and a half. By hard, honest labor I've dug all the large words out of my vocabulary and shaved it down till the average is three and a half. I never write *metropolis* for seven cents, because I can get the same price for *city*. I never write *policeman*, because I can get the same money for *cop*.

Speech in New York, September 19, 1906,
by S. L. Clemens (Mark Twain)

W HEN STUCK IN a traffic jam or tail-back, as happens so often now that they are coning off and digging up all the motorways in the United Kingdom simultaneously, you play the number plate game to pass the time. SVN makes Savanarola. PDD gives lampadedromy; and so on. It is a dangerous game for the Dutch, because of the abnormal proliferation of obscene three-letter Dutch words that occurs on the registration plates of native motor cars in the British Isles. In that impenetrably guttural language, the rude words seem to be three-lettered rather than four-lettered.

Leaving all licentious passages in the decent obscurity of a learned language, to avoid upsetting the sensitive, we do find on common number plates a wealth of obscene Dutch triliterals:

KAK means 'shit' in Dutch (cf. the French nursery talk, *caca*). Dutch also has *schijt*, closer to the Anglo-Saxon, and slightly less rude.

LUL means 'penis', though a better translation is 'prick', since *lul* has both the literal and the figurative meaning of the latter, as in, 'He's a real prick.'

ZAK means 'scrotum', really rather rude in Dutch, in fact not much better than *lul*.

KUT means the female *pudendum*, the quadriliteral beginning with C in English, so rude that one seldom hears it, even in the loucher districts of Amsterdam.

GAT means 'arse', literally 'hole'.

BIL is a quite mild term for 'backside'.

PIS is obvious.

GVD is an abbreviation for *God verdomme*, i.e. Goddammit, rather more serious in Dutch than in English.

FOK, oddly enough, is perfectly respectable in Dutch, being the present tense or imperative of *fokken*, to breed animals. A *schaap fokker* is someone who raises sheep, not a chap who does it with sheep or sheep-shagger, nickname of the Black Watch.

No doubt the shocking impact of these triliterals explains the form that Dutch car numbers take: two pairs of numbers and just a pair of letters.

Having a personalized number plate on your car that says something is a fashionable vanity and self-advertisement of the same sort as T-shirts proclaiming uninvitingly JOG FOR JESUS, or car stickers saying SAVE THE FERRET, or, even more dispiritingly, TERRY AND CHARLENE. The British government has just started to cash in on this modern form of self-display by selling vanity number plates. And quite right too, if there are feather-headed peacocks and mugs around willing to pay good money for them. There are. In December, 1989, a woman paid £160,000 plus £16,000 in commission for 1A, one of a collection of peculiar and prestigious number plates being auctioned at Christie's for the Driver and Vehicle Licensing Centre. She said it was a Christmas present for her daughter.

As usual the Americans, and in particular the Californians, are ahead of even the British in trendy vulgarity. In California such celebrity digits are known as Environmental License Plates (ELPs), and the proceeds from selling them are used to fund such environmental projects as wildlife parks. The state's Department of Motor Vehicles lists more than a million ELPs that proclaim in short the owner's status, job, self-esteem, hobby-horse, or bee in bonnet. The only restrictions are that the combination of up to eight letters and numbers must not duplicate previously issued plates, and must not be offensive or misleading. The plates seem to reflect the mood of the times, especially in that state where the mood changes ahead of the rest of the world. The *Los Angeles Times* reported that the most sought-after personalized number plate in California in 1970 was PEACE. By the mid-Eighties, in the new climate of Me-First-and-ZAK-the-rest-of-you, the most popular plates were GO FOR IT, IM A 10, and PORSCHE.

My specialist in Californian personalized plates had her

attention drawn to this obscure study when she found
herself stuck in a jam behind a plain white van with the
licence plate VAN BLANC. Then she spotted a BORN TAN
driven by a black woman. Is RGR8GRM 'Our Great Gran'
or 'Roger 8-Gram', a local drug-pusher? Dropping vowels
is a common ELP strategy, for example, JRNLST, NVG-
TOR, and LTLPAUL. Dropping consonants as well has
produced plates such as SGLFILE and MRXIMNT (Mr
Excitement, I fear). The loons use substitute characters
instead of conventional orthography: FSHN BIZ, EX-
SOLJA, JAGWAR. Substitution, addition, or deletion of
characters can represent accent or dialect: OIRISHI, HAH-
VAHD. Repetition of characters can represent joky stress:
BOOOOZE, ZOOOOOM (both those sound drivers to
steer clear of, SGLFILE if possible, on the Freeway). The
Californians exploit alphanumeric combinations: 5oISH,
9KIDS, THRTY7. Numerals and letters are used as homo-
phones: UBGD2ME, BOY1DER, T42ME4U, OBFUSC8,
ICALQL8. Their autos pun: 2CHE (ethyl, which presumably stands for Ethel). There are foreign phrases: MAIS
OUI, 2CHE PAS (*ne touche pas*), BET NOIR (on a black car),
JOI VIVR. There are codes and ciphers (which somewhat
destroy the point of blowing one's own trumpet in a traffic
jam); the actor William Conrad has a licence plate saying
DARNOC. The United Kingdom follows a few years behind California in these matters, so it's all going 2CUM
EAR. It is a modern, motorized revival of the Victorian
passion for after-dinner acrostics, puns, and other word
games. At least it will make the traffic jams marginally
more interesting.

While you sit there fuming, ask yourself what is the
other word (or words) in English that includes the letters
ABC in that order. I can manage dABChick, the little grebe.
But then I begin to suspect that the other word including
ABC is a chimera, like the third English word ending in
-NGRY, in addition to 'angry' and 'hungry', or words
including GNT or GHN consecutively (doughnut). I gave
mABCap a run, on the grounds that this may be the

etymologically correct derivation of mob-cap. You thought
that the floppy hat like a cauliflower, tied under the chin,
and worn by women, came from 'mob', because it was
worn by Tricoteuses and other female French revolution-
aries. I doubt it. *David Copperfield*: 'A mob-cap; I mean a
cap, much more common then than now, with side-pieces
fastening under the chin.' Mob is an abbreviation for *mobile
vulgus*, Latin for the fickle rabble. Swift thought that such
fashional abbrevs were destroying the English language:
'Abbreviations exquisitely refined; as Pozz for positively,
and Mob for mobile.' But mob-cap comes not from mob,
but from mab, which is short for Mabel. In the male
chauvinist slant of English, Mab was used to mean a
slattern or woman of loose character and slovenly dress;
and to mab as verb meant to dress untidily. And here we
are. Eureka. In a dictionary of unusual words published
in 1829: 'Mab, verb, to dress carelessly. Hence mAB-Cap,
generally called mob-cap, a cap which ties under the
chin – worn by elderly women.' Will that do? Simple
as ABC.

We might also consider ABChalazel, a botanical term
meaning located or facing away from the chalaza of a
seed. ABCoulomb is the CGS (centimetre-gram-second)
electromagnetic unit of quantity of electricity. A bABCock
test is the test for determining the butter value of milk and
milk products. A nAB-Cheat is old English slang for a hat,
nab meaning nob or head, and *cheat* from chattel or thing.
A sAB-Cat is modern slang for a saboteur. GrAB-Coup is
historical American slang for the snatching, by a losing
gambler, of all available money and then fighting a way
out. ABCee is a word for the alphabet, one way of writing
ABC. In 1552 Richard Huloet published his *ABCedarium
Anglo-Latinum*, in which he defined each English word not
only in Latin but also in English, so producing what can
be described as the first English dictionary. If these ABC
words seem a bit esoteric, and not the sort of words that
crop up in everyday speech, how about lAB-Coat, which
seems a fairly common garment, and crAB-Claws, which

you would not be astonished to find on a menu in a dockside dive in a fishing harbour?

Which hunt brings us by indirections to currying favour. Have you ever stopped to consider what you are saying when you talk about somebody currying favour? It has nothing to do with chicken vindaloo or any other curry, or with favour, for that matter. Favour is an ignorant English corruption of 'favel', meaning fallow-coloured, derived from the French *fauve*. Favel was the name of the fallow centaur in the early fourteenth-century satirical romance, *Fauvel*. This beast symbolized cunning and bestial degradation. Hence to curry Favel was to stroke or smooth down the brute, to enlist the services of duplicity, and to seek to obtain by insincere flattery, to ingratiate oneself by sycophantic officiousness, in short to behave like politicians (or journalists, for that matter) on the make. Puttenham's *English Poesie*, 1589: 'Sometimes a creeper, and a curry favel with his superiors.' Note how old 'creep' is in English as a term of contempt.

But this is not the end of the matter. In the ancient labyrinths of English, nothing ever is. Favel is said to be an acronym for the vices of the medieval church, and was used as propaganda in the arguments leading up to the Reformation. These intense religious and political conflicts are one of the reasons for the enormous changes and flowering of English in the sixteenth and seventeenth centuries.

F = Fornication, or some other word beginning with F
A = Averice
V = Venalite
E = Envie
L = Lecherie

It may even be true. After folks, there's nought so strange as words, which are the windy phantasms and creations of folk.

32

COLOURS

Red and Green

What value is given to cloth by adulteration with false colours? God likes not that which He Himself did not produce. Had He not the power to order that sheep should be born with purple or sky-blue fleeces? He had the power, but He did not wish; and what God did not wish certainly ought not to be produced artificially.

Women's Dress, circa AD 220, by Tertullian

H OW CAN WE tell that the various words for blue have quite the same meanings in languages and lands where the clear sky and the deep sea are quite different shades of blue? We can't. There is a problem about colour words. Colours speak all languages, but we cannot be sure that anybody else sees or hears them exactly as we do. Ruskin was right when he said that the purest and most thoughtful minds are those which love colour the most, and he influenced Proust with his glorification of colour.

Our colour words are very old and very curious. Romans used *purpureus*, which we translate as purple in English, as an enthusiastic epithet to describe things that do not look in the least purple to us. It was a colour, extracted with difficulty and therefore expensively, from three species of gastropod snails, that was steeped in status and taboo. In the Roman Republic there were rigorous sumptuary

restrictions on wearing purple. Only the censors and gen-
erals celebrating a triumph were allowed to dress in togas
or cloaks that were dyed purple all over. Consuls and
praetors had to be content with purple edges. In the Empire
the manufacture of royal or Tyrian purple was closely
controlled and restricted. An edict of the Emperors Valen-
tian, Theodosius, and Arcadius made it a capital offence
to manufacture royal purple dye outside the Imperial Dye
Works. By now the privilege of wearing the 'true' purple
was restricted to the Emperor. In AD 301 a pound of wool
dyed Tyrian purple cost 50,000 denarii, the equivalent of
a baker's wage for a thousand days' work. The only colour
word that has cognates spread through all the Indo-
European languages is red. It looks as though different
ages and different cultures see colours differently, and
deploy their languages to break up the spectrum into
different divisions.

The language and symbolism of colours are tangled old
undergrowth of civilization. The anonymous author of this
rhyme gives one version:

> Blue is true,
> Yellow's jealous,
> Green's forsaken,
> Red's brazen,
> White is love,
> And black is death.

There are numerous other and conflicting versions. Take
that favourite colour of the Romans, purple. Their word
comes from the Mediterranean shellfish they called *purpura*, perhaps chiefly *Murex brandaris*, from which they
squeezed the purple dye that they used as a status symbol
on their togas and as a sign of wealth and power. The
colour they had in mind seems to have ranged from blood-
red crimson to deep violet, depending on the technique
used. So we are not surprised to find *purpureus* used to
describe kings, and clothes, and Caesar, freshly spilt blood,
wine, plums, and, pushing it a bit, pears. These are all

purplish things, and Italian pears are better, or at any rate different. But the old eyebrow does flicker a bit when we find the Romans describing as purple the sun, moon, and stars, the raging sea, beautiful young people, the hair of Nisus (one of Aeneas' Trojan immigrants), swans, and even an oak tree in full leaf. I know they order these things differently in Italy. But purple swans and purple oaks are going too far.

You could say that they see colours differently under a Mediterranean sun, so that Homer called the sea wine-dark. You can say that the Romans were thinking of the sheen and glow of purple rather than the actual colour. You could try saying that Italians are colour-blind, or at any rate see colours through other than dim Anglo-Saxon eyes. You could try saying that they so loved the rich and vulgar colour that purple became a hurray-word meaning lovely as well as a descriptive colour word. Whatever you decide, you must agree that the Roman *purpureus* is different in significant connotations from our purple. And as for Homer, the sea is not the same colour as wine, whether red or white or muddy retsina. I incline to the view that Homer meant sparkling. Homer also describes oxen as wine-dark and purple. But then, Homer was blind.

Red as a word spread round the world from Sanskrit to Old Slavonic. It is used to describe the colour of things such as blood, sunset clouds, rubies, and glowing coal. In Old English the vowel was long, rēād, but it has been shortened, as it has also been in such words as bread, dead, and (the metal) lead. The original Anglo-Saxon long vowel is retained in English surnames such as Read(e), Reid, and Rede, denoting ancestral ginger-nuts in the family somewhere. It is a noisy, aggressive, bad-tempered colour, mercifully masked from those of us who are colour blind, so that we cannot see the berries on a rowan tree unless we stick our noses right up against them.

Red is one of the oldest words recorded in English, being given in glossaries as early as AD 700 as the English for Latin words of that colour. It was originally spelled, as it was pronounced, *read*. The Indo-European root from which it comes is found in cognates in most European languages, for example, *ruber* and *rufus* in Latin, *eruthros* in Greek. King Alfred uses *reade* in his translation of Boethius, one of the first books in English.

Red comes in one of the oldest proverbs in English: red sky at night, shepherd's (or in harbour towns, sailor's) delight; red sky in the morning, shepherd's (sailor's) warning. This is found as early as Wyclif's translation of Matthew XVI, 2, of about 1395: 'The eeuenynge maad, ye seien, It shal be cleer, for the heuene is lijk to *reed*; and the morwe, To day tempest, for heuen shyneth heuy, or sorwful.'

Red is the colour that appears at the lower or least refracted end of the visible spectrum, and is familiar in nature from blood, fire, sunset, old flowers such as the poppy and the rose, and ripe fruits. It covers a wide range of shades from bright scarlet or crimson to reddish yellow or brown, which tends to be called red particularly when referring to the hair of animals such as the fox and the bear, and for that matter that old but dwindling breed of cattle, the Red Poll. OK, Homer; you had a point with your purple oxen.

Because it covers a multitude of sins, red is the colour of sin, as in 'his sins were scarlet, but his books were read'. Because of its huge range, red tends to be distinguished by prefixed nouns or adjectives, to show what sort of red we have in mind: blood-red, brick-red, cherry-red, fire-red, flame-red, flesh-red, robin-red, rose-red, dark, dull, light, or lively red, fiery or foxy red, brown-red, orange-red, yellow-red, brownish or yellowish red, and so on, *ad* end of spectrum.

The chief symbolic meaning of red today is revolution and anarchy. This goes back long before the Russian Revolution. Red Square in Moscow was called *krasnaya* or red before the revolution, because for Russians red is synonymous with beautiful or pleasant, as purple meant rich and grand to the Romans. Blake: 'Red rage redounds.'

Tennyson, *Guinevere*: 'Red ruin, and the breaking up of laws.' This symbolic use of red for revolution goes back at least to the French Revolution, where the extremists, who were first in the queue to dye their hands in blood, were known as Red Republicans.

Before red became lefty, it was the colour of martyrdom for Christians, also symbolizing faith and charity. In ecclesiastical dress red signifies divine love (blood = heart = love). In blazonry, the art department of heraldry, red is called gules, and signifies magnanimity; blood-red is called sanguine, and signifies fortitude. In liturgical use red is the colour for red-letter days, marked red in calendars and orders of service, and also for martyrs and Whit Sunday.

In metals red is represented by iron (which rusts red), though in old ballads red was frequently applied to gold ('the gude rede gowd'). Iron is also the metal of war, and so blood, see Homer and subsequent writers. In Jungian symbolism red, like blood and dawn, stands for outer-worldly activity and existence. In popular folklore red is the colour of magic. Yeats in *Fairy and Folk Tales of the Irish Peasantry*: 'Red is the colour of magic in every country, and has been so from the very earliest times. The caps of fairies and magicians are well-nigh always red.'

Red-haired people are popularly held to be unreliable, deceitful, and quick-tempered. It is an old idea that somebody with red hair cannot be trusted, from the tradition that Judas was a red-head. Rosalind in *As You Like It*: 'His very hair is the dissembling colour.' Celia, defensively: 'Something browner than Judas's.' A man with black hair but a red beard was the worst of all, as in the old rhyme: 'A red beard and a black head, catch him with a good trick, and take him dead.' The superstition is widespread, as in the Armenian proverb, mistranslated in a bilingual version by dropping the prepositions that are necessary in English, though not in the original: 'Do not buy a red-haired man; do not sell one either.'

By ancient convention red is the colour of the English royal livery, because it is such a noisy colour, and perhaps for the primitive reasons for which the Romans made purple the imperial colour. Fox-hunters wear it, they claim (unpersuasively) because Henry II declared hunting the royal sport. They call their scarlet coats 'pink' in a Tallyho Henry convention. Thackeray in *The History of Pendennis*: 'Pen rode well to hounds, appeared in pink, as became a young buck.'

Do not ask why the Red Sea is named red, any more than why Homer thought the Aegean looked like wine. The Romans called it *Mare Rubrum*, following the Greeks, and apparently translating a Semitic name. It may be that it is the sea of reeds, or red because of the corals on its bed, or red from the dawn or sunset reflected on it. In book-keeping red traditionally indicates debt, although since computerization the colour no longer appears on British bank statements. At sea red signals port, as opposed to green for starboard. Red for danger on railways, and for stop at traffic lights. The British Army wore red until absurdly recently for going to war, perhaps to look grand, more practically to hide the blood in order to encourage the others. Red is a rum old colour in the language as well as in the spectrum.

Green is the colour of the Nineties, taking over as the red of the Communist world dissolves. As the environment moves to the centre of politics, we are going to get a lot more green words in our vocabulary. We already have the greenhouse effect and the greening of America.

The word green is Old English, with Teutonic but no other cognates. Unlike red, it has no deep Indo-European roots. Since green is Germanic, West Germany was the appropriate country for *die Grünen* to emerge about twenty years ago as supporters of the ecological party, which is committed to environmentalism and ecology as political issues. Since then their enthusiasm and the black propaganda of their establishment opponents has tarnished their green. Today in the United Kingdom the green label carries off-putting connotations of a bespectacled, humourless, environmentally-conscious prig, bullying those who disagree with him or eat what he disapproves of, and being even more of an undismissible bore as an election canvasser on the doorstep than 'workers' from the older parties. Here is a bosh-shot headline from *The Independent*, illustrating the growth of greenery and the hazards of punning head-lines: GREENS PREPARE TO WOO GRASS ROOTS LIBERALS. This brings to my mind an image of Nebuch-adnezzar on his herbal diet. The dead metaphors of green and grass roots are jerked to life by juxtaposition.

Green is a suitably healthy and self-righteous colour for the environmentalists, because of its connection with the new growth of spring after the black and white of northern winter. Old-fashioned prep school masters in England used to argue the following rickety syllogism: oxygen is necessary for life; green plants suck up oxygen; therefore green vegetables must be good for you, and in particular good for your bowels and the old English obsession with keeping 'regular'. Hence 'eat up your greens' became as much a maxim of the cold baths, Christianity, and cricket English character-building process as 'keep a straight bat (or a stiff upper lip)'. Green also has a symbolic connection with sexual activity in English slang, as in 'she (or he) is fond of her (his) greens'; while 'to give a girl a green gown' was a descriptive Tudor phrase for a romp in the fields. In art and religion green symbolizes hope, joy, youth, gladness, and resurrection, because of its connection with the spring of the year after the gloom of winter. Green's metal is copper; its stone is emerald; and its planet is Venus. In literature and folksong its roots are deep. Green studies lead you soon into the tangled undergrowth of Robert Graves's *White Goddess* and Frazer's *Golden Bough*.

Our new green words of the Nineties sprout from dark roots. They will take them some time to settle down: it took Newtonian physics more than a century to fix its vocabulary. I wish we could find a crisp, green word to replace the ghastly 'environmentally friendly', which manufacturers, in tune with the tide of the times, are sticking hopefully on their aerosols and bottles. One should always read such marketing slogans with narrowed eyes and a cynical cast of mind, asking: 'Why are these lying bastards lying to me?' Maybe 'environmentally friendly' is merely an advertiser's gimmick. But there is an idea there that asks to be clothed in words, not necessarily negative ones. It is agreeable to think of aerosols, beauty preparations, fuels, and such things being labelled 'harmless'. But this asks the question: harmless to what? The environment is a nebulous concept. The nearest synonym I can get to it is the cosmos. But I do not see 'eucosmic' or 'cosmophile' catching on. No doubt we shall evolve a suitable word, if the need for such a word is there. We usually do. Perhaps it will be something to do with green; perhaps green itself, charged with carrying the new meanings we need. We all play our part in producing these new words and meanings. There is everything to play for in our new green vocabulary, as there is in the larger, cosmic question of what we do about the cosmos.

33

BLUE

A Mix-up Out of the Blue

Are you a natural flavus, darling?

GED.

Blue, blue is the grass about the river
And the willows have overfilled the close garden.
And within, the mistress, in the midmost of her youth,
White, white of face, hesitates, passing the door.
'The Beautiful Toilet', by Mei Sheng, BC 140, rendered
by Ezra Pound

A WORD IN TIME

As purple was the imperial colour for Romans, blue is the sacred colour for Jews. In *Numbers* XV, 38, the Lord instructs Moses: 'Speak unto the children of Israel, and bid them that they make them fringes in the borders of their garments throughout their generations, and that they put upon the fringe of the borders a ribband of blue (*tekhelet* in Hebrew). And it shall be unto you for a fringe, that ye may look upon it, and remember all the commandments of the Lord, and do them; and that ye seek not after your own heart and your own eyes, after which ye use to go a whoring.'

In accordance with strict biblical and Talmudic concepts of holiness, these blue fringes must be coloured with *tekhelet*, a dye made from a snail, like the Roman *purpura*. This blue was the holy colour for the Hebrews in daily life. The first tractate of the Talmud (Berakhot 9a) asks: 'From which moment may one recite the Shema (the prayer of creed) in the morning?' And the first answer it gives is: 'When one can distinguish between *tekhelet* and white.' But by AD 760 the secret of making *tekhelet* had been lost. And ever since the tassels of the prayer shawls of the strictly orthodox have contained no blue strands, because in the strict eyes of the Law, there can be no substitute for *tekhelet*. Blue is holy, 'because *tekhelet* is like unto the sea and the sea is like unto the sky and the sky is like unto the sapphire, and the sapphire is like unto the Throne of Glory'.

One of the old and odd puzzles is how our word blue seems to have come from the Latin *flavus*, which meant pale yellow or golden to the Romans. The English and Latin lexicographers say that the words are cognate or 'probably related'. But they sound shifty and unhappy about it. Classical words for colours are notoriously few and indefinite, which is a puzzle in itself. But blue is so different from yellow that I wonder whether the colour shift may not have been caused by a simple misprint. When the choice is between conspiracy and cock-up, go for cock-up.

One of the key sources is the *Liber Mineralium* of Albertus Magnus or St Albert, which he wrote about 1250. In it Big Albert described the supposed medical and magical properties of minerals, and made personal observations on where they are found and in what form, and so on. And he seems to have been wearing yellow-tinted specs. For example, he describes *saphirus*, our sapphire, as a clear yellow (*perspicuus flavus*) 'like the sky on a fine day'. Albert described as *flavus* other stones that look blue to us, such as hyacinthus (whether corundum or zircon) and lapis lazuli. His book was immensely popular and influential among fortune-tellers, interpreters of dreams, and other intellectuals of the pop press. It was plagiarized and translated over and over again, in the same way that you can see an error perpetuated down the centuries in a newspaper archive.

For example, from *The Mirror of Stones*, first published in 1750, here is a straight lift from Albertus Magnus five centuries before: '*Zumemellazuli*, or *Zemech*, but in Latin is the stone *Lazuli*. This stone is *yellow*, of the Colour of the Sky when it is in its greatest Serenity, not transparent, and shines with golden Streaks; it sustains the Fire, and from its Beauty is called the celestial or starry Stone. Being prepared by Physicians, it cures melancholy disorders. There is also made of it a Colour called the Ultramarine Azure.'

In classical Latin *flavus* is used to describe honey, gold, sand, blondes such as Ganymede, and other things that are not obviously blue. How did the Roman yellow become our blue? We could try saying that the ancients were notoriously imprecise with their colour descriptions: for example Virgil described swans as purple, and there is Homer's wine-dark or *oinops* bull, purplish, and not to my eyes a very bullish colour. You could say that *flavus* changed its place in the linguistic spectrum during the Middle Ages. You could say that Albert's Latin was not very good. It has been suggested that he suffered from a rare form of Daltonism or colour blindness, in which the

A WORD IN TIME

light-sensitive proteins in the retina fail to distinguish between blue and yellow.

A better explanation is that the confusion between *flavus* and blue was a misprint, which can happen in the best regulated publications. As far as there were nationalities in those muddled medieval days, Albert was essentially German. Instead of using the classical Latin for blue, *caeruleus* 'colour of the sky', he used a Latinization of the local Germanic word for blue, *blau* or *blaw*, and wrote *blavus*. Whether he coined the word or picked it up does not matter. But the word *blavus* for blue was around in Germanic-speaking parts of Europe. Johannes the Monk, who died in 1313, in his life of St Odo described certain vestments: 'Of the colour which we in the vulgar tongue (*vulgo*) call *blavus*.' Salmasius (1588–1653), the commentator on many classical authors, places *blavus* as an adjective of colour between *purpureus* and *caeruleus* in the spectrum.

It was a very Germanic word. I think an early scribe or printer, not recognizing this unusual word *blavus*, pejorated it to *flavus*. In early type the character for F with ligature and serifs looks not unlike a B. And that was how their yellow became our blue. How often have I said to you that when you have eliminated the impossible, what remains, however improbable, must be human cock-up? And why do you suppose that we cry blue murder? Or should it be yellow murder? This is said to be a pun on the French exclamation *morbleu*, but it looks fishy to me.

Colour words are problematic. How are we to understand 'hyacinthine'? Hyacinthus was a Spartan youth loved and accidentally killed by Apollo, when the quoit they were playing with was blown by Zeus off course and onto Hyacinth's forehead. The myth said that Apollo created the hyacinth flower from the boy's blood, and the precious stone hyacinthus, probably our sapphire, was named after the flower. The Greek and Roman hyacinthus flower was the Martagon lily, or the iris, or something blue, like the sapphire. How do we explain this? Blue blood? Or red hyacinths? In the Odyssey, when Odysseus has managed to swim ashore on Phaeacia in a terrible state, his patroness Athene tidies him up by making him taller and mightier, and making his hair flow in curls like the hyacinth flower. The next line goes 'as when a skilled craftsman overlays silver with gold', suggesting that hyacinth was seen by the Greeks as golden. The colour confusion was translated into English by classicizing authors. Milton in *Paradise Lost*: 'Hyacinthin locks/Round from his parted forelock manly hung/Clustring.' And Pope, translating the passage about Odysseus' landfall from the *Odyssey*: 'His hyacinthine locks descend in manly curls.'

Another German called Magnus, Hans Magnus, proposed a Darwinian theory of gradual evolution in the human's colour sense in *Die geschichtliche Entwickelung des Farbensinnes* (1877). Goethe had already noticed that the Pythagoreans had not mentioned the colour blue. Hans Magnus examined the Bible, the Homeric poems, the hymns of the *Rig-Veda*, and the *Zen-Avesta* for references to colour, and noticed the absence of green as well as blue. He presumed that the authors were incapable of seeing these colours in trees and the sky, and suggested that the cause was only partly developed colour sensitivity in the retina. Hans Magnus suggested that the eyes of Homer, Virgil, and their contemporaries were still gradually evolving from the primitive state, when the retina was 'analogous to that of its peripheral zones at the present day', that is, every colour losing its true characteristics to appear as a 'gray, more or less light'.

Other scholars have tried to explain the colour blindness of the ancients with literary or linguistic theories. Father Dinet, Descartes' teacher, asked: 'Who can say that there may not have been other words which Homer and the Hindoo poets never used, or that the words they used had just the meaning that we now see in them?' Henri Cros and Charles Henry, nineteenth-century French artistic theorists, took a stiffer view: 'It is very certain that in remotest antiquity men did not apply the analytical powers of which we are capable to the evidences of sensation that obtained; but this was the result of intellectual and not physiological inferiority.'

It does seem to be the case that in many languages names for colours at the blue end of the spectrum emerge late. Can Hans Magnus have been right in suggesting that our retinal capacity for differentiating colours has fairly recently evolved from a primitive state of colour-blindness? In centuries to come will future generations experience colours that are now unimaginable? And will they then blame the absence of these colours from today's literature on an incomplete colour sense, or on some hitherto un-noticed computer-printer error? Homer is said to have been blind. But were both Homer and Virgil, and their contemporaries all colour-blind? It is an engaging theory, but not in tune with the best modern optical science.

It is indeed true that in most primitive languages the colour-names generally refer to the red end of the spectrum, and one word often suffices for the whole of the blue end, from green onwards. Thus the natives of the Carolines have only one word for black, blue, and green; among the Swahili, a single word, *Nyakundu*, covers brown, yellow, and red, and now they have had to borrow the word 'blue', having no equivalent word of their own; while even in a tongue as sophisticated as Japanese the word *aoi* sufficed until recently for any colour from green on through blues and violets. That last omission is extraordinary in a culture that distinguishes blues and greens so delicately in its painting and porcelain.

The same is largely true (as Gladstone noted in 1858) of our classical European languages, in which there is again a striking lack of words to cover the green-blue range, although there is still some confusion (as we have seen) as to the exact hue that the various names designated. This essential colourlessness of the blue end of the spectrum (typified by Homer's description of 'black water') persists in Italy, of all places, to this day. Norman Douglas described the difficulty he had in persuading the Calabrian peasants that the Mediterranean was blue; to them and their forefathers it had always been black. The confused colour terminology of the Greeks, and the slavish imitation of Greek usage by the Roman poets, and by classicizing English poets, have left ancient colours as a jungle for the lexicographer, into which the historian, archaeologist, biologist, or physicist ventures at his peril.

However the prospect of an ever expanding colour-range to delight our descendants is excluded by the physical characteristics of the human eye. We could just have evolved ocular tissues that were permeable or responsive to different wave-bands, like the separate photo-pigment of some freshwater fish, which reaches farther into the infra-red. The stickleback fish and the homing pigeon may extend their discrimination marginally into the ultra-violet (but to nothing like the degree found in insects). However, the longer the wave-length, the larger the diffraction pattern; so, quite apart from the chromatic aberrations, it would become impossible in principle to get sharp images. Perhaps we are not missing very much, as infra-red photography gives us little in the way of a new visual dimension, except in misty weather.

We all see colours differently through our different idioscopes and idiolects. Not all of us can see colour as vividly as Turner. When he was handed a salad at dinner once, Turner remarked to his neighbour: 'Nice cool green, that lettuce, isn't it? And the beetroot pretty red – not quite strong enough; and the mixture, delicate tint of yellow that. Add some mustard, and then you have one of my pictures.'

34

JANUS WORDS

The Attraction of Opposites

'Then you should say what you mean,' the March
Hare went on. 'I do,' Alice hastily replied; 'at least –
at least I mean what I say – that's the same thing, you
know.'
'Not the same thing a bit!' said the Hatter. 'Why,
you might just as well say that "I see what I eat" is
the same thing as "I eat what I see."'
Alice's Adventures in Wonderland, chapter 7, 1865, by
Lewis Carroll

THE ENGLISH HAVE an unjustified reputation for hypocrisy and duplicity. In fact, they seldom say exactly what
they mean not out of cunning, but because of laziness and
wanting to avoid a fuss. We are man-pleasers. We want to
be liked. We want a quiet life. So we are wizards at soft
soap and euphemism and white lies. The critic says: 'Your
review is in the post. It's quite short – about 500 words.'
She and the literary editor both know that what she really
means is: 'O God, I must really get down to writing the
thing tonight. It won't be much over 1,000 words.' The
literary editor replies: 'Greatest piece since Cyril Connolly,
if not Bernard Shaw. I hope to use it next week.' Both
parties know that what he means is: 'Not bad, with a
bit of creative subbing. It's going to gather moss in the
overmatter in my computer queue.'
Arnold Lunn, the author, controversialist, and founding

father of English skiing, invented the name PHROP in a
New Statesman competition to describe such a euphemistic
phrase, which does not wear its true meaning on its face,
but on the contrary means something like the opposite of
what it superficially appears to say. One of the reasons
that English is such a rich language for poetry is that it is
full of ambiguity and puns, that is to say, phrops. I prefer
to call them Janus words, after the Roman god of doors and
beginnings, whose sacred gateway in the Forum remained
open while Rome was at war, because they have two faces
which look in opposite directions.

The English are continually coining new Janus words,
for the most part unconscious of what they are doing.
Here are some current new ones that have come into the
language in our brisk new world of cut-throat commercial
values and the Devil take the hindmost:

> It's a question of market forces = I haven't a clue what
> will happen.
> Of course, I'm only a layman, but . . . = I'm about to
> tell you your job because you're so dim.
> It's time we faced up to today's world = We've failed
> with all our previous plans, so we have to dream
> up something new.
> It's a staggering fact that = I've only just realized that.
> Communication skills = You need to be able to operate
> a telephone and write complicated memos.
> They must realize that they're getting it very cheap =
> Let's squeeze a bit more out of them.
> Career-minded = You must be prepared to crawl and
> grovel.
> Charge what the market will bear = Let's squeeze some
> more out of them.
> That said/Having said that = This could go either way,
> so I'm covering myself both ways – take your pick.
> I don't mind constructive criticism = I like to be agreed
> with.
> What I don't understand is = What I understand per-
> fectly and don't agree with is.

It's difficult to quantify = This is a wild guess.

Friendly office = A decaying old building with Victorian furniture and a leaking roof.

It all boils down to the bottom line = Anything goes, so long as we can get away with it.

I worry about . . . = I'll support the big boss when he's made up his mind.

Ideal for a person studying for a recognized qualification = A badly paid, dogsbody post with a day or two off to attend training on days that suit the management.

Tact and understanding are essential qualities = You are going to have a peculiarly difficult group of people to work with, a cross between a Bolshie staff room and a news room full of prima donnaish hacks. You will need the patience of Job, the broad back of Hercules (and probably his club as well), and the unquenchable enthusiasm of St Ursula. I should think again, and become a traffic warden.

Even in our new world of unfettered market competition, the English still think that saying bluntly what you mean equals incompetence. Talking business with them is communication by code and innuendo, as indeed it is with the Japanese, but their codes are different.

Janus is the honorary foreign god of English. My ancestor, General Ioannis Metaxas, the Greek dictator at the beginning of the Second World War, was once invited to test a new flying boat. After flying a circuit or two, he was bringing the thing in to land on the runway when the commander of the air base intervened nervously: 'Excuse me, General. It would be better with this plane to come down on the water.' Metaxas swerved upwards, and touched down on the water. Then he switched off his engine, turned to his host, and said: 'Thank you, commander, for preventing me from making a stupid blunder.' Then he opened the flying boat's door and jumped down into the water. That was a near miss, or perhaps a near hit: at any rate, a splash-down. Our newspapers are always reporting another near miss between two aircraft over our airports. The expression is illogical, or at best an inveterate Janus word. A near hit or a near thing means that the hit or the thing was almost achieved. Logically, a near miss ought to mean that the target (or collision, or whatever) was nearly missed, but actually pranged.

Language is not entirely logical, thank Babel. There is deep ambiguity and contrariness in its roots. In many old languages, a word contains its opposite, and there is an antithetical or Janus sense in primal words. There is evidence that in the oldest languages opposites such as strong/weak, light/dark, large/small were expressed by the same root word. For example, in ancient Egyptian *keu* meant both strong and weak. In Latin *altus* means both high and deep; *clamare* means to shout, but *clam* means quietly or secretly; *recludo* means both I open and I close, which is what the Romans used to do to the gates of the Temple of Janus. In Greek *xenos* means both host and guest. Similarly in English until the Reformation, *host* used also to mean its correlative guest: 'They took me prisoner, not as *host*.' The Hostmen's Company of Newcastle upon Tyne, a dining and speech-making fraternity that still meets, has as its emblem an old engraving of two men in Tudor costume shaking hands, the same bubble coming out of each of their mouths: 'Welcome my oste.' In Greek *pharmakos* means both poison and antidote, an early example of homeopathic medicine.

> They put arsenic in his meat
> And stared aghast to watch him eat;
> They poured strychnine in his cup
> And shook to see him drink it up.

Some Janus words began life as quite separate words, and have grown to be the same in spelling and pronunciation by the tidal shifts of language over the centuries. For example, in modern English *to cleave* means on the one hand to chop apart, and on the other hand to stick together. Behind the face of Janus there are two quite distinct Anglo-

Saxon words, *cleofan* to split, and *cleofian* to stick fast. The former is derived from the vanished Indo-European root *gleubh-*, cf. the Greek *gluphein* to hollow out, as in *hieroglyph*, and perhaps from the Latin *glubēre* to peel. *Cleofian* is a quite different word, derived from another vanished root *kli-* to stick or adhere, as found vestigially in *clay* and *climb*. There was no confusion ten centuries ago, especially as the former verb is strong, with the past participle *clofen*, and the latter is weak, with the past participle *clifen*.

The most interesting and ambiguous type of Janus word is one that is made up originally from antithetical parts, known as enantiosemia in the linguistic trade jargon. Many primary words in old languages contain this ambivalence: strong-weak, command-obey, near-far, cut-bind, high-deep, inside-outside. Another name for such contradictory words is oxymoron, the Greek for pointedly foolish. A sophomore, literally, in its original Greek, a wise fool, is a recent American example that has been given the specialized meaning of a second-year college student. The Arabs, in their fascination with language and its quirks, have given a name, *addad*, to such two-faced Janus words or enantiosemia.

Some Janus words only look alike, but actually come from different roots. Other Janus words contain a primal ambiguity. But in English most Janus words are words and phrases that have started from the same root, and have grown opposed meanings over the centuries through the tides of idiom and illogicality and hypocrisy. Any word with a long, complex history has developed a great many different meanings for different groups and generations of people over the centuries; and some of those meanings are going to be opposites, or at any rate startlingly incongruous. The notorious Janus or chameleon word *nice* has in its time meant everything from silly to fastidious, and from agreeable to disagreeable. In the seventeenth century a nice man was a bad-tempered one, but a nice woman was, I regret to say, fast. Thus *affection* can mean both love and a disease. In the United States *liberal* means in favour of government intervention (political words are notorious playgrounds of Janus), but in other parts of the world it means opposed to government intervention. *Quite* means both moderately and extremely: 'She's *quite* pretty, but I shall never understand why Adam prefers her to Eve, who is *quite* lovely.' *Apparent* means at one time clearly and at another time an illusion. *Lose no time in* means both to do something promptly, and also not to do something at all. When sent unsolicited manuscripts by self-important busybodies, Henry James used as his stock reply the Janus phrase: 'I shall lose no time in reading your manuscript.' This is a phrase that on occasion comes in handy for hard-pressed literary editors.

Everyday English communication is thick with these insincere and coded expressions:

It is in the post (having ordered a special part from the manufacturer) = I have no intention of delivering it, let alone making it.

With respect = I am about to be bloody rude.

I am perfectly ready to admit . . . = You have made a trivial debating point there, but on the substantive point my prejudice is as irreversible as the Pontick Sea.

I am afraid Mr Whatnot is at a meeting = Under no circumstances can you speak to him, and he will never call you back.

You are the expert = You do it.

Subject to your views = If I have got this wrong, you are going to share the blame.

I wasn't a bit annoyed; I found the whole thing quite amusing = I am still seething, and intend to take my revenge.

Please edit this in any way you like = If you change so much as a comma, I shall be on the 'phone complaining.

Of course, I'm just a simple soldier . . . = When spoken by a senior officer, the subsequent dialogue usually

indicates that this phrop is not a Janus phrase, as
intended, but the literal truth.

The Janus words and phrops of estate agents, the lying
bastards, have entered British comic folklore. But exactly
the same antilogical process can be found in all areas of
British life and work. Advertising and the public relations
industries are erected upon the effort to persuade clients
and the public that black is, if not quite white, at any rate
a sexy and mature colour. You can observe the process at
work every day in job advertisements:

Business experience not necessary = We want to appoint
a retired colonel or government minister involved in
privatizations to this general manager post.
Business experience desirable = You will need to be
able to glide over office politics and sidestep board
directives.
Ample opportunities to develop new skills = This job is
in a real mess, and you will be expected to jump in
from a great height at the deep end.
Excellent training post = Not paid as highly as it should
be for the responsibilities.
Exciting opportunity = Actually incredibly boring, but
we're trying to make it attractive by Janus words.
Organizational approach = You should own a Filofax.
Organizational skills = You should own a Filofax, and
be able to use it and avoid losing it.
Liaise with all levels of the company = You are going to
be pig in the middle, and catch all the mud and other
unpleasantness that is flying.
Physically fit = The office is on the sixth floor and there
is no lift; we also have no intention of fulfilling our
quota of disabled people.
Temporary accommodation available = House prices are
extremely high round here.

Publishers' blurbs are impenetrable jungles of phrop and
Janus words, hung about with lianas of lies, white lies,

and misleading ambiguities. Even professions concerned with the truth go in for Janus worship. Heads of schools become experts at conveying their meanings indirectly when writing reports and references. 'Any headmaster will be lucky who gets Mr Smith to work for him.' 'Mr Jones left us as he came, fired with enthusiasm.' Without knowledge of Janus, you are lost without a paddle in the ocean of English indirections.

'Language, eight-armed, problematic, demiurgic, infinitely entrailed, must be honoured. Its riddling, jokey, mischievous, metaphoric, flawed, lapsible, parapraxic life must not be repressed, but tolerated, pleasured, submitted to, enjoyed, and so revealed for what it is.' Gale Strawson in *Quarto*, March 1982.

July 16, 1982, Peter Porter in *The Times Literary Supplement*:

> Which words
> Will come through air unbent,
> Saying, so to say, only what
> they mean?

Precious few words in English, Peter. They're all phrops and Janus words.

35

FORNICATION

Underneath the Arches

The big difference between sex for money and sex for free is that sex for money usually costs less.
Brendan Francis, quoted in *Playboy*, 1985

T HE ENGLISH ARE notoriously prudish and neurotic about sex. This explains much of the creative tension in their history, poetry, and jokes. Part of their hang-up comes from their mistranslation of the Latin *fornicatio* in the New Testament. The English take *fornication* to mean premarital and extramarital sex generally, and the teaching of Jesus Christ in the New Testament to be against all such activities. It no doubt suited the purposes of ferocious and fundamentalist puritans that this should be believed. But it is unscriptural and a misunderstanding of words. Jesus Christ in the New Testament condemns prostitution and adultery. He nowhere discusses copulation generally. The question does not arise.

In Hebrew society the family is central, and marriage is what maintains both the family and the People of God. The Israelites detested prostitution because it threatened the family, and because it was connected with the Canaan-ite and other surrounding idolatrous religions, many of which practised temple prostitution. This is how the Hebrew prophets came to describe the worship of idols literally and metaphorically as prostitution, whoredom, and infidelity to God. The harlot or *pornē* in Greek translation was a hated and feared type, and the lowest of the low. When Jesus wants to insult the chief priests and elders of the people at *Matthew* XXI, 31, he says: 'Verily I say unto you, That the publicans [i.e. the tax-collectors, the corrupt and hated officials of the occupying power] and the harlots [*pornai*, prostitutes] go into the kingdom of God before you.' In the Old Testament it is prostitution that is continually attacked, because of its explicit connection with idolatry. There is no condemnation of sexual relations that do not violate the marriage bond, although *Proverbs* VII reckons them imprudent: 'That they may keep thee from the strange woman, from the stranger which flattereth with her words.' Prostitution was an accepted part of the Hellenistic world in the Eastern Mediterranean, and the Roman Empire that succeeded it, from the fourth century BC onwards. Because of its roots in Judaism, Christianity made prostitution taboo for Christians. This explains why prostitution was banned, along with three ritualistic 'evils' from the first Council of the Early Church, held in Jerusalem, and described in *Acts* XV. It was decided that non-Jewish Gentile converts should be written to and enjoined 'that they abstain from pollution of idols, and from fornication, and from things strangled, and from blood'. That *fornication* translates *porneia*. In English it should be translated as prostitution.

Fornix in Latin means an arch or vault, the master invention of Roman architecture. And in Latin of the Golden and Silver Ages, *fornicatio* was a word meaning vaulting, used by architectural writers such as Vitruvius. In Rome and other Roman cities and towns, arches were everywhere, not just as the big monumental and triumphal arches, but at a humbler level supporting many buildings from the basement. And it was here, underneath the arches, that Roman prostitutes offered themselves for sale, as Isidorus explicitly notes. Hence in Latin *fornicatio* came to mean prostitution, behaviour that went on 'under the arches'. By the end of the fourth century, when Jerome translated the Vulgate at the request of Pope Damasus between 382 and 384, *fornicatio* was the regular word for prostitution, and Jerome used it to translate the Greek *porneia*. *Porneia* never means anything other than prostitution, except when it is used figuratively in the Old Testament for idolatry, and in translating back *fornicatio* as unchastity from the New Testament. Christian anti-sex tradition triumphed over classical scholarship in these translations, which are incorrect.

This gross mistake in translation had momentous effects that are still with us. It was used to express the extreme puritanical attitude towards sex and human sexuality, together with a downgrading of women, which engulfed the Early Church after the apostolic age. Fornication became a handy weasel word to condemn all kinds of sexual intercourse and behaviour which deviated from the Christian standard of chastity outside marriage and fidelity within marriage. *Porneia*, and *fornicatio* which Jerome used to translate it, have been vastly expanded to cover meanings far distant from the restricted meaning of prostitution in Greek and Latin. Thus the New English Bible translates *porneia* or prostitution 21 times as *fornication* (which in modern English has become a loose weasel word), once as 'sexual immorality', twice as 'immorality', once as 'lust', and once vaguely as 'base-born' (for the 'born of *fornication*' of the King James Bible of 1611). In the same way it translates *pornos*, a man who makes use of prostitutes or 'whore-monger', six times by the all-embracing '*fornicator*', once as 'given to *fornication*', three times by the vague 'loose livers' or 'who lead loose lives', and once by 'immoral person'. It is inaccurate translation, and therefore wrong doctrine.

Fornication has been hijacked in English for their propagandist purposes by the puritans and the imperfect scholars. It is defined by *The Oxford English Dictionary* as first: 'Voluntary sexual intercourse between a man (in restricted use, an unmarried man) and an unmarried woman. In Scripture extended to adultery.' The second meaning is the transferred metaphor of the Old Testament prophets: 'Especially in Scripture, the forsaking of God for idols, idolatry.' An English legal definition of *fornication* is 'voluntary sexual intercourse between two persons of the opposite sex where one or both are unmarried'. In English *fornication* slipped like the weasel word it is into meaning sexual immorality, and then simply sexual activity. To *fornicate* has come to mean the equivalent of the taboo four-letter word also beginning with f, as in *The Floating Opera*, 1956, by John Barth: 'The goal was to drink the most whiskey, *fornicate* the most girls, get the least sleep, and make the highest grades.'

Words of course do change their meanings, to suit the needs and obsessions of those who use them. But if you want to understand what the Bible actually says, you need to remember that when Jerome used *fornicatio* to translate *porneia*, he was translating a word that meant prostitution and nothing more or less. This explains numerous puzzling passages that have been twisted and misunderstood. For example, in St John's Gospel VIII, 41, Jesus argues that the Jews are not the children of Abraham, but the children of the Devil, because they are seeking to kill him. They reply, in the Authorized Version: 'We be not born of *fornication*; we have one Father, even God.' The Revised English Bible of 1989 gives: 'We are not illegitimate; God is our father, and God alone.' This is better: 'we are not the children of prostitution' in the original. A prostitute's children do not know who their fathers are.

There is a notorious and influential passage in I *Corinthians*, in which Paul is writing to his converts in the sea-port that was famous for its prostitutes in the ancient world. In chapter VII, 1–2 Paul writes: 'It is good for a man not to touch a woman. Nevertheless, to avoid *fornication*, let every man have his own wife, and let every woman have her own husband.' And verse 9: 'But if they cannot contain, let them marry: for it is better to marry than to burn.' The 1989 Revised English Bible distorts his meaning even worse than the Authorized Version: 'You say, "It is a good thing for a man not to have intercourse with a woman." Rather, in the face of so much immorality, let each man have his own wife and each woman her own husband . . . But if they do not have self-control, they should marry. It is better to be married than burn with desire.' This passage has had immense effect. It was incorporated into the Marriage Service of the Church of England Prayer Book from 1549 onwards in the summary of 'the causes for which Matrimony was ordained', viz. 'Secondly it was ordained for a remedy against sin, and to avoid *fornication*, that such persons as have not the gift of continency might marry and keep themselves undefiled.' In the Greek there is an odd plural at verse 2, 'owing to the prostitutions'. What Paul was saying to his Corinthian converts, perfectly reasonably, was: 'Since prostitution is everywhere in Corinth, I advise men to marry.'

In a society as poor and near the margins as Corinth in the first century, women turned to prostitution whether married or not, in order to have enough to eat and feed their families. When one Corinthian man had intercourse with a prostitute who turned out to be his father's wife, who had taken to prostitution, the Christian community were upset and wrote to Paul about it. He replied: 'Therefore put away from among yourselves that wicked person.' Revised English Bible: 'Root out the wrong-doer from your community.' Expulsion from the Christian community is recommended. 'I meant that you must have nothing to do with any so-called Christian who leads an immoral life [literally goes with prostitutes], or is extortionate, idolatrous, a slanderer, a drunkard, or a swindler; with anyone like that you should not even eat.'

First-century Palestine was as poor as Corinth, and there was as much temptation there for a poor woman to get desperate bread by selling her body. Jesus, when discussing the commandment 'Thou shalt not commit adultery' in the Sermon on the Mount, and again when questioned by the Pharisees on the legality of divorce, says in *Matthew* V, 32: 'Whosoever shall put away his wife, saving for the cause of *fornication*, causeth her to commit adultery: and whosoever shall marry her that is divorced committeth adultery.' Revised English Bible: 'If a man divorces his wife for any cause other than unchastity he involves her in adultery; and whoever marries her commits adultery.' This is the notorious 'Matthaean exception' which has exercised commentators and affected English divorce law. It is just another example of the old mistranslation. Jesus is not referring to *fornication* in its loose English sense of sexual activity or unchastity, but to *porneia*, prostitution, to selling the deed of love for money, as the temple prostitutes at the idolatrous shrines did. If his wife took to that, then a man could in Jesus' view rightly divorce her.

Biblical exegesis is a notorious playground for English amateurs, enthusiasts, and born-again Christians, who can twist it to suit their ends. The trouble with born-again Christians is that they are an even bigger pain the second time round. English sexual morals and attitudes have been significantly affected by the misunderstanding of *fornication* to mean something wider and looser than its biblical meaning of prostitution.

36

LILY-WHITE BOYS

Rabbie and the Gringos

A folk-song is a song that nobody ever wrote. The
only thing to do with a folk-melody, once you have
played it, is to play it louder.

Author unidentified

S OME SONGS ARE very old and very curious. You can find
vestigial echoes of human sacrifice and court scandal
centuries ago in nursery rhymes. As with most popular
folklore, passed on in different forms by word of mouth
rather than writing, it is difficult to prove anything, and
extravagant theories proliferate. One of the wildest goose
chases is among the green rushes or rashes. Not Burns's:

> Green grow the rashes O,
> Green grow the rashes O;
> The sweetest hours that e'er I spend
> Are spent among the lasses O.

And quite right too. But 'Green grow the rushes O' has
deeper roots than Rabbie as an enumerating or 'dilly' song,
found in various forms all over Europe, and carried over
the Atlantic to the New World with new versions.

You remember: 'Five for the symbols at your door, and
four for the gospel makers; three, three the ri-i-i-i-vals;
two, two, the lily-white boys, clothed all in green, O; one
is one, and all alone, and ever more shall be so.' The gospel
makers I can cope with. And I understand that three is a

suitable number for rivals, though I should like to know
whether we are referring to a particular eternal triangle or
event or play. The only five things at my door are five
uncollected full dustbin liners. So what are these symbols?
I think we should be told.

And who on earth or in heaven are these two lily-white
boys, clothed all in green, O? An archaic reference to the
Green Man and human sacrifice? Could they be the twin
Dioscuri, Castor and Pollux, appealed to by those in peril
on the sea and the poet Horace? Those twins certainly rode
on white horses, and appeared to sailors during storms as
the white lights of St Elmo's fire. In modern British slang
since about 1920 the lily-white boys signify a pair of not
necessarily youthful male lovers; but the slang comes from
the song, not the song from the slang. The earlier meaning
of lily-white boys, going back to the seventeenth century
at least, was first a chimney sweep, and then a Negro. But
this slang was also a jocular adaptation from the old
song.

The oddest etymological goose chase in the song is the
theory that it is the origin of *gringo*, the contemptuous
Mexican name for a Yankee. The orthodox academic explanation derives *gringo* from the Spanish word meaning
gibberish, which is a corruption of the Spanish *Griego* or
Greek. Compare the English (and Casca's) expression, 'It
was Greek to me.' But the lexicographers of *The Oxford
English Dictionary* are not prepared to support this (or
indeed any) derivation. Another amateur etymologist
suggests that *gringo* is a Mexican pronunciation of 'green
coat', which, we are asked to suppose, the Yankee cavalry
were wearing in those days. They always seem to be
wearing navy blue when I go to the cinema. There is
another theory advanced and confidently supported that
gringo is the Mexican pronunciation of the first two words
of 'Green grow the rushes, O', which was a popular song
among the American soldiers during the Mexican wars,
and at places like the Alamo. I love this explanation dearly.
But I have difficulty envisaging James Bowie and Davy

Crockett (or, for that matter, John Wayne) singing the song (whether in Burns's version or the dilly song) as Santa Ana advanced.

If it helps, the earliest recorded citation for *gringo* comes from 1849, the year after the end of the Mexican-American War. In William Audubon's *Western Journal*: 'We were hooted and shouted at as we passed through, and called *gringoes*.' I hope that *gringo* comes from 'Green grow the rushes, O'. But I have to tell you that a dark horse in the etymological stakes is Major Samuel Ringgold, a brilliant strategist and campaigner during the Mexican War. He was dreaded by the Mexicans, until he was killed at the Battle of Palo Alto in 1846. If you were a Mexican, pronouncing Ringgold's name with a trilled r, and dropping the last two letters as ugly and difficult to get the tongue round, it might come out as *gringo*. The advantage of such tangled territory for amateur folklorists is that at this stage nobody is going to be able to prove anything one way or the other.

It is time to leave the wild geese flapping, and pluck such domestic duck as we can find. The song is very old, and comes in many versions. A version appears in *Songs of Nativity*, 1625, and it is evidently a cumulative and enumerating song like 'One man went to mow' and 'Ten green bottles'. Its theme is clearly the Christian religion, maybe with pagan ghosts lurking from the old religion. It was probably connected with the great midwinter feast of Yule, and ceremonies with penalties and forfeits connected with the Twelve Days of Christmas. Here is a generally accepted version:

> I'll sing you twelve O
> Green grow the rushes O
> What are your twelve O?
> Twelve for the twelve apostles
> Eleven for the eleven that went up to heaven
> Ten for the ten commandments
> Nine for the nine bright shiners

Eight for the eight bold rainers
Seven for the seven stars in the sky
Six for the six proud walkers
Five for the symbol(s) at your door
Four for the gospel makers
Three, three for the rivals
Two, two for the lily-white boys
Clothed all in green O
One is one and all alone
And evermore shall be so.

All versions agree on one is one, which evidently refers to God Almighty, and is so taken by all folklorist exegetes. The lily-white boys are a problem. There are variants, for example, 'Two of these are lizzie both'. The most popular interpretation is that the lily-white boys are Jesus Christ and John the Baptist, both conceived in miraculous circumstances. Some say that there has been a corruption here, changing 'clean' to green. Sabine Baring-Gould, the antiquarian, and others go for the Dioscuri, alias the Gemini, as signs of spring. The song exists in Hebrew also, and this version is old. It has been suggested that the lily-white boys are the acolytes who carried the tables of the law. Robert Graves in his Tree Alphabet in *The White Goddess* argues that the letters D and T are twins, and the lily-white boys clothed all in green O. D is the oak which rules the waxing part of the year – the sacred Druidic oak, the oak of the *Golden Bough*. T is the evergreen oak which rules the waning part, the bloody oak. However, in ancient Italy it was the holly, not the evergreen oak, which the husband-men used in their mid-winter Saturnalia.

The most popular explanation of the three rivals is that they are the three persons of the Trinity, who are 'in glory equal, in majesty co-eternal', so that no one is greater or better than the others. On this reading 'rival' is used in its original meaning of *rivalis*, river-banker, somebody who uses the same stream with another; cf. Bernardo in the gripping opening scene of *Hamlet*:

If you do meet Horatio and Marcellus,
The rivals of my watch, bid them make haste.

Variants include three 'thrivers', 'tirers', and 'trivers', which, it has been suggested, are corruptions of 'wisers' as one printed version gives it. The rivals in this reading are the Magi or three Wise Men from the East, suitable visitors during the Twelve Days of Christmas.

All versions give four for the gospel makers, or sometimes 'preachers', Matthew, Mark, Luke, and John.

Five for the symbol(s) at your door is taken by some to be another corruption, this time for 'symbol to adore', and to refer to the five wounds in Christ's hands, feet, and side, on the cross. Another explanation is that 'symbol' is being used in its original fifteenth-century meaning, as it was used by Caxton, to mean a creed or summary of Christian belief. The symbol would be simply the cross. Another explanation is that the five symbols of Christ's wounds on a door indicated a safe house to Roman Catholic priests in the persecutions of the sixteenth century.

The most popular explanation for the six proud walkers is that it refers to the six water-pots used in the miracle that turned water into wine at the wedding-feast in Cana. Variants include six 'broad waiters', 'charming waiters', 'go waiters', and 'the minger waiters'. Others say that 'walkers' is a corruption of 'workers', and that the reference is to God's labour on the six days of Creation.

All versions agree on the verse about the seven stars in the sky, which presumably refers to the constellation of Ursa Major or the Plough, or less persuasively to the seven planets of classical astronomy. Another candidate comes from *Revelation* I, 16, where it is said of the Son of man: 'And he had in his right hand seven stars: and out of his mouth went a sharp two-edged sword: and his countenance was as the sun shineth in his strength.'

'Eight bold rainers' is the commonest version, but variants include 'rangers', 'archangels', 'the Gibley angels', 'the angel givers', and 'the Gabriel angels'. The most persuasive interpretation to my mind is the connection of eight bold rainers with the entire complement of Noah's Ark in *Genesis* VII, 13, where we are given the names of the males (Noah, Ham, Shem, and Japheth), but not of their wives. Like the marriage at Cana, Noah's Ark was a very popular theme in the religious drama of the Middle Ages. If you prefer to go for an angelic interpretation, you can note that an archangel is a member of the eighth order of the nine orders of the heavenly hierarchy, so that there may be a corruption of the eight archangels. The trouble with this explanation is that there are only four archangels in the Koran: Gabriel, Michael, Azrael, and Israfel. Christians do not specify how many archangels there are.

The most popular interpretation of the nine bright shiners is that the verse refers to the nine angelic orders of medieval theology: angels, archangels, cherubim, seraphim, thrones, dominions, virtues, principalities, and powers. A variant 'the nine delights' has suggested a reference to the 'nine joys of Mary'. Mathematical interpretations (thrice three as the perfect plural) and astronomical interpretations (planets plus the fixed stars plus the crystalline sphere in which, according to medieval astronomy, they all revolved) seem to me less plausible.

There are no variants and no problems with the ten commandments. The 'eleven and eleven that is gone to Heaven' in a variant are generally taken to be the Twelve Apostles without Judas Iscariot. And the twelve are, as the song itself says, the Twelve Apostles.

It is a fine old song, whose durability attests its magic. But it is wiser to sing it than to speculate too long about its meaning.

37

SLANG

Crime's Own Slanguage at Sea

The pusser cat.

Many of the slang words among fighting men, gamblers, thieves, prostitutes, are powerful words. These words ought to be collected – the bad words as well as the good. Many of these bad words are fine.

An American Primer, circa. 1856, by Walt Whitman

G ROUPS OF MEN shut away from the rest of the world are creators of slang, argot, and playful private languages. It helps to pass the time, and gives them the reassuring feeling of belonging to an exclusive masculine club. In this way prisons, boarding schools, lodges of Freemasons, and ships are prolific sources of slang, which seeps out to mystify and entertain the outside world. Crime has always been an important seedbed of slang. The word 'slang' itself is of mysterious but low origin, as one of its early uses shows: 'Such grossness of speech, and horrid oaths, as shewed them not to be unskilled in the slang or vulgar tongue of the lowest blackguards in the nation.'

The introduction to the 1811 edition of Francis Grose's *Classical Dictionary of the Vulgar Tongue*, renamed *Lexicon Balatronicum*, made the point about the coded secrecy of slang well: 'We need not descant on the dangerous impressions that are made on the female mind by the remarks that fall incidentally from the lips of the brothers or servants of a family. With our assistance improper topics can be discussed, even before the ladies, without raising a blush on the cheek of modesty. It is impossible that a female should understand the meaning of *twiddle diddles*, or rise from table at the mention of *Buckinger's boot*.' Naturally, some of Grose's first systematic record of English slang has changed over two centuries. Once the meaning of slang has leaked out to the general public, as it did in Grose's book, half the fun and use of slang has gone, and the slangsters move on to a new code. For Grose 'high living' meant 'to lodge in a garret or cockloft'; a 'faggot' was a stand-in soldier whom you hired to take your place at Adjutant's Parade (it wouldn't work in the Black Watch); and 'to lib' meant to lie together. But a 'pig' was still a policeman. And most of Grose's slang is criminal and Low Life, or, as Grose puts it whimsically, from the College in the Old Bailey.

This is still the case today. The gaudiest slang of the Nineties grows in the middens of crime, prison, the sex trades, and drugs. An argot or slang is the language of thieves and drop-outs and others on the shady side of the law, used as codes to veil their meaning, and shibboleths to test their freemasonry. The female mind is quite capable of taking care of itself these days (it always was). But omitting such obscenities as 'Buckinger's boot', the modern descendants of Francis Grose record at least a hundred names for the weed marijuana, for example: temple balls, Lebanese gold, Turkish pollen, brick, ganja, gangster, gunny, juanita, locoweed, maharishee, Maryanne, mother nature, turnip greens, bag of bones, bomber, exotic cigarette, and so on, *ad nauseam*.

The place to pick up the slang we shall all be speaking in the Nineties (so making it useless for its inventors) is not in the yuppie wine bars, but in Wormwood Scrubs, or whatever is your local nick. So here is the latest dope from my grass = grasshopper = shopper, or my nose or noah's = Noah's ark = nark, inside. There is a large lexicon of slang for drugs. For example: skag = heroin; snow = cocaine; whizz = amphetamines; blow = cannabis; acid = LSD; magic mushrooms = hallucinogens. Most of these are well known from the newspapers and other fiction. Modern media spread the slang much faster than in the days of Grose, when it had to be passed from mouth to ear.

My canary inside tells me that 'kanga' is the fashionable name for a prison warder; kanga = kangaroo = screw. This marks an interesting shift. Jim Phelan, who served a life sentence between the wars, and wrote of his experiences in *Jail Journey*, had a different equation: kanga = kangaroo = chew, i.e. a piece of tobacco suitable for chewing. He illustrated this by quoting a common expression in his day: 'Slip us a kanga.' This was a request for a surreptitious transfer of a piece of tobacco (contraband in Phelan's day) under the eye of authority. Tobacco is no longer contraband in British jails, and it tends to be smoked rather than chewed; so 'kanga' has changed its slang.

'Bomb disposal' is wrapping excrement in paper and throwing it out of the window rather than live with it all night; other inmates recover it in the morning. The absence of flush toilets is a Victorian peculiarity, possibly meant revengefully, of British prisons. 'It's on top' means that what was top secret is now common knowledge: every-body knows about it. A 'spin' is a search, especially a body search. 'Burglars' are those who conduct a spin. As is well known, 'snout' is tobacco. 'Diesel' is tea; I take this to be because of T(ractor) V(aporizing) O(il). 'Have a cup of TVO.' 'Scran' is food. This is a peculiarly long-lived slang word. It has been in English Low Life and nautical use for at least two centuries, and is of northern, possibly Icelandic origin. If you consult W. L. Lorimer's translation of The New Testament in Scots at *Matthew*, III, you will read of John the Baptist that 'locusts an bumbees' hinnie wis aa his scran'. Now John was certainly a member of the camel-hair-coated fraternity, and, like many others of his kind, wis pitten in the jyle. Could it be that the source of this particular piece of slang might be some old lag, repenting his errors and reflecting on other, earlier prisoners? If not a Scot himself, perhaps he met a Scotch Divine acting as a prison visitor, dispensing New Testaments for the edifi-cation of sinners. (No, it could not, Ed.) Slang is so transient, so volatile, and so unrecorded, that all specu-lations are possible.

The 'cabbage shop' is the workshop, because the monot-ony of such work as making ball-bearings turns men into cabbages. A 'banana' is a scar after a razor slash on the cheek. 'Draw' is cannabis; 'hooch' is illegally made alcohol, as it has been for a century, from the name of a small Alaskan Indian tribe meaning literally 'grizzly bear fort'; and 'burn' is tobacco. 'Slop-out', as is well known, is emptying the bucket in the morning (and it is time the practice passed into history); 'shady' is doubtful or dodgy (university rather than criminal slang originally, nearly two centuries old); and 'busy visit' is a visit from the pigs.

This is just a small sample of the slang at one of London's big prisons collected at the beginning of the Nineties. I hope that there is a Francis Grose somewhere recording all this, and its infinite variations around different coun-tries and different nicks. Slang has always had a short life but a merry one. Modern communications have made the shelf-life of slang even shorter than it always has been.

Naval slang is less ephemeral than criminal, because navies tend to value tradition more than prisons. Of course the new weapons and technologies of modern navies are producing their own new slang for the Nineties: 'mindfart' is a temporary mental aberration as an excuse for having trouble with the operation of a bank of switches; a 'down-bird' is a helicopter that has made a precautionary or emergency landing somewhere other than its intended destination, and which needs attention from the 'grubbers' (air engineering mechanics) of a 'downbird team' before it can fly again. But much naval slang goes back to Nelson and beyond. 'Baron' does not go back quite to Nelson as the Royal Navy's legendary source of gratuitous issue or general hospitality; but it is old. Anything free in the Navy is said to be 'on the baron' rather than on the house; and the process of taking advantage of a well-off civvy individual or organization is known as 'baron strangling'. 'Pusser' is an even older and more versatile word, meaning pretty well anything you want it to. 'Pusser's rum' is proper Royal Navy rum, unlike bogus brands that try to jump on the jollyboat by including the words 'navy' or 'naval' in their brand names. To illustrate the huge range of this word in naval slang: pusser's dust is cheap instant coffee; pusser's logic is a false economy; a really pusser officer is somebody who is absolutely formal in both dress and deportment; and, for indecent reasons (because she has two humps and is made for riding), a pusser's camel is a Wren, or member of the Women's Royal Naval Service.

Pusser, of course, is a naval pronunciation of purser, the paymaster and supplies officer of the old Navy, an appointment which is still made in the Merchant Navy. In the Royal Navy he is now formally entitled a ship's or establishment's supply officer; but everybody still calls him *the* pusser. 'A pusser' is any officer of the supply and secretariat specialization. Any badly tailored garment is said to fit like a pusser's shirt. It is a multi-purpose, pretty well an omni-purpose, word.

The first comprehensive survey of royal naval slang, entitled *Jackspeak*, opening portholes on the foam of perilous seas for outsiders, was published in 1989 by Rick Jolly, a surgeon commander in the Royal Navy. His professional interests lie in the topic of battle stress, and its particular effect on command. But he became hooked on naval slang as a green young surgeon lieutenant in Malta. His first patient was a tall and hearty Royal Marines corporal, who told him that he had 'caught the boat up'. As Dom Mintoff was at that time in the process of booting the Royal Navy out of Malta, Jolly was puzzled, but assumed that his customer was delighted to have been chosen for a sea voyage back to England. Or had he been selected for service in submarines, which are the only kind of 'boat' that go to service under the White Ensign in naval slang? So he congratulated him. The corporal looked puzzled.

'To catch the boat up' is a very old naval expression derived from the fact that Jack was not allowed ashore, even when sick, in the days of sail, for fear that he would desert. The naval hospitals at Portsmouth and Plymouth were positioned on creeks so that they could be reached by water without anybody going ashore. The sick-boat would circulate among the warships anchored offshore, take off those who were ill or injured, and then transport them up either Haslar or Stonehouse creeks. 'Up the creek' originally referred to the poor chance that Jack gave to anybody going to a naval hospital coming out other than feet first and wrapped up in a tarpaulin jacket. To 'push the boat out' refers to a celebration before sailing. But to 'catch the boat up (sc. the creek)' means to have contracted a social disease. These are deep waters of nautical slang, into which landlubbers venture in danger of misapprehension.

38

DOUBLETS

It's All Double Dust

Now, the melancholy god protect thee, and the tailor
make thy doublet of changeable taffeta, for thy mind
is a very opal.

Feste, *Twelfth Night*, II, 1600–1;
by William Shakespeare

C OLLECTED ANY GOOD dust lately? You know, the stuff
to which we all return. Golden lads and girls all must.
An avant-garde West German happening-entrepreneur is
collecting the stuff, to make an exhibition and a book out
of dust collected from sundry institutions. His letter asking
for dust runs, in part: 'What I have to say to you will seem
strange, but please bear with me – for three years now
I have been gathering specimens of dust from diverse
museums in Europe. My purpose in this undertaking is
conceptual: dust as a biblical metaphor, as a literary and
artistic symbol of fleetingness and finality; dust as tangible
token of possible association of ideas. Your co-operation
would constitute, as a welcome by-product as it were, a
bit of PR for your museum. An introduction touching on
the various implications of the subject of dust – themes,
inter alia, like cleanliness, hygiene, etc. – serves to impart
a culture-historical aspect to the scheme concerning the
angles to be examined, of a matter at first sight seemingly
so banal as plain dust.'

Dust, indeed, is not banal, but the stuff of the universe.

Chesterton, underrated by the poetry anthologists, put the matter better than the avant-garde dustman in his 'Praise of Dust', which ends:

> When God to all his paladins
> By his own splendour swore
> To make a fairer face than heaven
> Of dust and nothing more.

Language, like museums, gathers dust. But the dust is not dry. In it you can trace the history of a language. You will find revealing footprints in the dust of doublets. A doublet is the etymologists' name for a pair of words deriving ultimately from the same source, for example 'poison' and 'potion', 'fragile' and 'frail', and, surprisingly, 'grammar' and 'glamour'.

If you cannot tell the difference between a locust and a lobster, I am not going to let you order dinner in a fish restaurant. But the words come from the same root. In this case the doublet is already there in the Latin. *Locusta* in Latin means both the omnivorous insect, which according to Livy swarmed around the Pomptine Marshes south-east of Rome, and also the marine crustacean of the genus *Homarus*, with a greenish or bluish black carapace when raw, which turns a brilliant red when boiled. According to Suetonius, a biased witness, the Emperor Tiberius used to guzzle the lobster *locusta* on his island retreat at Capri. *Locusta* as lobster and *locusta* as locust are both held to be related to the Greek verb *lēkān* to leap. I never think of lobsters as being great leapers, though I know that Gérard de Nerval, the French Romantic poet, was found in the Palais-Royal leading a lobster at the end of a blue ribbon. When asked why, he gave the inspired answer: 'It doesn't bark, and it knows the secrets of the sea.' The Latin *locusta* lobster was transmuted into Old English as loppestre, lopystre, or lopustre. Nobody knows why the c was changed to a p. It happens, in the dust of language. The *locusta* locust kept its c in English. So, in a Lewis Carroll transmogrification, your locust became a lobster. In a complicated linguistic dance around this doublet, 'lobster' in English also means somebody who bowls lobs at cricket, and a stoat in East Anglian dialect. The latter comes from 'lob' meaning a country bumpkin and 'stert' or 'start' a tail. Because these lobsters come from different sources, they do not turn lobster/locust into a triplet or quadruplet.

'Glamour' and 'grammar' come from the same root word: a connection that may not be apparent to the little victims of the Lower Fourth as they are being belted around their ears by Old Chalky for getting their modal auxiliaries wrong. 'Grammar is derived ultimately from the Greek *grammatikē* (sc. technē), the art or science of letters. This branched into a variant 'gramarye', meaning occult learning or magic, originally in Scotland. The r changed to an l, and 'glamour' came into English, meaning originally magical beauty. The word was brought into general literary use by the enormously influential medievalizer, Walter Scott. It has become an overused and increasingly useless word.

In the rich dust-bowl of language 'Christian' and 'cretin' form a doublet. Recent scholarship has shown how surprisingly late the secret society of the Early Church adopted Christian as its name. Its meaning is obvious: a follower of Christ. But in the Romance languages 'Christian' came to be used also to mean a human being as opposed to a brute beast. In French *parler chrétien* means to speak an intelligible language (i.e. preferably French, and certainly European) rather than a barbaric babble. The deformed idiots of the high Alpine valleys were named 'cretins' in order to make the point that, although dwarfed and deformed, they were still human beings and God's children. La Bruyère was making the same point about the difference between Christians and beasts in his satirical description of the peasants in France in the reign of Louis XIV:

*L'on voit certains animaux farouches répandus par la cam-
pagne, des mâles et des femelles, noirs, livides, et tout brûlés
du soleil: attachés à la terre qu'ils fouillent et qu'ils rémuent avec
une opiniâtreté invincible; ils ont comme une voix articulée, et
quand ils se lèvent sur leur pieds, ils montrent une face
humaine; et en effet,* ils sont des hommes.

Marvellous. The history of language as well of a country
lies in its dust.

English is the Lego language. We stick it together, adapt
it, improvise it, and ad lib with more freedom than in any
other language. That is why English is becoming the world
language. One of the flexibilities we have is to use one part
of speech as a different part: a duplicate rather than a
doublet. We turn nouns into adjectives, for headline brevity, or because we cannot be bothered with or do not like
the existing adjectives. Thus we say a luxury hotel, when
the adjective luxurious is available; and a novelty act, when
we have novel. This stringing together of a Lego-chain of
attributive nouns can become a headline-writer's vice, and
misses opportunities for making distinctions. We write 'a
large vehicle fleet', when we could, by using the resources
of English more finely, distinguish between a large fleet of
vehicles and a fleet of large vehicles. The same distinction is
missed with 'a large girls' conference'. The context usually
makes clear which of the alternative meanings you have
in mind, but you should not rely on context to make your
meaning clear when you can do it precisely with the words.

Another very fashionable way that we put the Lego
blocks of language to a duplicate use is to take a noun and
turn it into a verb. There is nothing new about this process,
though it excites the condemnation of linguistic conservatives, who resist all change in language, and complain, for
example, of the modern use 'to tempest' (Mother Julian of
Norwich in the fourteenth century: 'He did not say: Thou
shall not be tempested. He did say: Thou shalt not be
overcome') or 'to cog' (a verb since 1499) or 'to receipt'
(since 1787). The practical, undogmatic, bolshie English

have been doing it since they began grunting inchoate
Anglo-Saxon at each other, turning nouns into verbs and
verbs into nouns as it suited them. But because of the vast
increase in new nouns, coming from the technology and
science explosion of our new world, the process is more
conspicuous. It is also accentuated by the passion of
headline-writers and such for snappy new words, never
mind the part of speech so long as it is short. In our brisk
new world, any noun can be verbed.

To give you an example of what is going on (regarded
by the conservatives as a pox on the face of English), here
is a (by no means exhaustive) list of nouns that have just
started to be used as verbs:

To debut; to trend; to platform; to ink; to dialogue; to
source; to bottom-line; to kangaroo; to black-box; to
rubbish; to down-market; to knee-cap; to dry-run; to
excerpt; to back-to-back; to impact; to fault; to capsule;
to shoehorn; to trash; to block (put an aircraft on
chocks); to shorthand; to format (from Computerese);
to author; to notice (i.e. review or write a notice of);
to milestone; to table; to shelve; to haircut; to version;
to signature; to video; to margin; to solo; to mainstream;
to dimension; to dividend; to weekend; to spreadsheet;
to palate; to rubber stamp; to envelope; to interface
(with); to colour-scheme; to brainstorm; to total (write
off); to plastic (use a credit card); to ticket; to trough
(eat like a pig); to amnesty; to nickle-and-dime; to
increment; to decrement; to slum; to sauce; to staff
(edit a proposal); to backstop; to hoover in; to arrow
upwards; to valet; to payroll; to yardstick; to front-end;
to resource; to grandstand; to target; to matrix; to
timetable; to armslength; to remainder; to legend (not
to pedicure, but to romanticize about); to careerpath;
to sideline; to transition; to doorstep; to guilt; to
bankroll; to joint-venture; to stretcher off; to hospital;
to white-line; boot-saling in progress; I neither vacuum
nor hoover, my char is tasked to do it; key-words can
be ANDed or ORed.

A different category of duplicates is made by tagging the suffix -ize onto nouns: capsulize, bulletize, hospitalize, initialize, vectorize.

Quite a lot of these adapted duplicate Lego blocks are likely to be ephemeral in their new roles. Many of them are coined by hacks desperate to grab our attention with a trendy new use. Some of them are charming; for example 'to plastic' is more fun than paying the bill with the boring old credit card. Quite a lot are obfuscations by professionals in order to impress us with their professionalism in illiterate technologies such as computer science: for example, I think, to target, to interface, to bottom-line. This is mere showing off, like the London probation officer who wrote a report for the magistrates stating that her client had 'a proneness to impulsivity'. But if we do decide to adopt some of these nouns permanently into the Lego-box of English as verbs, because they serve a purpose, by another ancient English trend we shall differentiate between duplicate noun and verb either by pronunciation and accent (use and use, Cathedral close and close the door, convert the heathen but a Catholic convert), or by spelling (half and halve, cloth and clothe, device and devise).

39

NEW WORDS FOR OLD

Adult Adulterations

Here are a few of the unpleasant'st words
That ever blotted paper.
The Merchant of Venice, III, *circa* 1597,
by William Shakespeare

W HEN HORNE TOOKE, who became a radical politician
and philologist, was at school in the middle of the
eighteenth century, his Latin master asked him why a
certain verb governed a particular case. 'I don't know,'
answered Tooke. 'That is impossible,' said the master.

'I know you're not ignorant, but obstinate.' But Tooke persisted in saying that he did not know, so the master beat him. The beating over, the master quoted the rule that governed the verb in question. 'Oh, I know that,' said Tooke at once, 'but you asked for the *reason*, not the *rule*.' He was clearly an admirably bolshie boy. He went on to found the Society for Constitutional Information (to campaign for parliamentary reform), and to be tried (and acquitted) for high treason for his support for the French Revolution.

We may think we know the rules of our language, but they keep changing, as the goalposts are moved, it seems without rhyme or reason. Words and constructions come in, or fade away, or change their meanings. There is usually a reason there, if you look closely. Euphemism and advertising are the reasons that *adult* has changed its meaning over the past few years. In many contexts *adult* has come to mean 'dirty', and this change affects the word in all its contexts, so that one's eyebrows flicker momentarily when one reads some totally decorous sports club magazine advertising 'adult tennis lessons'.

The things described as *adult* in Nineties idiom are clearly unsuitable for children. An *adult* movie actually means a pornographic film. An *adult* novelty is a toy or mechanism unpersuasively supposed to enhance sexual pleasure. An *adult* bookshop is one that sells explicit pornography: you would be making a ludicrous category mistake if you expected to find grown-up books there. As Ezra Pound said of Henry Miller's *Tropic of Cancer*: 'At last, an unprintable book that is readable.' *Adult* videos and magazines are the sort that an actual *adult* would be ashamed to be seen carrying. Here is one of the earliest examples of *adult* in its new clothes, from the early Eighties: 'The governor of California could be seen emerging from a restaurant in the middle of one of the gaudier blocks of strip shows, massage parlors and *adult* entertainments in this city.' *Adult* literally means grown-up, fully nourished, somebody who has ceased to grow vertically but not horizontally.

It is difficult to believe that the new meaning of *adult* represents the normal tastes of the fully grown *Homo sapiens*. The reason for the shift in meaning, which Horne Tooke would have recognized with glee and been beaten for again, is sleazy commercial euphemism.

Commercial euphemism is the reason for *unbundling*, another new word which is enriching the English lexicon. With its connotations of tidying up a mess, *unbundling* is a much more up-beat word than asset-stripping. Sir James Goldsmith, who claims to have invented the word, and the other semantic scholiasts of financial takeovers, argue that *unbundling* is not the same as asset-stripping at all, at all: 'Asset-stripping, which happened mainly in the Fifties and Sixties, is when you take over a moribund company with the intention of closing it down, selling off its dead bones, and putting people out of work. *Unbundling* means that you intend to retain the core business, and spin off the rest, without anything being closed down.'

Goldsmith claims to have coined *unbundling* during his sensational bid to take over BAT (British-American Tobacco Co.) in 1989. He and his colleagues had been discussing how to describe their bid in a positive way. 'Disconglomeration' gave the required meaning of breaking up a conglomerate, which has recently become a boo-word. But it was a mouthful. Goldsmith thought 'disaggregate' sounded too surgical, and it was not quite what he had in mind. At the last minute he came up with *unbundling*, with its implication of coming in to tidy up a complex jumble of assets that are not being run properly, like a nanny tidying up the nursery after the children.

In fact, in City jargon asset-stripping and *unbundling* are not exact synonyms. There are no exact synonyms. But their meanings overlap to a great extent, and *unbundling* sounds friendlier in the present climate of idiom. In fact also, Sir James Goldsmith was not quite the first to coin the smiling participle *unbundling*. I think *unbundling* was first used in the computer world (source of much new jargon), when IBM introduced separate pricing for software, which until then had been included in the price of equipment (hardware). The intention, according to the salesmen, was that customers would have a choice: they would no longer have to pay, even implicitly, for the cost of items they did not want. It came as no surprise to anyone that the final cost of installing a computer system went up considerably. The *à la carte* menu in a restaurant is another example of *unbundling* that has been with us, though not in name, for a long time.

After sex and death, money is the richest source of euphemism in English. Even in a period when market forces are seen as the only engine for society, the money-makers still feel the need to hang the noblest label they can devise on their activities. Hence *unbundling*, which sounds less rapacious than asset-stripping. Hence the personnel manager's classic expression of the most difficult disclosure of all: 'I'm afraid we're going to have to let you go.'

Euphemism literally means 'speaking well of'. It is a very old superstition that you improve things by speaking well of them. Euphemism is the use of a mild or vague expression as a substitute for blunt precision or disagreeable truth. It seems to be a necessary part of human nature and the mechanism of language. In Old English the Anglo-Saxons called a lavatory (literally, a place for washing) a *gang*, 'a going place'. Euphemisms reflect contemporary social attitudes and taboos. The Anglo-Saxon name for a prostitute was a 'sinner'. In the sixteenth century she became a courtesan (a lady courtier); in the eighteenth century a *fille de joie* (a French fun girl); in the nineteenth century a scarlet woman (reference to *Revelation* XVII); today she is a call girl. Death has become our great taboo. When Arthur Koestler committed suicide, he called it 'self-deliverance', and the term has been adopted officially by Exit, the organization that campaigns for the legalization of suicide.

The ancient process of political euphemism is changing our meanings of *sensible* and *stupid*. Until very recently *sensible* as euphemism meant ugly or unfashionable, as applied to female clothes, shoes, and so on, with implied sexist transference to the wearer: 'Her breasts, neatly harnessed under a dark sweater, did not swing as she walked. She wore the ultimate in *sensible* shoes.' Politicians have started to take the word over. For them *sensible* is used to mean 'anything I suggest or support'. Conversely, *stupid* is used to mean 'anything suggested or supported by a person or group opposed to me'. There is nothing to surprise Horne Tooke in the reason for this change, which is as old as politics, and language itself. You can read the politicians in Aristophanes and Plato commandeering favourable value words, their contemporary equivalents of *adult* and *sensible*, to describe their party and their obsessions, and selecting disgraceful boo-words for the opposition. Twisting language to suit your cause is an integral part of party politics and advertising.

Not euphemism, but ignorance and tautology are responsible for the new phrase of the Nineties, to *head-butt*, as done by Rambo street-fighters, particularly if they come from Glasgow. To *butt*, from the Old French *boter*, has meant to strike with the head or horns for four centuries. Only in the past year or two have we started to use the pleonastic *head-butt*. The only reason that Horne Tooke might find for it is that to *head-butt* is not only performed with one's own head, but it is also directed at one's unfortunate opponent's head.

Not euphemism, but obsolescent metaphor is the reason for the new Nineties verb in British idiom, to *doughnut*, meaning to surround with encouraging camouflage and propaganda, as in: 'Her supporters *doughnutted* the Prime Minister in a tight circle to give the impression of a crowded and enthusiastic Chamber.' This came in overnight at the end of 1989 with the televising of the House of Commons. The House of Lords had already been televised for some years; but its members are less nimble and less partisan than Members of Parliament. The word refers to the old-fashioned shape of *doughnuts* as thick rings, or, in the geometrical jargon, tori (tores, or perhaps toroids), as found in the tuck shop at Greyfriars and other boarding schools of English legend and folk memory. In modern British *doughnutteries* and other temples of stodge, *doughnuts* tend to come spheroid or blob-shaped, and covered with chocolate or other goo, as often as they come toroidal. Members of Parliament seldom make time to read for pleasure, and their memories of fiction tend to go back to their schooldays, and to be at quite a low level, in those golden days when *doughnuts* really were *doughnuts*. Horne Tooke would like to know where this musty old metaphor came from. The televising of other parliaments? Or show-biz and the pop world of boxing and pseudo-celebs, where a tight ring of assistants and fans and groupies is used deliberately, as a prop, to make our man look the centre of attraction for television's distorting eye?

40

NOUNS OF ASSEMBLY

Collector's Items

'Ay, lad, but there are other forests besides Woolmer, and other lands besides England, and who can tell how far afield such a knight errant as Nigel of Tilford may go, when he sees worship to be won? We will say that you were in the deserts of Nubia, and that afterward at the court of the great Sultan you wished to say that you had seen several lions . . . How then would you say it?'

'Surely, fair sir, I would be content to say that I had seen a number of lions, if indeed I could say aught after so wondrous an adventure.'

'Nay, Nigel, a huntsman would have said that he had seen a pride of lions, and so proved that he knew the language of the chase. Now, had it been boars instead of lions?'

Sir Nigel, 1906, by Arthur Conan Doyle

W E NOW HAVE a yaah of yuppies, a wheeze or a pong of joggers, a bonk of tennis stars, a jam of tarts, an edification of editors, and a conviction of Thatcherites. Undertakers come together as an unction or a heep (*sic*), or, if there are a lot of them, an extreme unction or an 'umble 'eep. When taken collectively, tourists roasting in the sun on the Costy Bravy make a peel. Categorized by nationalities, Germans make a gross, Italians an explosion, the French an *ennui*, the Irish a point, the Scots a fifth or a half-and-half, and the English a puke or a riot. A self-congratulation or vanity of chat show presenters; a vacuum of socialists; a contradiction of liberals; a fanfare of strumpets; a strabismus of VDU-operators; a twaddle of public speakers; a Dallas of royals; a flush of tabloids.

These nouns of assembly, collective nouns, or group terms are an old, poetic game in the English language. They are found more copiously in English than in any other language, because of the old English love of riddles and word jokes (available in a language with so many roots and near-synonyms), the old English love of tests to sort the gents from the cads, and the old English passion for blood sports. Their origins are lost in the forests and hunting fields of the Dark Ages. Nouns of assembly perform the same function as Cockney rhyming slang, or most other slangs, by providing a code and a shibboleth to separate insiders in the know from outsiders in the dark. In this case the insiders were the upper, or at any rate the hunting, classes, who invented nouns of assembly for the birds of the air, the beasts of the field, the fish of the river, and then, carried away by the game, for different groups and conditions of men.

These group terms are first found in medieval word lists, which were the earliest forms of dictionary. Until Dr Johnson, English dictionaries tended to be lists of difficult, or at any rate unusual, words. One of the earliest medieval word lists of group terms is found in *The Boke of St Albans*, printed in 1486. This is the *locus classicus* for the venereal game of group terms for animals. The popular, antiquarian view is that it was compiled by a Dame Juliana Berners, who makes the point of snobs and élitists down the centuries that it is crucial to select the correct term for each animal, since this is what distinguishes 'the gentylman from the ungentylman'. As often, the popular, antiquarian view is wrong. Little is known of the authorship or compilation of *The Boke of St Albans*. The 'Dam Julyans Barnes' of the hunting treatise, who is cited *passim* as the originator of group terms in English, and whose name has been translated by the antiquarians into the better known 'Dame Juliana Berners', seems more likely to be connected with the additional material in the *Boke* rather than with the hunting treatise and the group terms. She is certainly neither the authoress nor the compiler of the whole *Boke*. She cannot be identified further, in spite of the strenuous efforts of the romantic antiquarian industry to create a more detailed existence for her.

Dull historical facts seldom destroy romantic legends. Conan Doyle had been reading what he took to be Juliana's *Boke* when he wrote his historical novel, *Sir Nigel*. Sir John Buttesthorn, the Knight of Duplin, and England's greatest authority on the hunt, instructing Nigel, the keen young beginner, on the way to become a yuppie in the hunting field, says: 'There is so much to be learned that there is no one who can be said to know it all. For example, Nigel, it is sooth that for every collection of beasts of the forest, and for every gathering of birds of the air, there is their own private name so that none may be confused with another.'

You can break terms of assembly down into various categories, if you want to play Aristotle and categorize:

Ancient phrases making medieval comments (often historically interesting): an abomination of monks, an exaltation of larks, an incredibility (i.e. in its old meaning an incredulity) of cuckolds.
Onomatopeia: a murmuration of starlings, a gaggle of geese.
Alliteration: a porridge of prisoners.
Collectives made by adding an ending such as -y or -age: a froggery, a brigandage.
Characteristics, insults, comments, editorialization: a pride of lions, a skulk of foxes, a clash of Heads (e.g. at the Headmasters' Conference or the Girls' Schools Association).
Outstanding characteristics: a puke of babies, a crash of teenagers, a push of sales reps, a hector of orators.
Habitat: a warren or bury of rabbits, a shoal of minnows.

Appearance: a turmoil of porpoises, a bouquet of pheasants.

Unfavourable comment on disapproved group: a murder of crows, a cowardice of curs, a hover or pounce of Customs men, a gotcher of policemen, a whack (now obsolescent, thank God) of Headmasters.

Noises that people make: a honk of Sloane Rangers, a shout of Evangelists, a roar of Members of Parliament, a bellow of Sergeant-Majors, a strangulation of Counter-Tenors, an orgasm of prima donnas.

Mistake, from ignorance, madam, pure ignorance: a singular (*sanglier*) of boars, a school (shoal) of fish, a charm (from the archaic 'chirm', i.e. chatter) of goldfinches.

Jokes, puns, play on words (the best bit of the venereal game): an anthology of pros (prostitutes), a failing of students, a stock of clergy, a diapason of organists, a slick of garage mechanics, a scrape of gynaecologists, a balls-up of pawnbrokers, an *ex cathedra* of professors *emeriti*, a faction of reporters, a rip-off of repairmen, a cancellation of trains (because of an earlier incident on the Circle Line).

Dam Julyans Barnes (whoever she was) has nothing to do with them. But group terms are an endearing compartment of the English language and idiosyncrasy.

41

FASHION WORDS

Bodies, Boots, and Bags

While clothes with pictures and/or writing on them
are not entirely an invention of the modern age, they
are an unpleasant indication of the general state of
things. I mean, be realistic. If people don't want to
listen to *you* what makes you think they want to hear
from your sweater?

Metropolitan Life, 1978, by Fran Lebowitz

FASHION CHANGES ALL the time, to persuade us to buy
new clothes we don't need, and to keep the rag trade
in business. The etymology of the word suggests change.
I have the New Look; *you* have let down your hem; *she* has
had that frock since 1933. And the vocabulary of fashion
changes faster than most other jargons. *Jeans* are so called
because the kind of material from which they are made
was originally manufactured in Genoa, in French Gênes.
Denim is the *serge de Nîmes*, the manufacturing town in
southern France that first made the stuff.

Teddy is a newer word from the lexicon of fashion,
meaning a woman's undergarment combining chemise
and panties. The experts suggest that it is related to *teddy
bear*, which came from President Theodore Roosevelt, who
might have been surprised to have ended up as the latest
thing in knickers. A *teddy* is not meant to be seen, except
by close friends. The new name for a kind of stretch

A WORD IN TIME

camisole that is worn to be seen by all and sundry is a
body.

The language of fashion is constantly shifting, in order
to sound new. Take a plain fashion accessory, such as
pocket-handkerchief. Its etymology is anything but plain. A
pocket is a little poke, from the French *poche*, a sack, as in
a pig in a poke, which one should think twice about
buying. *Chef* is French for head (from the Latin *caput*); and
a *couvre-chef* or kerchief is a head-cloth or bandana. One
you keep in your hand to sneeze into or wipe your nose
with is a *hand couvre-chef* or *handkerchief*. So a *pocket handkerchief* is originally a 'little-sack-hand-cover-head'.

In her time the most influential name in English fashion
was Queen Elizabeth (the First). Her wardrobe was a
wonder of the world in a period when you wore your
fortune on your back for display. Her richly embroidered
gowns were displayed with other treasure to dazzle the
eyes of visitors to the Tower of London. The inventories
of her clothes in the British Library, the Public Record
Office, and the Folger Shakespeare Library in Washington
DC are treasuries for historians of dress, art historians,
social historians – and wordsmiths. Here you can trace the
curious route that links the silk called Caffa to the town
on the Crimean coast called Feodosiya. The town was once
called Kaffa, and was of some importance on the medieval
trade routes from the East, whence came the coveted
silk. And, Good Grief, what is this *body* doing in Queen
Elizabeth's vast wardrobe? Surely the Virgin Queen didn't
flirt her underclothes like a modern yuppette? Of *course*
she did. *Plus ça change, plus c'est la même chose*, in language
as in fashion.

In Queen Elizabeth's wardrobe, down among the loose
gowns, a *body* was an inner garment for the upper part of
the body, quilted and strengthened with whalebone. In
the second half of the sixteenth century a *body* refers to
both this stiffened inner garment and to the upper part of
a woman's gown fitted close to the body – what we would
now describe as a bodice. It seems to have originally been

– 248 –

called in full a *French body*. In 1577 Jérôme Lippomano
wrote: 'French women have inconceivably narrow waists;
they swell out their gowns from the waist downwards by
whaleboned stuffs and vertugadins [farthingales, I think],
which increases the elegance of their figures. Over the
chemise they wear a corset or bodice, that they call a *corps
piqué* which makes their shape more delicate and slender.
It is fastened behind which helps to show off the form of
the bust.' When your couturier, dress-maker, or woman's
mag tells you that the very latest thing for the trendy is
a slinky little *body*, you tell them to tell that to Queen
Elizabeth.

Bodies have been in fashion, on and off, ever since
Queen Elizabeth. You can find them *passim* in the letters of
Somerville (Edith Oenone) and Ross (Violet Martin), the
Irish cousins who entertained the world at the turn of the
century with their books about an *Irish R.M.* For example,
a letter from Violet to Edith of June 6, 1887: 'I have gone
out in a shirt without a *body*.' And Edith to Violet: 'Mother
was rather horrified at hearing the shirt and body was £1
10s or thereabouts.' There are profuse references to blouses
and *bodies*, but no mention of jerseys, cardigans, sweaters,
and our other modern protections against the Irish mist.
There is an old joke dating from at least the beginning of
this century about the child learning her catechism. 'Who
made your vile *body*?' 'Mother made my *body*, and Auntie
made my skirt.' *Body* may be the latest thing, but it has a
long tail.

At the other end of the body in fashion jargon, *green
wellies* are coming into the language as well as on to the
legs of snobs, who want to flaunt country landowner, or
at the very least country cottage, pretensions. You meet
men and women in *green wellies* striding around the streets
of Kensington, as if they were just off to the stables, for
the same reason that you see them furtively spraying
their new Range Rovers with Old Muckspreader's Genuine
Country Dirt Aerosol. Queen Elizabeth the First would
have recognized the use of clothes as propaganda to pro-

claim a message. In fact, now that the common herd has caught up with the idea that *green wellies* are the thing, real trendies have moved on to navy blue or yellow Wellington boots, with their intimations of their wearer nonchalantly handling the tiller in a Force 9 gale in the Firth of Clyde.

Language follows the *bodies* and the boots. *Green-welly* is coming in as epithet to describe attitudes and institutions of people who wear such things. For example, people are beginning to refer to such universities as Bristol, Exeter, York, and St Andrews as *green-welly* universities, because of their large proportion of students (called Yaaahs) from middle-class homes and independent schools. This presumably distinguishes them from the blue-boot universities, Oxford and Cambridge, and the red-brick-welly universities, the rest.

Let us not go into the very shiny, pointed-toe wellies, which, with fishnet tights, make life good for sadomasochists. In defence of *green wellies*, with the sense of social superiority they are meant to convey, I was told by a pretty basic ship's chandler in Lowestoft harbour that *green wellies* are much longer lasting and better value than the old-fashioned *black wellies* I was after.

Wellies come, as you know, from Arthur, the First Duke of Wellington, who, because he lived so long and became such a national hero, became the eponym of more words than anyone (except, perhaps, Napoleon). His original Wellington boots were nothing like ours, but either a high boot covering the knee in front and cut away behind, or a somewhat shorter boot worn under the trousers. They were made of leather, of course, not rubber or plastic, and were tightly tailored to fit, not galumphing tree-trunks. Here is a contemporary description of the original fashion: 'No gentleman could wear anything in the daytime but Wellington boots, high up the leg, over which the trousers fitted tightly, covering most of the foot, and secured underneath by a broad strap.'

Our own dear *wellies* came widely into use and into the language during the Second World War. In the Fifties and Sixties at boarding schools the instruction to wear Wellingtons was given out by the Headmaster at the end of breakfast, in the same way that the wearing of greatcoats on parade in the army is signalled by three Gs on the trumpet after reveille. *Welly*, the word, as affectionate diminutive, came into English in the Sixties: 'Perhaps it wasn't done for a parson to wear *welly* boots under his cassock.'

As nomenclator the Iron Duke also gave his name to a greatcoat (just below the knees), trousers (fashionably vast in longitude and latitude), a hat (with a yeoman crown), a tree of the Sequoia family, the *Wellingtonia* (because it is very tall), a term in the card game Nap which doubles the call 'Napoleon', Wellington College (opened in 1853 as a public school for the sons of officers), and Wellington School in Somerset (less socially OK, and the one that Jeffrey Archer actually went to). Aircraft recognition instructors used to point out that the silhouette of the Wellington bomber from the side looked like a Wellington boot lying on its back with its foot (corresponding to the stabilizer fin) stuck up in the air. The Wellington bomber shared with penguins the ability to look hopelessly awkward and waddling on land, and to be magically transformed into a swift and graceful thing in its natural element.

The Iron Duke has been dead for a century and a half. But his name goes marching on, in muddy fields undreamed of by him. If he did say, 'The battle of Waterloo was won on the playing fields of Eton', and the attribution was refuted by the Seventh Duke, he would have been referring to bare-knuckle and bloody fist fights behind the Fives courts. No doubt the irascible old duke would have a pithy comment on our modern *green-welly* brigade: 'I never saw so many shocking bad boots in my life.'

Like *body* and *wellies*, *handbag* is a fashion accessory that is changing its meaning. *To handbag* as an active verb, meaning to belt around the ears with one's bag (metaphorically or literally) somebody with whom one disagrees or who has committed *lése majesté* in some other way, is a new word of the Thatcher linguistic revolution that may stick in the vocabulary even after the original *handbag*-wielder has taken up less violent exercise. It conjures up a vivid image. It is vulgar. It may be affected by analogy with the verb 'to sandbag', to fell with a sandbag, and a 'sandbagger', a ruffian using a sandbag as a weapon. Metaphorically, 'to sandbag' can be used to mean to persuade someone by harsh, but not necessarily stunning, means. In other words, *handbag* has the qualities to establish itself in the language.

Handbag is the non-U word, like toilet, notepaper, and perfume, if you bother with the snobbish Ross, Mitford, and Betjeman categorization. The U word is plain *bag*. Cheltenham ladies carry *bags* and abhor *handbags*. The act of hitting with one's *bag* has not developed any class distinction of U or non-U. But as a verb, to *bag* already has several meanings: to put in a bag, to kill game, to steal, and, in Oz, to denigrate somebody. In other dialects and registers of English, for example Nigerian English, *bag* is coming in as a conveniently short word for headlines to mean to win or get: 'Youth bags prison sentence'; 'Queen bags top Nigerian award.' There is the British English schoolchild's slang: '*Bag* me a place'; '*Bags* I go first.' With all this linguistic activity from old *bags*, to *handbag* is better for our new use.

The word *handbag* is quite recent, not much more than a hundred years old; and it originally meant a light travelling *bag* carried by members of either sex. George Bernard Shaw in a letter of November 9, 1896: 'I want to buy a *handbag* for the journey.' The most famous *handbag* in literature so far was one of those sexually indeterminate light carrying bags. 'Where did the charitable gentleman who had a first-class ticket for this sea-side resort find you?' 'In a handbag.' 'A *handbag*.' The outraged hoot is forever Edith Evans.

The secondary meaning of *handbag* as a lady's *bag* for accessories, with the increase in casual wear now sometimes carried by men, especially on holiday and in hot climates, is comparatively recent. The earliest citation in *The Oxford English Dictionary* is from a magazine called *Vanity Fair* in 1913: 'The latest novelty in *handbags*.' Note that novelty, another key word in our neophiliac century.

For such a universal and useful object, *bag* has had surprisingly little impact on English. It is first found in *The Ancrene Riwle*, the devotional manual in prose written for the rule and guidance of certain English recluses in the early thirteenth century: 'Hit is beggares rihte uorte beren *bagge* on bac; & burgeises for to beren purses.' The locality of *The Ancrene Riwle* is consistent with a Scandinavian origin for the word, but it is not certain that the Old Norse *baggi* is a native word. Similar forms are found in Romance languages, such as the Old French *bague*, and the Provençal *bagua*, baggage, whence comes the medieval Latin *baga*, a sack or chest. But the source of these cognates is not known, nor is their relation to the West Flemish *bagge*, a pannier carried on the back. The last of these is the origin of the *bag* in bagpipe.

A *bag* of bones is an old country metaphor meaning emaciated. The *Bag* o' Nails as an English public house sign might be a corruption of Bacchanals, but is more likely Baggers' Nale, a bagger being the old name for somebody buying corn and other goods and carrying them away to sell elsewhere, and nale being Chaucerian English for an ale-house. In the *bag* is as good as certain; in racing parlance in Australia it means that a horse will not be running. The bottom of the *bag* is the last expedient. To be left holding the *bag* (or baby, or can) is to be deserted by one's comrades and left with the entire onus of what was originally a group responsibility. To empty the *bag* is to spill the beans and tell everything, cf. the French *vider le sac*. To give the *bag* these days means to give an employee the sack; formerly it meant the reverse, an employee who left without giving notice being said to have given his master the *bag*. To let the cat out of the *bag* is to spill the beans, and something near the reverse of a pig in a poke. In United States slang, to set one's *bag* is used to describe somebody setting out to secure political office or preferment.

In proverbs, empty *bags* will never stand upright, meaning that extreme need makes survival impossible. Benjamin Franklin: 'Poverty often deprives a Man of all Spirit and Virtue; 'Tis hard for an empty *Bag* to stand upright.' There's many a good cock comes out of a tattered *bag* is a cockfighting metaphor, used, for example, by a farmer whose buildings were out of repair and mucky, but his stock in good condition. '"There's many a good cock come out of a tattered *bag*," said the dark shape, slowly. There was an instant of silence, and then Simon said, "And a good tune played on an old fiddle."'

There is *bags* of scope for new *bag* metaphors and proverbs in the language. Mrs Thatcher's alleged way with her *handbag* is a welcome addition.

42

MODERN PROVERBS

Catchphrase Them While You Can

I do not say a proverb is amiss when aptly and season-
ably applied; but to be forever discharging them, right
or wrong, hit or miss, renders conversation insipid
and vulgar.

Don Quixote, II, 1615, by Cervantes

M OST OF OUR modern proverbs and catchphrases come
from television (particularly telly ads and jingles),
and therefore have lives as short as that ephemeral medium. 'The sky's the limit', 'Come on down', 'I bet he
drinks Carling Black Label', 'Refreshes the parts other
beers cannot reach', 'Nice to see you, to see you nice', 'So
it's goodnight from me and it's goodnight from him',
and the doubly tautologous 'Hello, good evening, and
welcome', are already showing signs of age. As Hamlet
said, the proverb is something musty. These contemporary
quotations will not last a year longer than their pro-
grammes or advertising campaigns. Already such recently
universal slogans of the British television-watching generation as 'Go to work on an egg', 'Put a tiger in your
tank', and 'Drinka Pinta Milka Day' (claimed to have been
invented by Fay Weldon when she worked in advertising)
are boring gibberish to the young. Such sayings have the
brief lives of mayflies because they aren't really saying
anything. They are meaningless proverbs, such as 'One
does not moisten a stamp with the Niagara Falls', and 'She

that knows why knows wherefore'. They are fashionable parrot squawks with no solid bottom of sententious or proverbial meaning.

Consider the way that the catchphrase 'Nice one, Cyril' has died the death, when only a few years ago it was in the top ten of vacuous vocables of modern British squawks. This started life, like many of these things, as an advertisement on television. In 1972 there was a campaign for sliced bread called Wonderloaf on British television. In it two bakers, wearing T-shirts labelled 'Nottingham' and 'Liverpool', were claiming to be able to tell who it was who had baked a particular specimen of Wonderloaf in one of their local bakeries around the country. Could it be their colleagues in Leeds? High Wycombe? Could it be one of Cyril's? (The ancient Christian name Cyril, from the Greek *kyrillos*, *kyrios* lord or ruler, is considered silly in modern Britain, for no apparent reason.) The truth was that the bakers in the ad couldn't tell for sure who had baked the loaf, but they concluded resoundingly: 'Nice one, Cyril.'

Mercury, god of quirks, knows why it caught on. The repeated sibilant was fun to say? Cyril is an agreeably funny name in modern Britain, like Clarence or Bernard? 'Nice one, Cyril' is a putty phrase, which can be used in almost any situation or context, particularly in sexual ones. For a few years it raged through the nation as a catch-all catchphrase, with the universal popularity of the revenge taken in Kipling's short story, 'The Village that Voted the Earth was Flat'. Tottenham Hotspur soccer fans adopted it as a chant to encourage their current player, Cyril Knowles:

> Nice one, Cyril,
> Nice one, son,
> Nice one, Cyril,
> Let's have another one.

Then the catchphrase died, as suddenly as dead meat (there goes another dying modern catchphrase). The advertising campaign had stopped. The fickle populace had moved on to other slogans and squawks. The prodigious, continual output of the modern media means that we change our sayings, and grow bored with them, far more often than in the days when they were passed on only by word of mouth. The shelf-life (there's another semi-catch-phrase that is approaching its sell-by date) of catchphrases was centuries longer when they were passed around only by word of mouth.

Almost all political catchphrases are equally ephemeral. Such crudities as 'On your bike' and 'Like the Roman, I seem to see the River Tiber foaming with much blood' will not make it into the central core of English phrases that last; though people will continue to read Virgil, of course. Once politicians die or cease to have power for other reasons, the herd public recognizes their familiar slogans for the self-serving, sensational banalities that they were, and drops them.

How many of today's popular political slogans can you think of that will still be with us in ten years' time? *The Art of the Possible*, the title of R. A. Butler's memoirs, though he did not invent the definition of politics which is the antithesis of 'conviction politics'? Bismarck was the coiner of 'The Art of the Possible' in modern times, though Rab found John-the-Baptist forerunners of the phrase in Cavour, Salvador de Madariaga, Camus, and Pindar. 'If you don't like the heat, get out of the kitchen' was Harry Truman's characteristically down-to-earth reason for retiring from the presidency. But he was quoting his resident military jester, Major General Harry Vaughan. And I reckon General Vaughan was repeating an American old wives' saying. It is a political catchphrase that shows signs of considerable longevity, because of its universal folksy common sense.

'There's no such thing as a free lunch' has recently been popularized by Milton Friedman as a proverbial explanation of monetarism or laisser-faire liberalism. But the saying in fact goes back more than a century to American bars, which provided free lunch if you bought a drink, but not if you didn't. It looks a stayer. 'I'd rather have him inside the tent' is another American political catchphrase that shows staying power. Interesting how the long-running political catchphrases are mostly American, *hein*? When J. Edgar Hoover reached seventy, pressure was put on President Lyndon Johnson to make the old crocodile, who ran the Federal Bureau of Investigation and had far too much secret political power, resign. Johnson, with characteristic cowboy indelicacy, replied: 'No; I'd rather have him inside pissing out than have him outside the tent pissing in.' I guess 'inside the tent', like 'one of us', may be a stayer as political catchphrase.

The political catchphrase that shows surprising staying power, even though the source of the metaphor has been obsolete for nearly a century, is that greasy old 'pork barrel'. It has even crossed the Atlantic to the United Kingdom, which never went in for pork barrels, except metaphorically. It is a vivid political metaphor, more used in the United States than in Britain, but still applicable in any elected democracy. We British might as well try to get it right when we use it. As metaphor, the pork barrel means a state or national treasury into which politicians and government officials dip for 'pork', i.e. funds for local projects, in order to gain popularity and win votes. The classic annual American pork-barrel bill is the Army Civil Functions Appropriation Bill, formerly known as the Rivers and Harbors Bill. It is managed by Federal not State machinery. It contains funds for dozens of projects in every State. And it is, accordingly, the hardest for the administration to cut item by item. A Democratic Senator, expert in pork barrels, defined the process of the Bill: 'As groups win their battle for special expenditures, they lose the more important war for general economy. They are like drunkards who shout for temperance in the intervals between cocktails.' Every year whoever is President denounces dozens of last-minute pork-barrel amendments slipped into the Bill, which authorizes expenditure of hundreds of billions of dollars a year, without time for debate.

Typical pork-barrel amendments are funds for cranberry and blueberry research in the fruit-growing States, money for the study of crawfish, subsidies for sunflowers, and money to prevent pigs attacking exotic plants in Hawaii.

Old American history lies behind the useful metaphor. Fat hogs were developed in the United States as cheap food for slaves and the urban working class. The pork was salted and kept in barrels through the winter. *The Farmer's Almanack* of Boston in 1801 illustrated the practice: *'Better spare at the brim than at the bottom* is an old proverb, and should teach us to mind our pork and cider barrels.' Before the Civil War, salt pork used to be distributed periodically to the slaves on an estate out of huge barrels. I have found no contemporary description of what it tasted like, but I should guess fatty, salty, and nasty. A commentator described how the phrase became our aged metaphor: 'Oftentimes the eagerness of the slaves would result in a rush upon the pork barrel, in which each would strive to grab as much as possible for himself. Members of Congress in the stampede to get their local appropriation items into the omnibus river and harbor bills behaved so much like Negro slaves rushing the pork barrel that these bills were facetiously styled pork-barrel bills, and the system which originated them has thus become known as the pork-barrel system.' The term was astonishingly popularized in the United States by a dire short story called 'The Children of the Public' published in 1863, and containing a pig-fish of a mixed metaphor:

> We find that those who work honestly, and only seek a man's fair average of life, or a woman's, get that average. And thus we find that when an extraordinary contingency arises in life, we have only to go to our pork barrel and the fish rises to our hook or spear.

Of course we don't have pork barrel politics in the United Kingdom. We have it on the authority of the former Prime Minister, Harold Wilson, now Lord Wilson of Rievaulx, in his book *The Governance of Britain* (dire, also): 'In Westminster, the Government has complete control over expenditure. Thus, in Britain, pork-barrel expenditure is ruled out.' Oh yeah? I have collected examples over the past few years of the British Press denouncing a Tory government for treating nationalized industries as enemies, while opening up a pork barrel for private firms, and denouncing a Labour Prime Minister for regional pork-barrelling by promising to build two aluminium smelters, using subsidized electricity, in development areas, which tend to vote Labour. Politicians sucking up to greedy constituents are part of the political process in all democracies, not just the United States. The pork barrel is related to log-rolling, another charming settlers' and homesteaders' metaphor from the sticks. In the New World the neighbours helped a new settler roll the logs away from his clearing. The practice has not been known literally in Britain since the Dark Ages, when we cleared our forests. But log-rolling, like the pork barrel, is a catchphrase that has caught on as a metaphor wherever English is spoken, and shows signs of sticking in the central core.

43

NEW JARGON

Shell-Fruit To Them All

your didactic minimalism, use of borrowed space and linear economy, clearly depicts the equine quadruped with great negative force.

quite!

GED.

You and I come by road or rail, but economists travel by infrastructure.

Margaret Thatcher, interview in
The Observer, May 26, 1985

I T IS A noble enterprise to try to improve the jargon of the European Community and other such economic and political bureaucracies. It is worthy of much improvement. A number of bodies have been formed to do this: for example, CECG (Consumers in the European Community

Group) and ERICA (European Research into Community Affairs). I do not see how POSA (Proliferation Of Silly Acronyms) helps their case. But the DJ (Day of Judgement) is going to be confusing, since the EC (European Community) officially classifies both sheep and goats as sheepmeat. In the new Eurojargon nuts are called 'shell-fruit', flowers are classified as 'non-edible vegetables', and cows are 'adult bovine animals' (so are buffalo). The Euro-definition is that milk 'shall mean exclusively the mammary secretion obtained from one or more milkings without either addition thereto or extraction therefrom'.

Let us hope that these new crusaders for plain speaking are not introducing flagellation measures to an equine quadruped entirely devoid of its original capacities. Two cheers for them. Plain English is usually preferable to the other sort, though not always; not, for example, if you are a politician dealing with a deeply embarrassing question, or an insurer writing a policy that has to take into account every contingency. We must all try to dock our speech and writing of prolixities, simplify and clarify, say precisely what we mean and not a word more or less. But it is populist rubbish to demand that everything (Einstein's Theory of Relativity, *Finnegans Wake*, any Act of Parliament) can be rewritten in language that the average punter can understand. Reading European Community documents or Acts of Parliament (or *Finnegans Wake*) is a minority sport. MEPs (Members of the European Parliament), press officers, and journos (and literary critics?) are there to interpret and explain what they mean to the rest of us. *C'est leur métier.*

Like most old words, jargon has many meanings. When it first came into Chaucer from Old French it meant the twittering of birds. Then it came to mean unintelligible and ugly-sounding language, like the jargon of structuralists, or thieves' cant. Then it came to mean deliberate obfuscation, the use of long words to show off or to conceal the poverty of meaning, and circumlocution generally. It has acquired other meanings also on its long journey into English, but those are the principal ones.

Specialists such as brain surgeons, computer hackers, linguistic philosophers, and Eurocrats naturally develop their specialized jargons in order to communicate rapidly with other specialists and to cover all contingencies without spelling them out in full. If we insisted that everything they said and wrote be translated into plain, monosyllabic English that the average man or woman waiting (interminably) for the 27 bus could understand, they would never get anything done. If you are legislating or administering policy, you are not usually writing for the average man. You are writing like a lawyer to take into account every conceivable possibility and loophole that might let something through. So you write 'equine quadruped' instead of horse in case some wide *garçon* from Marseilles starts evading Euroduty by turning Shetland ponies or zebras into salami without paying horse tax. You classify flowers as 'non-edible vegetables' to prevent globe artichokes being moved around freely across tariff barriers by counting them as flowers. Where does this leave dandelions, the leaves of which when young make a delicious, sharp salad? No doubt the regulations about moving things around the world are daft. Regulations often are. But the jargon is carefully designed.

The same mistaken populism demands that all literature should be understood by everybody. 'It is no use pretending that in an age like our own good literature can have any genuine popularity.' As in most good debating motions, there are a lot of value words in there. It all depends on what you mean by good/literature/genuine/popularity. And I am not sure what we mean by an age like our own, which in this respect is much like all previous ages. This may sound élitist, or even Fogeyish; but the truth is that what is usually meant by good literature, e.g. *King Lear*, *Finnegans Wake*, or Auden, is always going to have a small readership compared with the simple-minded pap that is at the top of the bestseller lists for a while, and then the memory of it is forgotten as if it had never been. The reward of literary 'jargon' is longevity. Of course popular genres can be well done (Georgette Heyer, P. D. James, Le Carré). But the demand that everybody should understand and enjoy everything written is philistine rubbish.

Contrary to the gloom of populists, language reactionaries, and dyslexicographers, much of the new jargon that our scientists coin is vivid and charming. Modern physicists seem particularly inventive. 'Charm' itself is a happy neologism to describe the property of some elementary particles, proposed to account for their unexpectedly long lifetimes compared with other particles of matter. It is a charming word. 'Quark' has literary origins, being associated with 'Three quarks for Muster Mark!' in *Finnegans Wake*. Murray Gell-Mann, who introduced the notion of 'strangeness' and thence quarks, and named them, explained how he hit upon the word in a private letter to the editor of *The Oxford English Dictionary Supplement*: 'I employed the sound "quork" for several weeks in 1963 before noticing "quark" in *Finnegans Wake*, which I had perused from time to time since it appeared in 1939. The allusion to three quarks seemed perfect. I needed an excuse for retaining the pronunciation "quork" despite the occurrence of "Mark", "bark", "mark", and so forth in *Finnegans Wake*. I found that excuse by supposing that one ingredient of the line "Three quarks for Muster Mark!" was a cry of "Three quarts for Mister . . ." heard in H. C. Earwicker's pub.' It is apt and agreeable that such elusive little things as quarks should have so elegant and unforgettable a name.

You need imagination, lateral thinking, and an ability not to take your speciality as the most important thing in the world to coin good jargon. An American physicist is in the process of using these qualities as name-giver. He has discovered that the motion in certain superfluids is damped by tiny whirlpools, which he wants to name 'boojums'. You remember:

But oh, beamish nephew, beware of the day,
    If your Snark be a Boojum! For then
You will softly and suddenly vanish away,
    And never be met with again!

In some laboratory somewhere, I hope that a scientist with a sense of style is coining new connotations for the Snark himself, Jabberwocky, and many other memorable names in English Literature.

It is not necessary to be a physicist to be good at creating new jargon. Physicians are pretty good at it, apart from a vain tendency to name their discoveries after themselves, from the Finkelstein Test to Sistrunk's Operation. For example, 'kamikaze protein' is an imaginative name for the newly discovered protein that appears able to repair cancer damage to DNA molecules in the body's cells before dying itself, and may offer hope for the prevention and treatment of cancer.

Paradoxically, it is the specialists in non-physical disciplines, chaps who work with words rather than things, who seem to be less good at devising jargon. It would be difficult to argue that the jargons of modern philosophy, sociology, or linguistics are elegant or perspicuous, or, in some cases, serve any useful purpose, other than blinding us with obfuscation. Much of the jargon of Lit. Crit. is woolly and ugly, perhaps because Lit. Crit. is not really a genuine science. Here is a recent piece of the new Sociologese from two of the discipline's eminent professors: '. . . availability information . . . dual gender perspective . . . governmental passivity . . . employer biased manpower services . . . computer use ineffectivity . . . massive personnel burn out . . . public sector effectivity . . . work environmental and effectivity consequences . . . priorated . . . the parameters, structure and function of society's organizations.' Blood pressure rises and brow furrows as you wade through the strings of flatulent abstract nouns.

Like many specialists, sociologists and social scientists use their jargon partly to impress each other and pull the wool over the eyes of outsiders. Nevertheless, behind their jargon, many of them do useful work. Here are the latest terms of Sociologese, making their way across the Atlantic from the United States to the United Kingdom, the direction in which most new jargon travels:

Access: as a verb, means to use; social service clients 'access' a service.

Aftercare: treatment provided after treatment that was supposed to solve the original problem; but usually didn't.

All-time: pointless and fruitless Journalese as well as Sociologese; as in, 'Botham played his last Test innings this year, and perhaps of all time'; or, 'British coal announced last month that men in the Selby showcase colliery had broken their own all-time British output and productivity record.'

At-risk: persons likely to have a particular problem.

Capability: possibility; available resources; specialized staff; political desirability; or ability to achieve a political goal; pretty well anything you want it to mean.

Catchment area: a geographical term implying that the social services agency is expected to catch anyone living in the area who needs its specialized services.

Common language: the jargon of social services and sociology; it plays a leading role in accusations by sociologists that journalists and politicians just will not try to understand what they are trying to tell us.

Crisis stabilization: getting emotionally troubled people to calm down, as only social workers can.

Front-end: this comes from Computerspeak, or possibly from motor-manufacturing. Front-end is the first stop in a social services problem, e.g. mental health officials trying to get 'clients' to seek services in local centres instead of mental institutions.

Hospitality: a euphemism for shelter for the homeless.

Impact: a buzz-word, meaning to have an effect rather

than to make contact; to wreak havoc, as in: 'The budget will impact our services severely.'

Income maintenance: an allocation of cash (or other grant) to poor people; much social services jargon is generous euphemism to avoid calling a spade a spade for the self-respect of the clients.

Interface: another piece of social services jargon taken from Computerese; it means the co-operation of agencies in the social services field, as opposed to face-off, when they are in dispute.

Intervention: more positive than the word in politico-military jargon: 'Early intervention is necessary to stop the problem from impacting more people' means getting services to somebody before things get worse.

Negative exit: a client who leaves a social programme before the problem is solved, such as a juvenile running away from a detention home, or some project abandoned because of lack of success or money.

Positive peer cultures: putting children with problems in the company of children with fewer problems.

RFP, sc. *Request-For Proposal*: a request for money; in the United States there are college courses in RFP writing.

Reference: in Sociologese now a verb, like 'to impact', another one probably from Computerese: 'Can we reference our conversation last week?'

To surface: to come to the attention of. 'A husband-wife dispute surfaced about the child' means that social workers became aware (or were informed by others) of such a dispute. In Journalese to say that something has surfaced means that the journo is guessing or repeating gossip from not very impressive a source.

Let us not bounce into the absurd and philistine reaction that all sociology is useless because some Sociologese is vacuous. In spite of his notorious jargon, even the dreaded Talcott Parsons has added to the sum of human knowledge in his efforts to create a general theory of social action that will encompass, as a logical system, all dimensions of human behaviour from individual motivations to macro-social processes in one grand, conceptual scheme. (As you can see from that last sentence, Sociologese is catching.) Moreover, do not forget that Max Weber's Sociologese has given us two of the most popular new jargon words of our century, status and charisma (the latter adapted from the original theological jargon).

INDEX